Examining GCSE Geography

R Bateman and N Rowles

Hutchinson

London   Sydney   Auckland   Johannesburg

Hutchinson Education Ltd
62–65 Chandos Place, London WC2N 4NW

Century Hutchinson Australia Pty Ltd
PO Box 496, 16–22 Church Street, Hawthorn,
Victoria 3122, Australia

Century Hutchinson New Zealand Ltd
PO Box 40–086, Glenfield, Auckland 10, New Zealand

Century Hutchinson South Africa (Pty) Ltd
PO Box 337, Bergvlei 2012, South Africa

First Published 1988
Reprinted 1989

© Dick Bateman and Nick Rowles
Designed and phototypeset by Gecko Limited, Bicester, Oxon
Illustrations by Taurus Graphics, Abingdon
Printed and bound in Singapore by
Singapore National Printers Ltd

British Library Cataloguing in Publication Data

Bateman, R.
   Examining GCSE geography.
   1. Geography — Text-books — 1945 –
   I. Title   II. Rowles, N.
   910   G128

ISBN 0 09 172904 1

Acknowledgements

The authors wish to thank the officers of the Associated
Examining Board, the South Western Examinations Board and
the Southern Examining Group for their help and support over
the years, and Trevor Day for much constructive criticism. Many
GCSE students have played an important role in the writing of
this book, and their contribution is gratefully acknowledged.
Particular thanks are due to Paul Barber, Nathan Burlton,
Michael Gale, Vanessa Gale, Jason Milkins and Chris Trueman.
Last, but by no means least, the authors would like to give their
devoted thanks to their wives and families for their unerring
support and encouragement.

The following examination boards have kindly granted permission
for the use of questions from past examination papers:
Associated Examining Board, South Western Examinations
Board and Southern Examining Group.

The publishers wish to thank the following for permission to
reproduce copyright material:

British Railways Board; Collins Educational (*Worldwide Issues in
Geography*); The Department of Trade and Industry (Crown
copyright); Esselte Studium ab (*Heinemann Atlas 2 & 3*); Mary
Glasgow Publications (© *Geofile* No 31, April 1984); The
Geographical Association (*Geography* magazine); Heinemann
Educational Books Ltd (*Farming and the Countryside*, Dunlop
and Macdonald: *Place and People No 4*); Harper & Row
(*Geography: A Modern Synthesis*, P Haggett); Longman Group
Ltd (*Geographical Studies – Western Europe*, Randle; *Geography
of East Africa*, Hickman and Dickens; *Certificate Geography of
West Africa*, Higsan; *Africa: A Modern Study*, Pritchard);
Macmillan Education Ltd (*Temasek Geography for Secondary
Schools* Book 3, Lock and Wan); Thomas Nelson & Sons Ltd
(*Europe*, D Waugh; *The British Isles*, D Waugh; *Man and his
World*, Dawson and Thomas); Oxford University Press
(*Development in the Third World* © 1983, M Morrish); George
Philip & Son Ltd; Plessey; Time Magazine; Reuben K Udo
(*Geography of West Africa*); United Nations (*UN Statistical
Yearbook 1985*); Unwin Hyman Ltd (*The Developing World: The
World Now*, A Reed); Frederick Warne/Penguin Books Ltd
(*Geographical Studies – Western Europe*, I G Coghill); Yorkshire
Water Authority. Special thanks are due to the Ordnance Survey
for allowing the publishers to reproduce map extracts on which
they hold copyright. Their help is gratefully acknowledged.

The publishers' thanks are also due to the following for
permission to reproduce photographs:

Action Aid; Aerofilms; Michael J Allan Photography; J Allan Cash
Photolibrary; Barnabys Picture Library; Ron Boshier; Bradford
Economic Development Unit; British Coal; Camera Press;
CEGB; Christian Aid; Colorific Photo Library Ltd; The
Telegraph Colour Library; Gatwick Airport Limited; The
Hutchinson Library; Landform Slides; National Remote Sensing
Centre; Bob Naylor Photography; Tropix Photographic Library;
West Air Photography; Richard Woodhouse.

The publishers have made every effort to trace the copyright
holders but if they have inadvertently overlooked any, they will
be pleased to make the necessary arrangements at the first
opportunity.

*This book is dedicated to John Taylor, late Headmaster,
Skelmersdale R.C. Primary School.*

Contents

Matrix relating book contents to syllabuses

Topic	UNIT	AVERY HILL (WITH MEG) 1	WJEC 1	WJEC B	SEG A	NISEC 1	NISEC D	NISEC C	NISEC B	NEG A	NEG D	NEG C	NEG B	MEG A	MEG D	MEG C	MEG B	LEAG A
Knowledge, skills, values and Enquiry	1.1	●	●	●	●	●	●	●	●	●	●	●	●	●	●	●	●	●
	1.2	●	●	●	●	●	●	●	●	●	●	●	●	●	●	●	●	●
	1.3	●	●	●	●	●	●	●	●	●	●	●	●	●	●	●	●	●
	1.4	●	●	●	●	●	●	●	●	●	●	●	●	●	●	●	●	●
OS Mapwork	2.1				●					●	●					●		
	2.2				●					●	●					●		
	2.3				●					●	●					●		
	2.4				●					●	●					●		
Earth movements	3.1				●			●						●	●	●		
	3.2				●			●						●	●	●		
	3.3				●			●						●	●	●		
	3.4				●			●						●	●	●		
Surface processes	4.1	●	●	●	●	●	●	●		●				●	●	●	●	●
	4.2	●	●	●	●	●	●	●						●	●	●	●	●
	4.3	●	●	●	●	●	●	●		●				●	●	●	●	●
	4.4	●	●	●	●	●	●	●						●	●	●	●	●
Air processes	5.1	●	●		●			●	●	●				●	●	●	●	●
	5.2	●	●		●			●	●					●	●	●	●	●
	5.3	●	●		●			●	●	●				●	●	●	●	●
	5.4	●	●		●			●	●					●	●	●	●	●
Population	6.1		●	●	●	●	●	●	●	●	●	●	●	●	●	●	●	●
	6.2		●	●	●	●	●	●	●	●	●	●	●	●	●	●	●	●
	6.3		●	●	●	●	●	●	●	●	●	●	●	●	●	●	●	●
	6.4		●	●	●	●	●	●	●	●	●	●	●	●	●	●	●	●
Settlement	7.1	●	●	●	●	●	●			●	●	●	●	●	●	●	●	●
	7.2	●	●	●	●	●	●			●	●	●	●	●	●	●	●	●
	7.3	●	●		●	●	●	●	●	●	●	●	●	●	●	●	●	●
	7.4	●	●		●	●	●	●	●	●	●	●	●	●	●	●	●	●
Agriculture	8.1	●	●	●	●	●	●	●	●	●	●	●	●	●	●	●	●	●
	8.2	●	●	●	●	●	●	●	●	●	●	●	●	●	●	●	●	●
	8.3	●	●	●	●	●	●	●	●	●	●	●	●	●	●	●	●	●
	8.4	●	●	●	●	●	●	●	●	●	●	●	●	●	●	●	●	●
Industry	9.1	●	●	●	●	●	●	●	●	●	●	●	●	●	●	●	●	●
	9.2	●	●	●	●	●	●	●	●	●	●	●	●	●	●	●	●	●
	9.3	●	●	●	●	●	●	●	●	●	●	●	●	●	●	●	●	●
	9.4	●	●	●	●	●	●	●	●	●	●	●	●	●	●	●	●	●
Communications and transport	10.1	●	●	●		●	●	●		●	●	●		●	●	●		●
	10.2	●	●	●		●	●	●		●	●	●		●	●	●		●
	10.3	●	●	●			●	●	●		●	●		●	●	●		●
	10.4	●	●	●			●	●	●		●	●		●	●	●		●
Quality of life	11.1	●			●	●					●	●		●		●		●
	11.2	●				●					●	●		●		●		●
	11.3	●		●		●					●	●		●				●
	11.4	●		●		●					●	●		●				●
Development	12.1	●		●	●	●				●	●	●				●	●	●
	12.2	●		●	●	●					●	●	●	●	●	●	●	●
	12.3	●			●	●	●				●	●		●	●	●	●	●
	12.4	●			●	●	●				●	●		●	●	●	●	●

How to use this book

The book has four major components:

1 An Introduction and Map Skills section (chapters 1 and 2).

The introductory chapter deals with the structure of GCSE examinations, showing the contributions of Knowledge and Understanding, Skills, Values, and Geographical Enquiry to 16+ Geographical Education.

2 Content chapters 3–12 giving information about topics common to most examination board Geography syllabuses. The authors' impression of how these topics relate to the units in this book are shown in the matrix on page 4.

3 Questions similar in style to those set by GCSE examiners. They are copyright-free to allow flexibility of use in the classroom and for homeworks. Each set of questions has an analysis to show the contribution of Recall, Understanding, Skills and Values to the final mark.

4 Mark schemes similar to those used by GCSE examiners to make a first assessment of how candidates have responded to the examination questions. Each mark scheme shows teachers and pupils how the marks could be awarded.

The content pages

The first two pages of each unit in chapters 2–12 are content pages. They are designed to help in revision and to provide a foundation for further, issue-based ideas. No attempt has been made to deal with all concepts found in 16+ Geography courses but most key points have been introduced.

The content pages can be used for note making and as a source of ideas for group discussion.

The assessment pages

The second two pages of chapters 2–12 are assessment pages with GCSE-type questions. These pages can be used in several ways.

(a) *For individual work* (either singly, or as a class)
   (i) As an introduction to examination techniques. The individual can work through the questions, referring back to the relevant content pages as necessary.
   (ii) As a straightforward test, against time, to give examination practice without reference to content pages (or mark schemes).

(b) *For pair or group work*
The questions can be used to prompt discussion in class or in small groups. Candidates often interpret examination questions in different ways. It is helpful for all candidates to see how others respond to questions of varying difficulty. Two methods are:
   (i) The pair or group can work through the questions looking back at the relevant content pages for ideas on how to answer the questions as fully as possible.
   (ii) As a group test, against time, without reference to content pages (or mark schemes), but with the candidates allowed to discuss each question to try to find the best answer.

The mark schemes

The mark schemes can be used:
(a) For individuals to mark their own answers. This is useful, but helps full understanding less than (b).
(b) By a pair or small group to mark another group's answers, comparing each answer to the mark scheme and discussing how many marks should be awarded.

This discussion process is very helpful to all candidates. It strengthens everyone's understanding of the topic and makes candidates more aware of what examiners are looking for in the answers. The important thing is not to mark someone else's work in order to criticise it. The idea is to show areas of weakness so that improvements can be made next time.

1. GCSE: Aims, skills, values and examination styles

There are four main aims of upper school Geography:
1 To gain **knowledge** and **understanding** of geographical topics.
2 To learn the **skills** needed to gain and make best use of this knowledge and understanding.
3 To learn to appreciate the **values** which geographers think are important.
4 To gain the **confidence** needed to make first-hand investigations of places and the processes which change them.

These aims should be met through a study of places at different scales. Your local area is one obvious choice. Most courses also involve a study of regions in the United Kingdom (UK). The UK is the whole of Great Britain (England, Wales and Scotland) plus Northern Ireland.

Other places included in many syllabuses are Western Europe and parts of the world with which the UK has historic links, such as the USA and Canada. Important geographical ideas, such as how people cope with their surroundings, the reasons why some areas are rich and some are poor, and how employment is changing, should be studied at all these scales. (See Photographs A and B.)

It is often difficult to understand abstract ideas like these. So as to make them more 'real', an example is given below of the sort of geographical study you might be expected to do in the classroom. This example is about jobs in a British county.

"Map C and Table D provide information about the county of Avon in the south west of England. In some ways what they show is true of the rest of the United Kingdom (UK).

The table shows that there is a trend away from jobs in the manufacturing industry towards those in service industries like retailing, insurance and tourism.

Most new manufacturing industries are 'footloose'. They can be located anywhere there is electricity and good roads. They are usually found in an industrial estate on the edge of a city where the main roads go into the

(i)

(ii)

(iii)

(iv)

A Coping with difficult surroundings   *(i) Bridge over a flood plain in Burma   (ii) Spraying against malaria in Dubai   (iii) Irrigated plots and green houses in the desert, United Arab Emirates   (iv) Terraces in China*

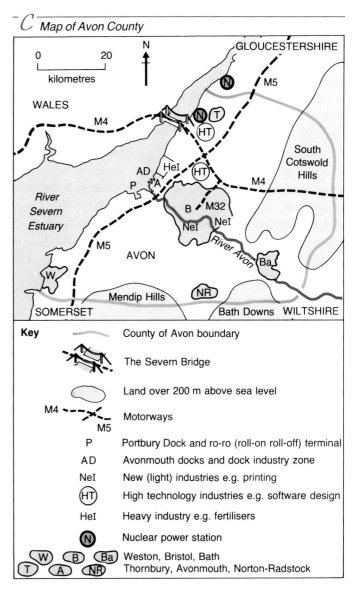

C Map of Avon County

B *Some rich, some poor – modern and traditional Kenyans*

city. Their products are small, easy to move, and produce little pollution, so the factories can be located near residential areas. They tend to have fewer workers than the old factories they have replaced.

Modern jobs demand different, often more advanced, skills to those of the past. For instance, automation, including robots, is replacing much of the repetitive work on production lines. This has caused some loss of jobs in larger manufacturing firms as they have tried to get up to date and have brought in new machinery.

The new service industry jobs are mainly concentrated in large shops, offices and restaurants, often in the middle of the city. Many of them need special skills such as word processing and computer literacy."

D Avon County employment

Classification of Employment	% in Avon 1917	% in GB 1971	% in Avon 1981	% in GB 1981
Agriculture, forestry and fishing	1.4	1.6	1.4	1.6
Mining and quarrying	0.3	1.8	0.2	1.5
Food, drink and tobacco	5.0	3.9	4.5	2.8
Coal, chemicals and metals	3.3	2.4	2.8	1.9
Textiles, leather and clothing	1.8	5.3	1.5	2.8
Engineering	5.4	7.0	5.0	5.0
Aerospace and vehicles	10.9	9.9	7.1	7.2
Bricks, pottery and furniture	1.0	0.8	1.7	1.8
Paper and printing	5.5	3.6	3.9	3.9
Other manufacturing	0.9	0.9	0.7	0.8
Construction	7.5	5.7	6.7	4.8
Gas, electricity and water	2.2	1.7	2.1	2.1
Transport and communications	7.0	7.1	6.9	6.6
Distribution	14.2	11.7	13.8	13.9
Insurance and banking	3.5	4.5	6.3	5.5
Professional education and health	14.1	14.5	15.2	15.3
Leisure and catering	10.3	11.2	13.0	14.3
Public administration	6.1	6.4	7.3	8.0
Total*	100	100	100	100

*slightly out because of rounding up

ASSESSMENT, KNOWLEDGE AND UNDERSTANDING

The questions in this book are attempts to demonstrate what is meant by the National Criteria for GCSE. All GCSE examinations have to conform to these criteria. Certain objectives must be tested and these will give the candidate the opportunity to show what he or she 'knows, understands and can do'. All the examinations must test these objectives, and in examinations where questions are optional, each question must give the same value or weighting to each objective. The objectives can be put into four groups:

Recall (R)
Understanding (U)
Skills (S)
Values (V)

The questions in this book are marked out of 25. This total is split into marks for the four groups. An example is given below:

Recall   6 (24%)   Understanding   12 (48%)
Skills   4 (16%)   Values   3 (12%)

In Chapters 3–12, these allocations are summarised in columns headed R, U, S, V, at the side of each question. The questions in Chapter 2 do not show these allocations since they are almost entirely concerned with testing skills. Some examination groups have specific skill-based questions or papers. Skills and values are explained in Units 1.2 and 1.3.

The major difference between the GCSE and previous examinations at 16+ is the increased importance of using facts rather than just memorising them. Nevertheless, some **recall** of knowledge is still required. 'Recall' means being able to remember facts, ideas and locations. In this book the recall sections refer to the information given in the unit to which a question refers. For example:

(i) In which county is Bristol?
(ii) What are the four ways in which the GCSE course should help Geography students?

Understanding covers a number of separate objectives:

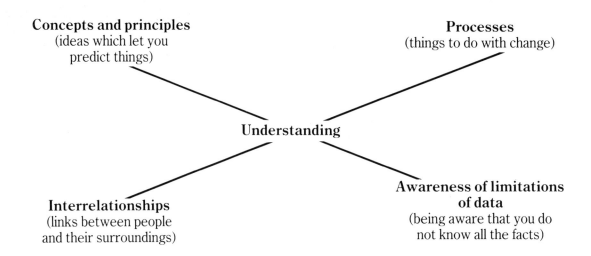

Concepts and principles
(ideas which let you
predict things)

Processes
(things to do with change)

Understanding

Interrelationships
(links between people
and their surroundings)

**Awareness of limitations
of data**
(being aware that you do
not know all the facts)

The questions will ask you to show an understanding of geographical **concepts** and **principles** and also an ability to apply them.

A **concept** is an idea which ties together lots of facts so as to make sense of them. A **principle** is a concept which allows you to predict what may be true about a place you have not studied. 'Ports have refining industries' is a principle. It means that a port (like Avonmouth, Singapore or Duisburg) might be expected to have industries like flour milling and sugar refining. GCSE questions will ask you to explain certain concepts and principles. They may also ask you to apply this knowledge to a new situation. For example, 'What do you understand by "high technology industry"? Explain why you think it is located where it is in the County of Avon.'.

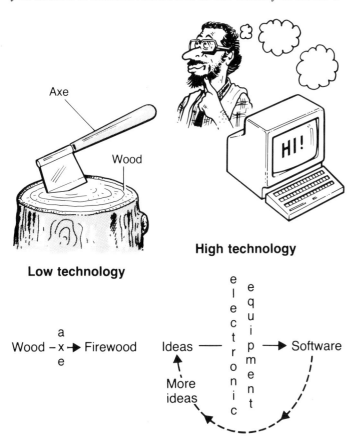

Low technology

High technology

$$\text{Wood} \xrightarrow[\text{e}]{\text{a}}_{\text{x}} \text{Firewood}$$

Ideas — electronic equipment → Software

More ideas

Processes are the forces at work in the environment which create and change our surroundings. These processes may be physical, like river action, or human, like building roads. For example, 'What factors have encouraged development of "footloose industries" near residential areas?'

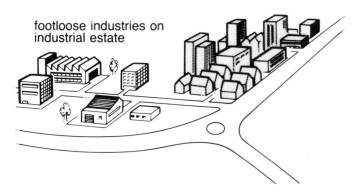

footloose industries on industrial estate

Interrelationships are the links between people, their activities and their environment. These relationships may be concerned with either physical or human geography or both. A typical question might be 'Why should Avon's two cities, Bristol and Bath, both be on the River Avon?' Study this photograph of a glaciated Highland area, and explain the advantages and disadvantages for human use.

E

Alternatively, the building of a new transport system would be expected to have a profound effect on the human geography of an area. For example, you could be asked to consider the changes resulting from the building of the Severn Bridge on the Severnside area.

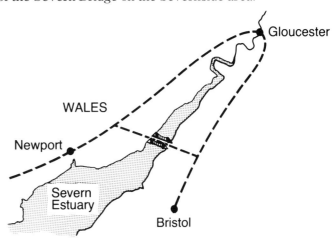

WALES

Gloucester

Newport

Severn Estuary

Bristol

For some questions you must show that you appreciate the limitations of geographical data and that many conclusions can only be tentative. It is often difficult to find complete explanations for things. For example, the percentage of people employed in 'Food, drink and tobacco' has gone down over the past 10 years both in Avon and in Great Britain, while the percentage of people employed in 'Leisure and catering' has gone up. Why do you think this is so?

SKILLS IN GCSE GEOGRAPHY

The skills needed for GCSE Geography can be divided into ten groups. They are important in many other subjects as well as Geography. All these skills have a long-term value, as you will find when you leave school for work or further training. Examples of each of the ten groups are shown below:

1 Research skills

These include:

(a) knowing where to look for information (in textbooks, the Yellow Pages, newspapers and so on)
(b) being able to pick out the facts you really need when searching through lots of information.

A When writing up your research, always give your sources, for example, 'From an article by F. Bloggs on page 5 of the East Middleshire Echo, 6/12/1990.'

Textbooks Magazines

STEPS IN GEOGRAPHY

MOTOR BIKE WEEKLY

Newspapers Yellow Pages

NEWCASTLE ECHO

BRIGHTON AND DISTRICT

B Research skills

Court cases reported in today's 'Evening Post'			
Nature of case	Verdict	Location of Incident	Neighbourhood of accused
Burglary	Guilty	Upton	Downton
Common assault	Not guilty	Carlton	Royston
Drunk and disorderly	Guilty	Shafton	Kelston
Speeding	Guilty	Marton	Leyton

2 Thinking skills

These include:

(a) analysing information (sorting the information out so you know what it means)
(b) interpreting data (deciding what the data tells you about the topic you are studying).

C Thinking skills

"...My results seem to be suggesting that there is a high rate of passenger vehicles moving inwards and a low rate outwards. The commercial vehicles do not show the same effect. There is a far higher rate of lorries flowing inwards but a lower rate of vans. At first this puzzled me, but this is what I think....

There is a higher rate of lorries going in due to the factory taking in supplies in the morning. There is a higher amount of vans going out because of shop deliveries from the shopping centre. The passenger vehicle flow is going into the shopping centre for the morning shopping..."

3 Writing skills

These include:

(a) sticking to the point without 'waffling'
(b) summarising the main points of a long piece of writing, such as an official document or text from a book, into a few short paragraphs
(c) planning and writing a long piece of work which is the result of a sensible investigation into the real world (In this, your findings may be surprising. The real world is very hard to make sense of.)

(d) describing things accurately as you see them, not just to fit the ideas you started with.

D Examples of GCSE writing

Striding Edge is an example of an arete. It is a sharp ridge leading to the summit of Hellvelyn in the Lake District.

During excavations at Somerdale, workers uncovered a Roman Villa. Relics uncovered included coffins, coins and jewellery.

Litter survey along cycle track

Plan
1 Map of cycle track.
2 What I set out to do: Walk along and record litter.
3 Survey record.
4 Map showing major litter sites.
5 Interpretation of findings.
6 Limitations.
7 Conclusion.

The factory waste outlet lies opposite the marina and constantly during the day the wastes of the factory flow into the river.

4 Mapping skills

These include:
(a) reading maps of various types
(b) drawing maps to suit the area and topic being studied.

E Mapping skills

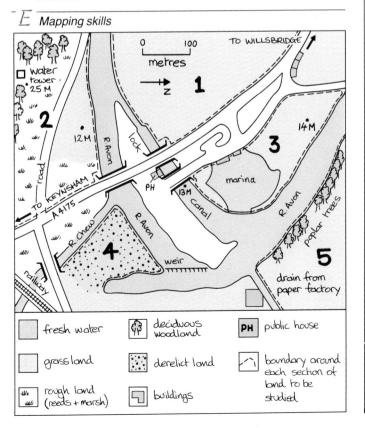

fresh water

grassland

rough land (reeds + marsh)

deciduous woodland

derelict land

buildings

PH public house

boundary around each section of land to be studied

5 Graph skills

These include:
(a) drawing line graphs to show how things are changing with time
(b) drawing bar (column) graphs to show the relative sizes of things
(c) drawing scatter graphs to show how two things seem to be linked
(d) interpreting these graphs.

F Graph skills

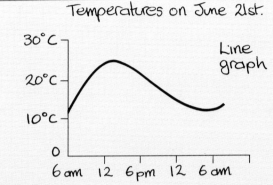

Temperatures on June 21st.

Line graph

The temperature rose quickly to a maximum at about 2pm then fell more slowly to a minimum at about 4 am.

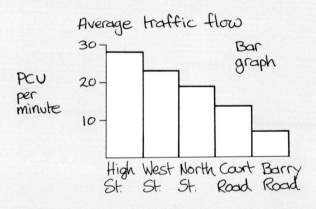

Average traffic flow

Bar graph

High Street had most traffic with 28 PCU/minute. Barry Road had least, with 6 PCU/minute. (PCU = Passenger Car Unit)

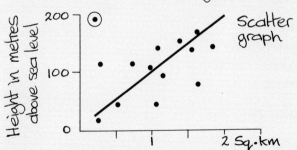

Scatter graph

Estimated area of individual woods on OS Map extract (1:50 000)

It looks as if the higher the site, the larger the woods are, but notice ⊙ which is high but small in area.

6   Diagram skills

These include:

(a) making simple drawings which show how landscape features are formed

(b) constructing accurate drawings from statistics.

G Diagram skills

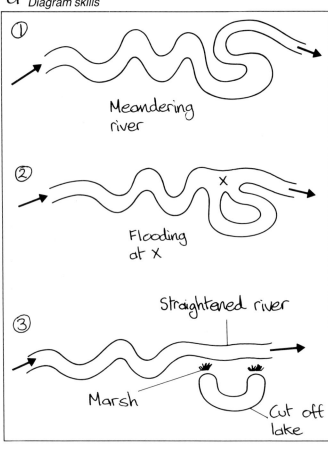

H Constructing accurate drawings from statistics

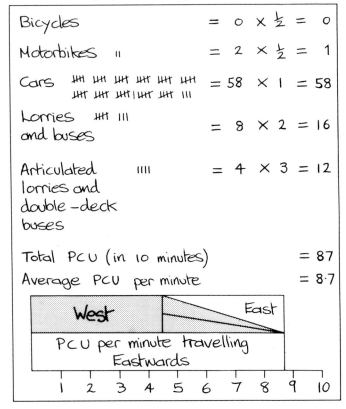

7   Photograph interpretation skills

These include:

(a) identifying features and looking for relationships between the landscapes shown by aerial and satellite photographs and images

(b) linking photographic information with that from large scale maps of the same area.

I Photograph interpretation skills

8   Sketching skills

These include:

(a) drawing simple sketches of a landscape (with labels)

(b) drawing simple sketches of buildings.

J Sketching skills

9   Fieldwork skills

These include:

(a) making sensible observations of features in the environment
(b) identifying major features in the environment
(c) thinking of definite questions or problems to study in the field
(d) planning how to investigate a question or problem
(e) collecting relevant data by research and direct observation
(f) analysing, presenting, interpreting and concluding the study.

10   Application skills

These are the skills involved in applying any or all of the above to issues or problems in the real world.

L Application skills – planning future land use

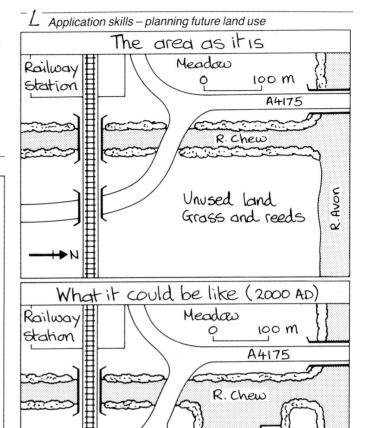

K Fieldwork skills

a Sydenham meadow is pasture land on the north bank of the River Avon.

b It consists of a flood plain and a river terrace.

c It could become a new site for contract builders. Where should they build?

d Cross section to be drawn after a foot survey of the site.

e R. Avon

key brambles   grass

f The most sensible solution is for the houses to be built on the river terrace, where floods do not reach.

On the eastern bank the river could be diverted to make a small lake. The lake could be used by 'radio-controlled boat' enthusiasts. A shop could rent out boats to the public at a fair price. All the profit would be spent on the upkeep of the boats and lake.

11   Labelling

Labelling is an important skill with points **4**, **5**, **6** and **8** described above. Labels should be small but clear, and should not clutter an illustration. It can even be useful to keep labels clear of illustrations, as shown opposite.

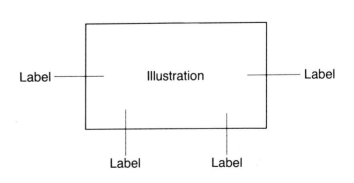

VALUES IN GEOGRAPHY

The GCSE National Criteria for Geography say that pupils should form **values** when studying the subject. What are values?

Knowledge and understanding in Geography are to do with questions like '*Where* is this place?' and '*What is going on* in this place?'. **Skills** in Geography are to do with the question '*How can we study* this place?'. **Values** are to do with your own judgement. Values questions often start off with the word 'Should'. They may ask whether, according to your judgement, a place should be where it is, or should be as it is. Diagram A shows some examples of questions to do with values.

Think about these three questions:
'Should you be able to set up a noisy timber cutting business in your back garden without getting permission from anyone?'
'Should food aid be provided for all hungry people or would that stop them growing food for themselves?'
'Should there be money back on all drink cans to encourage people not to litter the environment?'

These questions show that values can be to do with money or people's feelings or both. Even if your next-door neighbours offered you money to make up for any noise from their wood cutting business, you might prefer the peace and quiet to the extra money.

A Should or would?

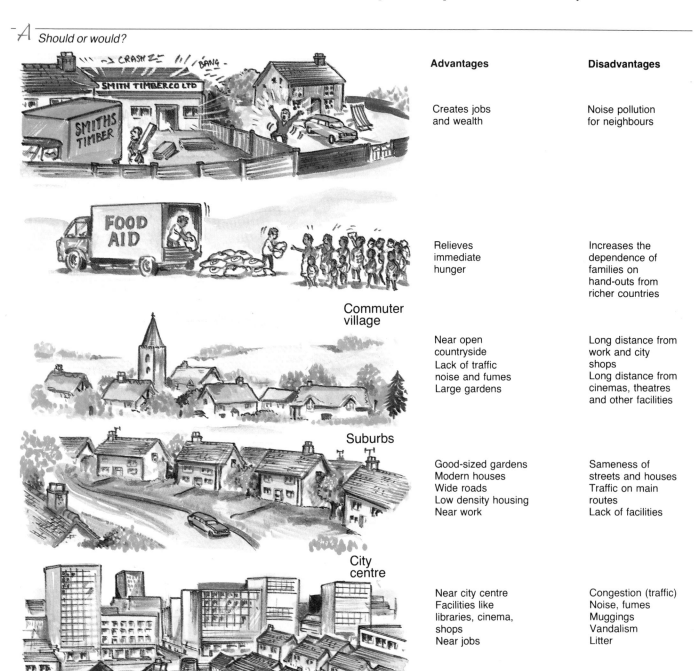

	Advantages	Disadvantages
	Creates jobs and wealth	Noise pollution for neighbours
	Relieves immediate hunger	Increases the dependence of families on hand-outs from richer countries
Commuter village	Near open countryside Lack of traffic noise and fumes Large gardens	Long distance from work and city shops Long distance from cinemas, theatres and other facilities
Suburbs	Good-sized gardens Modern houses Wide roads Low density housing Near work	Sameness of streets and houses Traffic on main routes Lack of facilities
City centre	Near city centre Facilities like libraries, cinema, shops Near jobs	Congestion (traffic) Noise, fumes Muggings Vandalism Litter

When you learn about values you become more aware of how things really happen. For instance, you will discover that how people *feel* about something is often as important as how much it will cost. The cheapest place for a sewage treatment works might be in the middle of a housing area but would people want it there? Studying this problem would make you aware of the importance of the people involved and the officials who make such decisions. The people involved are said to have a 'vested interest'. Do you think it would be fair if people with a vested interest were in charge of making the decisions about a problem?

When talking about values it is important to be clear about the difference between facts, which are definitely true, and opinions, which are what people think are true. Values are almost always opinions.

By thinking about values you can learn to see an issue as a whole, from *many* viewpoints, rather than from the first one you come across. You will then be better able to make a **balanced judgement** about what you think should be done.

'Evaluate' is a word that is sometimes used to ask what your values are about an issue. It is important to know how it differs from words such as 'describe' and 'explain'. To describe is to say **what** you think the facts are. To explain is to say **why** you think the facts are like that. To evaluate is to say **how important** you think each of the facts are.

Diagram B shows some of the viewpoints about what would seem to be a small decision, where to put a new telephone box in a street. Describe the viewpoints, explain why they are held and evaluate them (say how important they are). Putting things in order of importance is one way of evaluating them.

B *Where should a new telephone box be situated?*

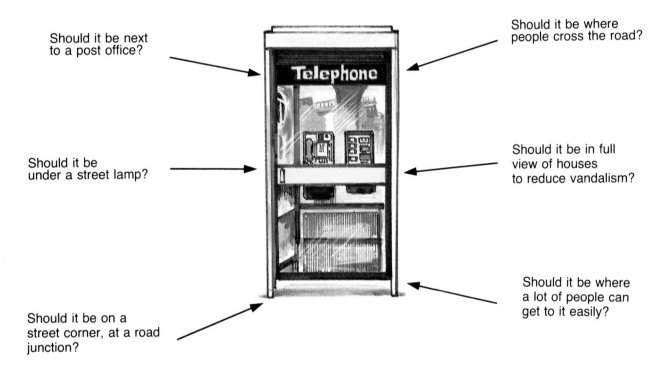

Should it be next to a post office?

Should it be where people cross the road?

Should it be under a street lamp?

Should it be in full view of houses to reduce vandalism?

Should it be on a street corner, at a road junction?

Should it be where a lot of people can get to it easily?

Study the information in Passage B and Sketch C. Then discuss the following questions with your friends. (Note the difference between describe, explain and evaluate.)

1 Describe any three facts about this issue and any three opinions.

2 Explain the attitude of the fertiliser plant workers when their government told the company to stop dumping waste in the harbour.

3 What might have happened if the fertiliser company had decided to shift its waste products elsewhere, where they would harm no-one?

4 How do you think the government should have handled the issue so as to keep the place prosperous. (You will realise that you really need more information to be definite about things, so use words like 'perhaps', 'may have' and 'possibly', rather than words which suggest you are absolutely sure.)

5 Evaluate which action, in your opinion, was at the heart of this problem. Was it the pumping, the riots or something else?

A

Group work can be a great help in sorting out facts, opinions, attitudes and values. In the end, though, everyone has the right to make up their own mind.

B "How a harbour died"

'But Jobim knew enough about certain kinds of people, about how stupidity and brutishness and greed could combine to drive a person to do things that even a moment's rational thought would perceive as destructive, to self as well as others. It was the promise of great profit at little expense and no risk, of quick money in the hand right now and don't worry that there won't be any more when the fish are gone. Someone else can weep over that. I'll get mine while I can, and other people can worry about themselves.

It was the same mentality that led the company that made fertiliser in the city to pump its chemical wastes into the harbour. The company got rid of its wastes, which was economical and good. The government, however, began to think that it wasn't a good idea to keep pumping chemicals into the harbour where people swam and fished so it told the company to stop.

The workers had rioted and tried to burn down the government building, because they said the company couldn't afford to haul its wastes elsewhere, and if it had to do so, some workers would lose their jobs and all would lose an impending raise in pay. The government backed down; the company continued to pump wastes into the harbour.

Two and a half years later, the harbour died. The chemicals had formed a poisonous sludge that coated the bottom and choked all the vegetation and shut off the oxygen in the water and killed every living thing. Guests at the luxury hotels, who swam in the harbour, began to come down with ghastly skin ulcers.

The government ordered the hotels to close and told the chemical company to stop pumping chemicals into the harbour. But the chemical company had made no plans to haul its wastes elsewhere, and so, compelled to stop using the harbour, it closed down.

Because there were no longer any hotels to stay in or restaurants to eat at or waters to swim in, the tourists and vacationers stopped coming to the city, and all the gift shops and boutiques closed and pitched their workers into the streets.

The workers at the chemical company had gotten their raise in pay, and for a few months had enjoyed the money. But because of their insistence on that new money they had lost everything. And it was not just they who were punished, but all the other workers who had lost their jobs. And eventually, 'all' became everybody, for the city was deprived of a reason to exist, and slowly but inevitably it ceased to exist.

Nowadays it was a dusty cluster of empty buildings in a ring around the still-dead harbour, with the skeleton of the chemical company standing on a promontory as a reminder to passersby of the fragility of things.'
(From *The Girl of the Sea of Cortez*, by Peter Benchley, published by André Deutsch, 1982.)

C

Before

many fishing boats and touring yachts in harbour

fertiliser factory

lots of lorry traffic on main road

several large hotels

lots of holiday makers

After

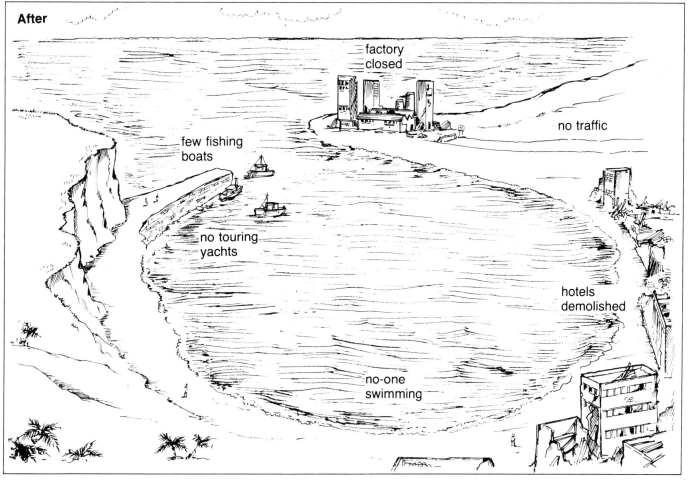

factory closed

no traffic

few fishing boats

no touring yachts

hotels demolished

no-one swimming

GEOGRAPHICAL ENQUIRY

All GCSE syllabuses include a minimum of 20 per cent of the final examination mark for coursework, which usually includes some kind of geographical enquiry. Many other names are given to this part of the syllabus. Here are some of them:

Geographical investigation
Enquiry-based practical unit
Individual study
Fieldwork study
Practical observation

All Examination Groups say that some **fieldwork** must be included in a geographical inquiry. Fieldwork is a first-hand study of a geographical feature. Diagram A shows some topics suitable for fieldwork.

Some Groups ask for more than one enquiry. At least one of these must include fieldwork. The others may be studies using **secondary material**. This means things that other people have written or drawn. (It is called secondary because it is 'second-hand' knowledge.) Diagram B shows some ways of studying secondary material.

-A-

-B-

Learning to do your own fieldwork is useful. Firstly, you gain skills (often painfully, by getting things wrong, and having to do them again!). Secondly, you learn to appreciate what other fieldworkers have had to do to gain the knowledge that goes into their writing, sketches, diagrams and maps. Thirdly, you learn that no matter how hard you try, no-one's first-hand studies are perfect. When you have finished your fieldwork you will know that there are lots of ways it could be improved if you had the time. The same is true of all fieldwork that has been done for the first time. It should not stop you. Just think, 'If I get it wrong, I will get it right next time!'.

Geographical enquiries should have a plan. Sensible planning is essential if you are to do any job properly. The notes and drawings in Diagram C will help to explain each of the stages:

1 Finding something to do
2 Thinking of a title
3 Deciding how to do the fieldwork
4 Collecting the data
5 Presenting the data
6 Interpreting the data
7 Being honest about any sources of error
8 Conclusion (What have you found out? How useful is it?)
9 Ideas for follow-on studies
10 Sources of any secondary material used.

Most projects have to be between 1000 and 2500 words long. With drawings this means between 10 and 25 sides of A4 paper. However, no-one is going to count every word. The people who mark it will not worry if it is short but good!

The best approach is to decide on something you know you can do, plan it carefully, do it honestly and write it up quickly. Show it to as many people as you can to get their comments. Make your own mind up about it and change it where necessary. Then hand it in and get on with something else. Do not spend weeks and weeks trying to get it perfect – you never will!

(7)

Too much traffic to count

(8) Conclusion: Apart from a few odd results, the wider the road the greater the traffic density.

(9) Follow on study: Enquire into the odd results.

(10) Sources: textbooks, TV, radio, photos, maps, software, magazines, newspapers

—C————

(1) Make sure you can do it without spending too much time, effort and money. Collect data close to where you live. Try to make it useful. All things <u>can be</u> interesting.

What should be done about the traffic hazard at Mylane?

(2) Write the title as a short question. 'Is the wind direction the same at various heights above an observer?'

(3)

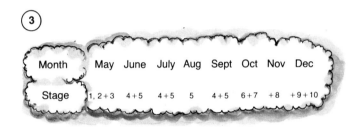

Month	May	June	July	Aug	Sept	Oct	Nov	Dec
Stage	1, 2 + 3	4 + 5	4 + 5	5	4 + 5	6 + 7	+ 8	+ 9 + 10

(4)

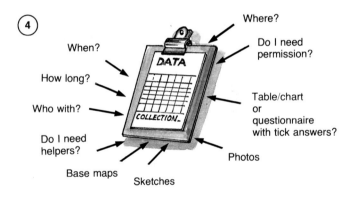

When? How long? Who with? Do I need helpers? Base maps Sketches Photos Table/chart or questionnaire with tick answers? Do I need permission? Where?

(5)

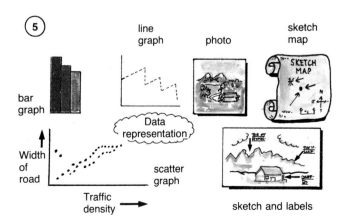

line graph   photo   sketch map

bar graph

Data representation

Width of road

Traffic density

scatter graph

sketch and labels

(6) Interpretation: putting into words what the data shows.

An example of a geographical enquiry (in note form)

1   Finding something to do
I am interested in the weather. Weather studies are on the syllabus. I have been taught to read meteorological instruments. I listen a lot to local radio. Why not see if the radio weather forecast is correct for the school area.

2   Finding a title
I must put it as a question. It must be precise. I must listen to hear exactly what is being forecast, then think what I can record on my own and then choose my title. 'How accurate is the local weather station's 07.55 hrs daily forecast for Mytown High School site?'

Add any important details as a sub-title, for example: 'With reference to temperature, wind direction, wind force, pressure and rainfall)'.

3   How to plan the fieldwork, collecting secondary material and write-up
Draw up a table for recording data from the radio forecast and from your own fieldwork on school Stevenson screen instruments. Record data from regular 7.55am forecast on local radio.

Take readings each morning break at 10.30 hrs.

Repeat for each school day in June, July and September (50 days approximately).

Write up in October. Take more readings in October or November if needed. Ask friends, relatives and teachers for comments.

(Geography teachers are allowed to help you up to a point if they have the time!)

Hand in at Christmas.

Start to write up introduction by saying why I chose the topic and title and how I planned to do the job.

Also give a brief description of school area. (Put in map and photocopy of aerial photo to make it clear.)

4   Collecting the data
Each morning at 7.55am. Fill in the forecasted temperature, wind direction, wind force, pressure and rainfall on the table.

At 10.30am fill in the same things from first-hand observations at school. (Use own judgement of wind force and direction.) Table D shows what the first few readings will look like.

5   Presenting the data
Put completed table in the write-up to show how data was collected.

Draw bar and line graphs from data. Show any differences between the two sets of data (Graph E).

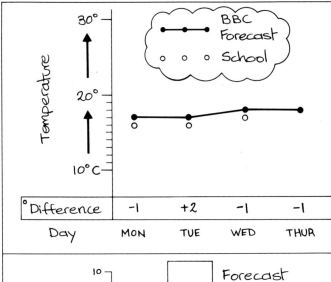

E   Line and bar graphs

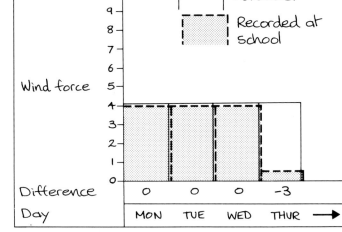

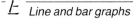

D   Collecting the weather data

Day	Forecast Temperature	School Temperature	Difference	Forecast Wind force	School Wind force	Difference	Forecast Wind direction	School Wind direction	Difference	Forecast Pressure	School Pressure	Difference	Forecast Rainfall	School Rainfall	Difference
1. June 2	17	16	1	4	4	—	SW	SW	—	1020	1015	5	—	—	—
2. June 3	17	16	1	4	4	—	SW	SW	—	1018	1013	5	—	—	—
3. June 4	18	17	1	4	4	—	SW	SW	—	1019	1014	5	—	—	—
4. June 5	18	18	—	4	1	3	S	S	—	1010	1014	4	—	—	—

6   Interpreting the data

Look carefully for any patterns in the differences in the data from day to day. Show it clearly in the write-up in words or drawings. Experiment with ways of showing just what I mean. (Invent drawings like F to help.)

F   Possible reasons for temperature and pressure differences

Temperature . . .   Places 100 m higher than others have 1°C lower temperatures.

Pressure . . .   The higher you are, the lower the pressure.

165 m asl   SCHOOL

65 m asl   100 m difference

So this MAY explain the lower temperatures and lower pressures than forecast

---

The two sets of results seem close but school temperatures and pressure are usually slightly lower than the forecast ones. Maybe this is because the school site is 100m higher than the weather centre. In textbook it says 100m = 1°C and 5mb difference near sea level. This fits the results.

One or two wind directions and forces are very different, though mostly they are similar.

Calculate the percentage difference between my results and the weather centre data. (Table G.)

G

WEATHER	TOTAL COMPARED	SIMILAR RESULTS	%
Temperature	50	44	88
Wind force	50	39	78
Wind direction	50	36	72
Pressure	50	41	82
	200	160	80

∴ % difference = 20%   Similarity = 80%

---

7   Sources of error

Wind directions and forces were difficult because they seem to change from minute to minute.

Didn't take readings at weekends. Might have missed some differences.

Forgot to listen to forecast four times!

School barometer pinched by science teacher for a week for teaching. No readings taken!

8   Conclusions

(i)   The weather centre's forecast is pretty accurate. 85 per cent of the readings taken were exactly the same, when the 100m difference in height was taken into account. Rainfall was exactly right, it only rained three times and they were all forecast.

(ii)   The main differences were in wind direction and force now and again. I cannot explain them but they were changing all the time when I took my readings. Maybe I should have taken five readings at one minute intervals and worked out an average. (No time to do this anyway.) Maybe local conditions cause these differences.

(iii)   General conclusion is that the forecast was pretty good and a useful guide to local weather.

9   Further study ideas

Could look into the differences in wind force and direction to see if the weather centre actually gets them wrong or whether local conditions cause the differences.

10   Sources of secondary data

Textbook: *Examining GCSE Geography*, Bateman and Rowles, Hutchinson 1988

Atlas

OS 1:50 000 sheet 172

Local radio weather forecast

Mytown weather centre

My geography teacher.

2. Mapwork

TYPES OF ORDNANCE SURVEY MAP

The Ordnance Survey (OS) produces accurate, official maps of the whole of Great Britain. There are six types of OS map, each with a different scale. The scale tells you what real distance on the ground is represented by a length on the map. For example, 1 cm on the map represents 2.5 km on the ground on a 1:250000 map.

To read a map you need to understand these things:

(a) scale
(b) distances
(c) grid references
(d) directions and bearings
(e) symbols and the key
(f) heights.

A brief reminder of these skills is given in Diagrams A to F.

A Straight line distances

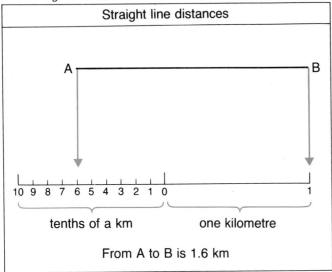

Straight line distances

From A to B is 1.6 km

tenths of a km — one kilometre

C Four figure grid references

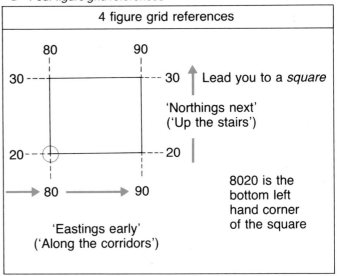

4 figure grid references

Lead you to a *square*

'Northings next' ('Up the stairs')

8020 is the bottom left hand corner of the square

'Eastings early' ('Along the corridors')

B Non-straight lines

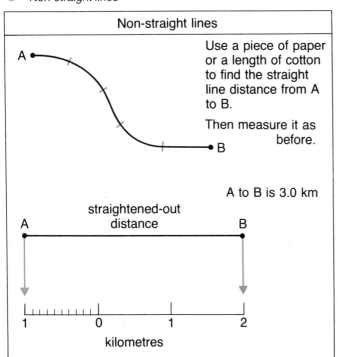

Non-straight lines

Use a piece of paper or a length of cotton to find the straight line distance from A to B.

Then measure it as before.

A to B is 3.0 km

straightened-out distance

kilometres

D Six figure grid references

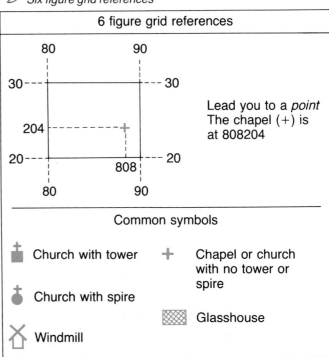

6 figure grid references

Lead you to a *point*
The chapel (+) is at 808204

Common symbols

Church with tower

Church with spire

Windmill

Chapel or church with no tower or spire

Glasshouse

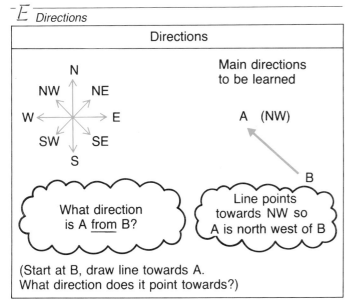

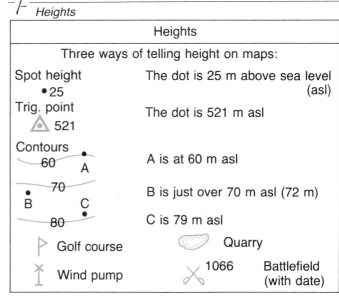

The six types of OS map are shown below.

1 Routemaster maps are at a scale 1:250000 (1 cm to 2.5 km). Nine of them cover the country.

2 Landranger maps are at a scale of 1:50000 (1 cm to 0.5 km). 204 of them cover England, Scotland and Wales.

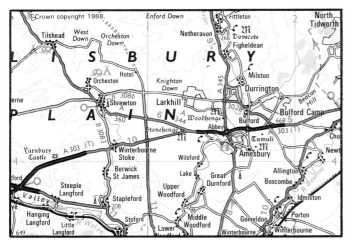

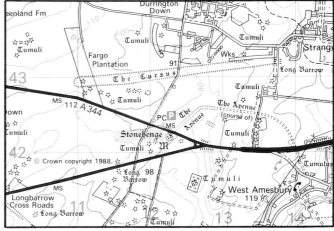

Characteristics

Routemaster maps have colour shading and contours to show height. Roads have distances shown along them between markers. Telephone, radio and tourist information is also shown.

Uses

They are designed for motorists to find the shortest, quietest or most scenic route between places. They can be used by business people or holidaymakers.

Characteristics

Landranger maps have contours at ten metre vertical intervals which show ground height very accurately. Footpaths which are rights of way (the public has a right to use them) are clearly shown. The pattern of roads in towns and villages is shown.

Uses

They are all-purpose maps for people who want to get to know an area well. They are widely used in schools and by walkers, cyclists and motorists wanting to see details of their route.

3   Pathfinder maps are at a scale of 1:25 000 (1 cm to 0.25 km). There are 816 of them.

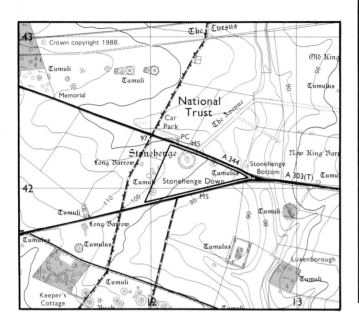

Characteristics
Pathfinder maps show the same things as Landranger maps but in twice the amount of detail for a smaller area. They also show field boundaries.

Uses
They are very useful for anyone wanting details of an area for walking, cycling or surveys of farms or villages.

4   1:10 560 maps (1 cm to 100 m).

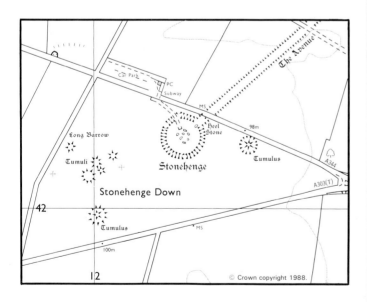

Characteristics
1:10 560 maps show local areas of 10 km by 5 km. They have ten metre interval contours.

Uses
They are used for detailed study of urban or rural field patterns. Town planners use them to make local plans.

5   1:2500 maps (1 cm to 25 m).

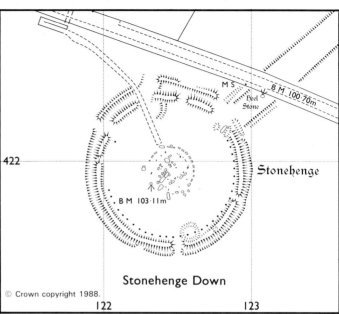

Characteristics
1:2500 maps show the areas of fields, the width of roads and have many spot heights to show the exact height of the land between the contours.

Uses
They can be used by farmers or engineers who need to know details within fields or streets.

6   1:1250 maps (1 cm to 12.5 m).

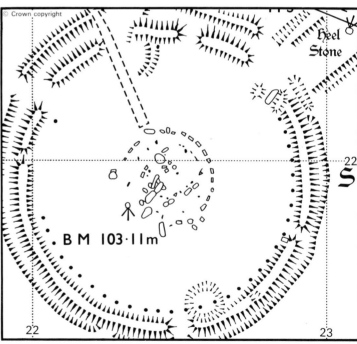

Characteristics
1:1250 maps are the most detailed OS maps on general sale. They show details of individual houses and gardens.

Uses
They are used by town planners to study plans for house extensions and other proposed changes.

1   (i) What are the scales of the following maps?

      Landranger ....

      Pathfinder (2) ....

  (ii) Suggest a use a geographer might find for each of these two types of map. (2)

....

....

....

....

2 Study the map extract 458/127 on page 29.
    (i) What is the scale of this map extract? (1)

....

  (ii) What is the distance in kilometres from the church at Lawley (668087) to the church at Little Wenlock (647068) in a straight line? (1)

....

  (iii) What is the distance, to the nearest kilometre, along the River Severn from easting 61 to the bridge at 645044? (1)

....

  (iv) What is situated at each of the following grid references?

     679015 ....

     672034 ....

     703025 (3) ....

  (v) State the four figure grid reference for the council offices at Dawley. (1)

....

  (vi) State the six figure grid reference for

     the junction on the A442 just east of Stirchley

....

     the highest point of the Wrekin. (2) ....

  (vii) Name the main land use in square 6207 (1).

....

  (viii) In what direction does Little Wenlock (6406) lie from Leighton (6105)? (1)

....

  (ix) Describe the human features visible in the area shown in square 6805. (7)

....

....

....

....

....

....

....

....

....

....

....

....

....

  (x) What is the height of the triangulation pillar on top of the Wrekin? (1)

....

  (xi) What is the difference in height between the top of the Wrekin and the trig. point at 646004? (1)

....

  (xii) What direction is the church at Buildwas from Little Wenlock? (1)

....

Note: These questions are all 'skills' exercises (see page 8).

MAPS AND LANDFORMS

Ordnance Survey maps provide a source of information on the **landforms** in an area and how people make use of the land (**land use**). Together these form the **landscape** of the area shown on the map.

Here are some ways to use the landform information. As you see, contours are a valuable source of evidence.

1 Contour patterns showing slopes

A Identifying different slopes

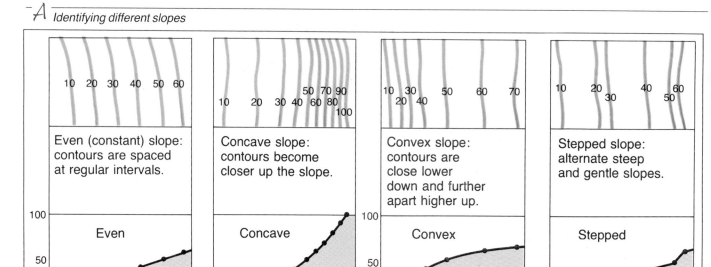

2 Contours and gradients

A gradient is a measure of how steep a slope is. A low gradient shows a gentle slope, a high gradient shows a steep slope.

B Gradients

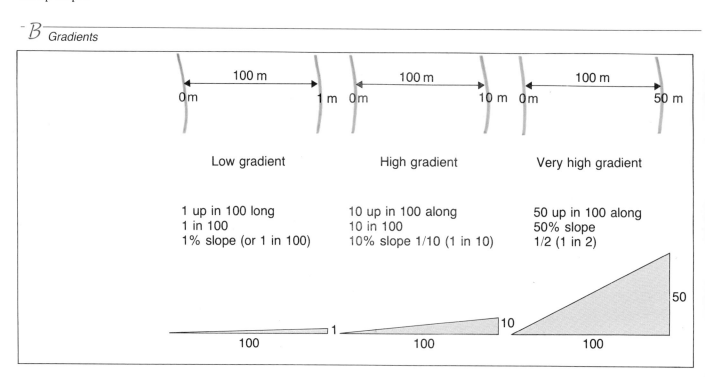

3   Cross sections and intervisibility

By plotting from contours you can draw a cross section to see what the surface looks like. 'Intervisibility' is whether it is possible to see between two points on the ground. To find out, you draw a cross section between them. In the cross section below, you can see A from B but you cannot see C from B.

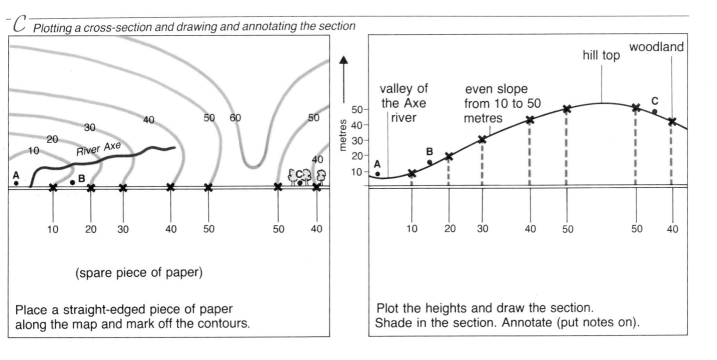

C Plotting a cross-section and drawing and annotating the section

(spare piece of paper)

Place a straight-edged piece of paper along the map and mark off the contours.

Plot the heights and draw the section.
Shade in the section. Annotate (put notes on).

4   Contour patterns and landforms

The contour pattern and cross section in Diagram D and Sketch E show typical lowland scenery.

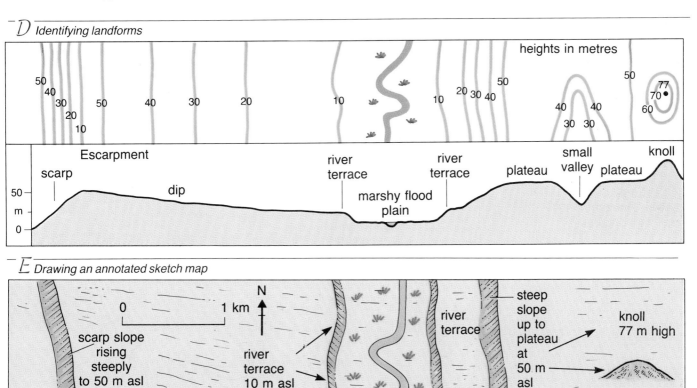

D Identifying landforms

E Drawing an annotated sketch map

F Identifying landforms: glaciated highlands

Contours

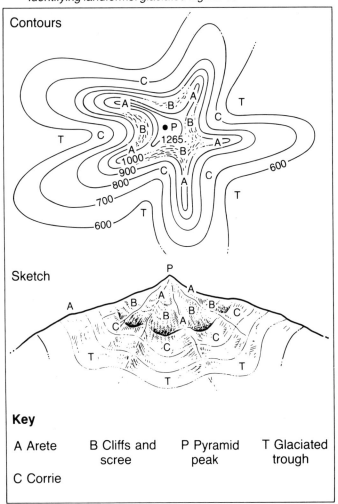

Sketch

Key

A Arete   B Cliffs and   P Pyramid   T Glaciated
             scree   peak   trough

C Corrie

G Identifying landforms: coasts

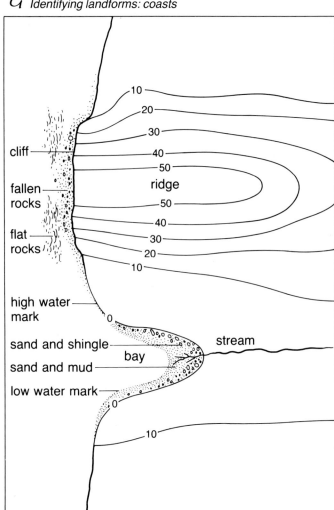

5 Drainage basins and watersheds

A drainage basin is the land drained by a river and all its tributaries. A watershed is the ridge of high ground which separates drainage basins.

H Drainage basins and watersheds

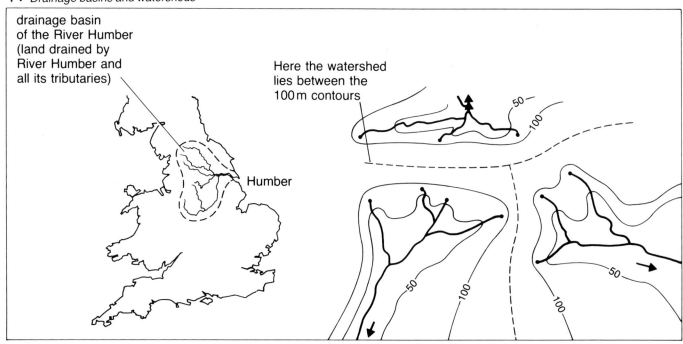

drainage basin of the River Humber (land drained by River Humber and all its tributaries)

Humber

Here the watershed lies between the 100 m contours

Assessment MAPS AND LANDFORMS

Study map extract 458/127 below.

1   Look at the following squares and name the type of slope found there.

6208 ....

7001 ....

6607 (3) ....

2   Draw a section along the bridleway from 646019 to 658001. (3)

3   Draw an annotated sketch section across the valley of the River Severn along easting 63 from 630020 to 630070.
Mark in the main physical and human features. (8)

4   How does the shape of the valley's cross section at Ironbridge (6703) differ from the one you have drawn? (3)

....

....

....

5   Would it be possible to see Huntington (6507) from the other side of Woodgreen 6108?
Explain your answer. (2)

....

....

6   Draw an annotated sketch map showing the relief of the area between eastings 61 and 65 and northings 07 and 09. (6)

xtract 458/127

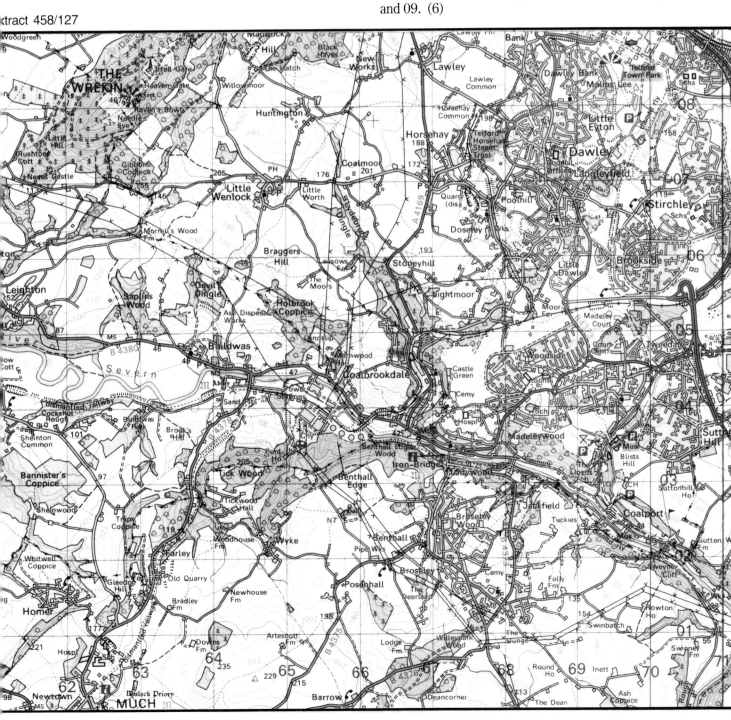

Ordnance Survey can be used in many ways to find out about land use. Five of these ways are shown here. Other types of map can also provide evidence of land use, and some important ones are shown in point 6 below.

1 Showing distribution of land use

Distributions should always be shown by a simple map like Map B below. It shows that in the area shown on Extract A, woodland is found on steep slopes or on the plateau.

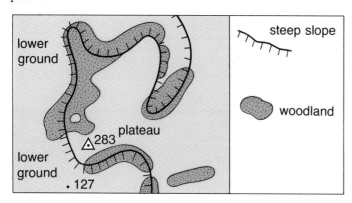

2 Patterns of settlement

Rural settlement is either isolated like Goffin's Farm, in hamlets like Woodrow Barton or in villages.
Upton Pyne is a linear village. It extends along the line of a minor road.
Stoke Canon is a nucleated village. It is more compact with a centre.

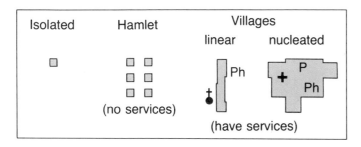

Urban settlement patterns show their age.
Old centres have short streets with no particular pattern.
Victorian parts (100 years old) have straight streets.
Newer suburbs have crescents and cul-de-sacs.

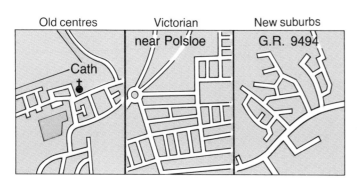

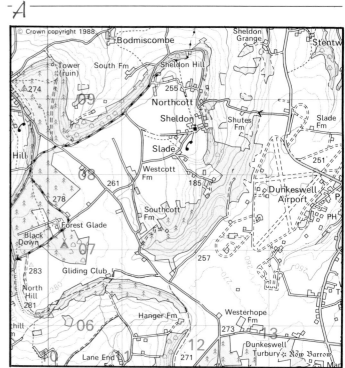

- A -

- B -

3 Communication patterns

Railways and motorways need low gradients, so they follow valleys wherever possible. They have cuttings and embankments to keep the route as level as possible (south of Strathculm).

A and B class roads usually follow gentle gradients along the river terraces (between the flood plains and valley sides). They are sometimes found on steeper gradients but are less straight, to reduce the slope.

Minor roads can go straight up steep slopes and often do so with sharp bends (near Pottshayes Farm).

4 Evidence of ancient human activity

Tumuli (one tumulus, several tumuli) are ancient burial mounds. Many have been ploughed up. Those which are left are often found on high moors. They date back over 2000 years.

A villa shows that Romans lived in an area. They also left evidence in Roman signal stations, Roman roads (very straight) and Roman temples.
Sites and dates of battles are also shown.

Note: *Map extracts A, B, C, D and E are all taken from the Ordnance Survey 1:50 000 Landranger series, Sheet 192 (Exeter and Sidmouth)*

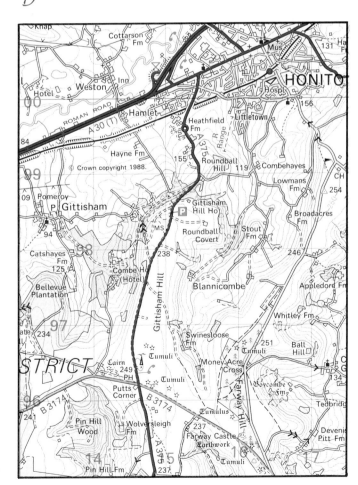

5   Evidence of industry

 A quarry shows that the rock in an area has a commercial use. Granite and sandstone are used for building. Limestone is used for roads and limestone and chalk are used for making cement.

 shows a colliery with a coal spoil heap.

 shows a factory or public industry like a sewage works (often by a river).

 shows storage tanks and an oil refinery.

6   Other types of map

There are various other types of map which are useful for people studying particular types of land use. Some are listed below:

(a) Land utilisation survey maps
(b) Soil survey maps
(c) Town plan maps
(d) Leisure maps
(e) Road maps (e.g. AA or RAC)
(f) Maps of industrial layouts (e.g. steelworks).

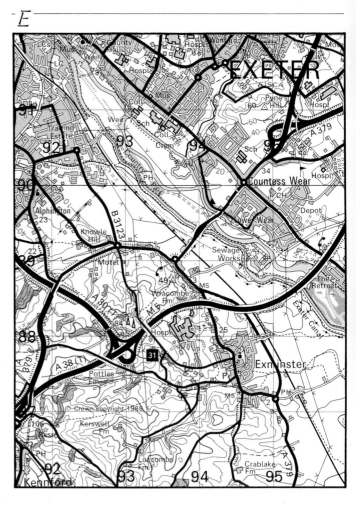

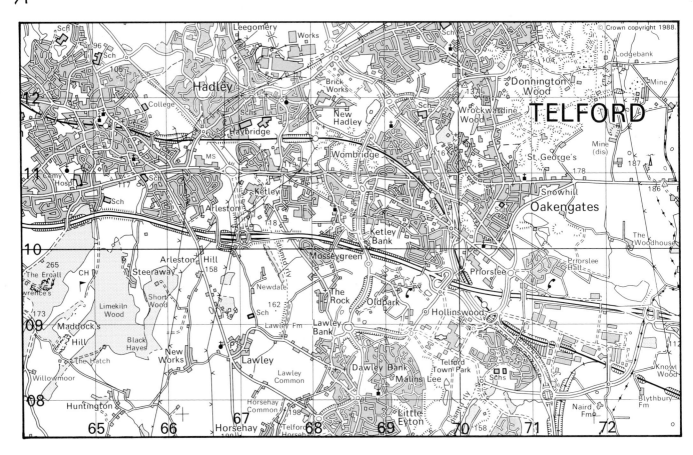

Assessment MAPS AND LAND USE

1 Study the following sketch map based on OS map extract number 453/127 (page 29).

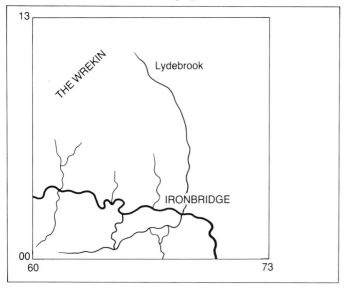

(i) Mark on the sketch map the main areas of woodland. (4)

(ii) Describe the distribution of woodland on the map extract. (2)

....

....

....

....

(iii) Suggest reasons for the pattern you have shown. (3)

....

....

....

....

....

2 Study the areas of Wellington (Map A squares 6412, 6411, 6512, 6511) and Brookside and Stirchley (page 29, squares 6906, 6905, 7007 and 7005).

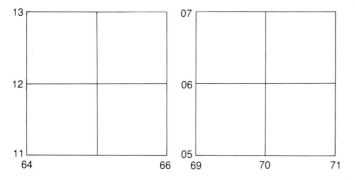

(i) Sketch the layout pattern on the grids provided. (4)

(ii) Describe and explain the different urban settlement patterns of these two areas. (4)

....

....

....

....

....

....

....

....

3 Study Map A opposite. How has past economic activity influenced the built up area of Telford? (3) Illustrate your answer with a sketch map. (5)

....

....

....

....

....

....

MAPS, PHOTOGRAPHS AND IMAGES

Three types of photograph are helpful in geographical map studies:

1 Satellite photographs

These are more correctly 'images', as they may be recorded electronically. They are taken from space by man-made satellites such as Landsat and Meteosat. Landsat is designed to send back information to show differences in ground surface coverings such as forest or farmland. Meteosat is designed to show differences in cloud cover and type. Such images give an overview of hundreds or thousands of square kilometres of land and sea and show patterns which may not be noticed by ground level map makers.

2 Aerial photographs

These are taken from the air by aircraft.
They will be either (a) vertical: pointing straight down at something or (b) oblique: pointing down at an angle at something.

Aerial photographs usually show areas of between one and ten square kilometres. The outer detail of buildings can be seen. Building types which look the same on maps (factories, houses or offices) can be recognised as different. People and vehicles can be seen and counted. Shadows show the angle of the sun, which can be used with the map to tell when in the day the photograph was taken. (Long shadows pointing west indicate the morning; short ones pointing north are at noon; long ones pointing east indicate the evening.) Leaf cover on trees is a clue to the season. Farm machinery, animals and work in progress may give clues to the type of land use.

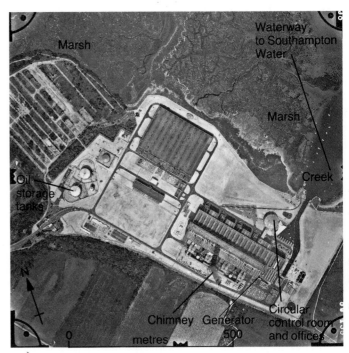

A Vertical aerial photograph of Fawley Power Station. The power station is on the marshy coastal plain to the west of Southampton Water in OS grid square 4702. The chimney shadow points to the north east. The Sun must have been in the south west. The photograph must have been taken in the afternoon. Notice the oil storage tanks, the generating buildings and the control room.

B Landsat image of the Solent region. The dark blue built up areas of Southampton and Portsmouth show up clearly. In the countryside the brown areas are forest and the green shows arable field crops near the coast. Fawley Power Station can just be made out as a blue built up patch near the spit on which Calshott Castle is built.

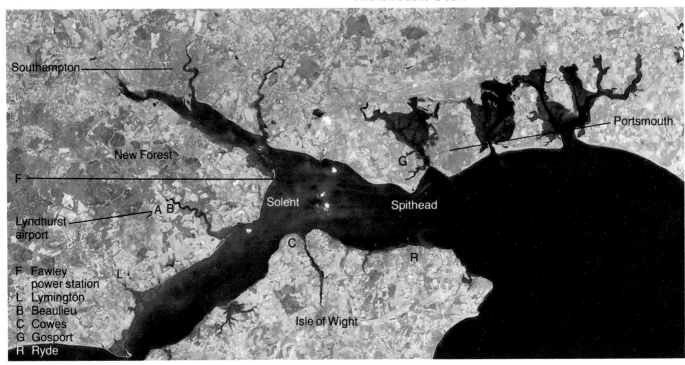

3 Ordinary photographs taken at ground level

These photographs show a smaller area than aerial ones but in much more detail. Street, shop and town names may be seen. Types of crop and their stage of growth may be obvious in the countryside.

Landsat image B and Photographs A, D and E show Fawley Power Station, an oil fired power station owned by the Central Electricity Generating Board (CEGB). These different sources can be used to give useful information about the power station and its location, as shown on Map C.

C OS map of Fawley Power Station site

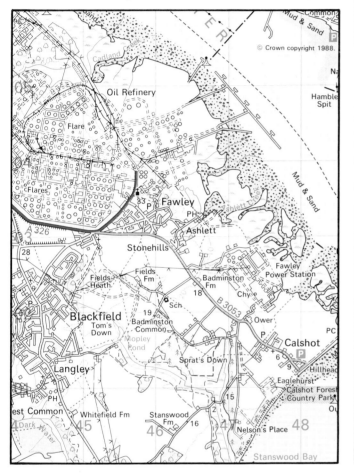

© Crown copyright 1988.

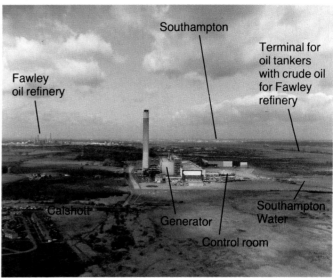

D *Oblique aerial photograph looking north west towards Fawley Power Station and Southampton. This photograph shows the site and situation of Fawley Power Station. It is sited on a marshy coastal lowland near a creek. Its situation is 2 km south east of Fawley Oil Refinery on the western shores of Southampton Water. The terminal for the oil tankers which bring oil for the refinery and power station can be seen in the photograph. It is shown in GR 4704 on the map extract. The village of Calshott (4701) is seen in the foreground of the photograph.*

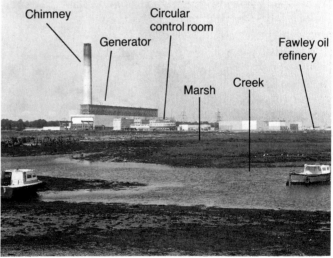

E *This photograph shows how close Fawley Power Station is to the creek on Southampton Water. Details of the generator, the control room and the boundary fence are clear. Fawley oil refinery is seen on the right of the photograph. The photograph was taken looking north west from a point at about 480 022 on the map extract.*

Guide to satellite imagery

Satellite images are made up from data which is 'sensed' by recording devices within the satellite. Images can either be shown in 'true colour', where the colours of objects appear as they would in a normal photograph, or in 'false colour', where different colours are given to different characteristics of the photograph. Satellites often sense areas using infra red light instead of visible light, as infra red light can pass through cloud cover and so can provide an image of the land surface even on cloudy days.

Landsat image A shows an infra red image, and the key to the false colours is as follows:

Black – deep sea
Blue-grey – built-up areas
Green – shallow sea
Red – pastoral farming of mature crops
Light grey – newly ploughed land
Brown – woodland
Grey-green – moorland

Study OS map extract A to help with these questions.

1 Study Landsat image B.
  (i) Name the place marked X on the Landsat image. (1)

....

  (ii) What information does the Landsat image give about the land use at Z? (2)

....

....

....

....

2 Study the vertical aerial photograph C.
  (i) Name the island shown. (1)

....

  (ii) Study the places marked A, B, C, D and E. Write against each of the letters the correct feature from the list below:

Offshore deposition   Woodland   Sandy beach
Built up area   Power station   Island lake

A .... (1)

B .... (1)

C .... (1)

D .... (1)

E .... (1)

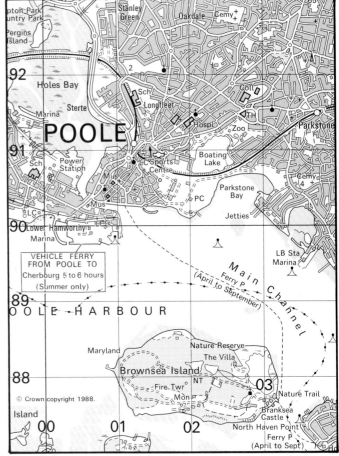

A

B

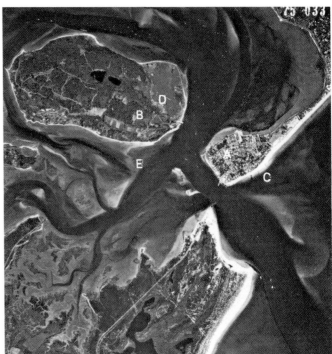

C

3 Study oblique aerial photograph D.
Find features A, B and C on the photograph. Give the four figure grid reference for each feature and write one fact about it. (6)

....

....

....

....

....

....

D

4 Study Photograph E, taken from ground level in Parkstone, Dorset.
    Draw a simple sketch of the area shown on Photograph E, labelling
  (i)   holiday homes
  (ii) a spit
  (iii) sand and mud flats. (3)
  Give your sketch a suitable title. (1)

....

5 Use any information available on this page to give your opinion of Poole Harbour's advantages and disadvantages for recreation and tourism. (6)

....

....

....

....

....

....

....

E

Unit 3.1
TECTONIC ACTIVITY AND PEOPLE

'Tecton' was the word Ancient Greeks used for a builder. **Tectonic activity** is the movement of the Earth, which builds its surface into certain shapes and features.

Although we think of the ground beneath us as solid, in some parts of the world it moves! Map A shows how the continents have moved apart over the last 200 million years. This movement is very slow, about one centimetre per year. In 1 000 000 years this is 10 000 metres or 10 kilometres. In 200 million years the movement is 2000 km.

In some parts of the world the movement is much faster. Pressure to move builds up in the Earth's crust and the rocks suddenly tear, moving everything on top of them. The force of such **earthquakes** is measured on a scale invented by an American, C.R. Richter, in 1935.

B Simplified Richter scale and effects of earthquakes

Force	Effects
Below 3.5	Noticed by instruments only
3.5 to 3.9	Slight vibrations, hardly noticed
4.0 to 4.4	Vibrations like a lorry passing by
4.5 to 4.9	Vibrations shake loose objects
5.0 to 5.4	Trees sway; church bells ring
5.5 to 5.9	Building walls crack; plaster falls
6.0 to 6.4	Traffic stops; chimneys fall
6.5 to 6.9	Weak buildings collapse
7.0 to 7.4	Ground cracks; many buildings fall; gas, electricity and water supplies badly affected
7.5 to 7.9	Few buildings left standing; service pipes ruined; fires; dams burst; floods
Above 8.0	Total destruction; ground rises and falls in waves

The highest ever recording was 8.9 for an earthquake in Alaska in 1960.

A simple version of this scale is shown in Table B with descriptions of what earthquakes of each force can do in an area where people live.

The place at the centre of an earthquake is called the **epicentre**. It gets the shock waves first. The shock waves then spread through the Earth's crust to places further away.

Map C shows areas where the Earth's tectonic activity is most intense. These areas are at the edges of **tectonic plates**. Tectonic plates are large sections which make up the Earth's crust. They float on the hot molten rocks of the mantle beneath. They are moved by convection currents caused by very high temperatures deep within the mantle. At the boundaries of the moving plates earthquakes occur and **volcanoes** erupt. Where ocean plates meet continental plates, great ranges of **fold mountains** are raised up.

A Map showing how continents have moved

A

Laurasia

Gondwanaland

B

| Trench | | New ocean floor |
| Rift | | Zones of slippage |

A
180 million years ago the continents looked like this. The arrows show which way the continents were moving.

B
Now the continents look like this. *But* they are still moving. The arrows show the direction of movement.

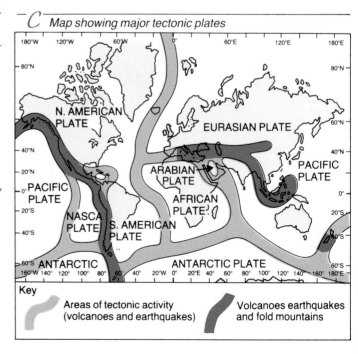

C Map showing major tectonic plates

N. AMERICAN PLATE

EURASIAN PLATE

PACIFIC PLATE

ARABIAN PLATE

PACIFIC PLATE

AFRICAN PLATE

NASCA PLATE

S. AMERICAN PLATE

ANTARCTIC

ANTARCTIC PLATE

Key

Areas of tectonic activity (volcanoes and earthquakes)

Volcanoes earthquakes and fold mountains

Volcanoes occur where molten rock from deep inside the Earth is forced up to the surface. This often happens where the edge of one plate is being forced down under another. As this happens, the soft rocks of the ocean floor are scraped off by the plate on top and are folded up to give fold mountains. As the rest of the ocean floor descends, it melts and, under great pressure, is forced up to the surface through cracks in the crust. Diagram D shows how the volcanoes and fold mountains of South America are being formed in this way.

In the middle of the oceans, the opposite situation gives volcanic activity. Here the plates are moving apart. Magma from the mantle rises up through the cracks between the plates. Islands like Iceland were formed like this (Diagram E).

Earthquakes and volcanoes have enormous power and can cause great loss of life and destruction of property and people living nearby. Yet many people do live in areas of tectonic activity. Diagrams F and G show some of the problems caused by earthquakes and volcanoes.

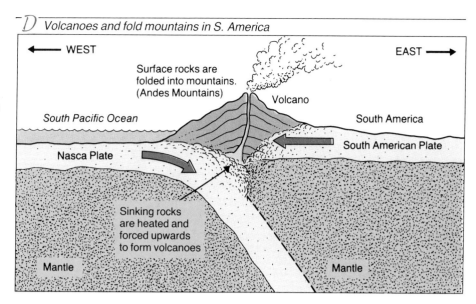

D | Volcanoes and fold mountains in S. America

← WEST   EAST →

Surface rocks are folded into mountains. (Andes Mountains)

Volcano

South Pacific Ocean   South America

Nasca Plate   South American Plate

Sinking rocks are heated and forced upwards to form volcanoes

Mantle   Mantle

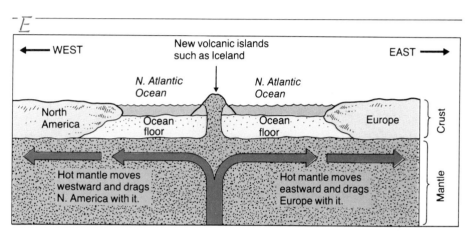

E

← WEST   New volcanic islands such as Iceland   EAST →

N. Atlantic Ocean   *N. Atlantic Ocean*

North America   Ocean floor   Ocean floor   Europe   Crust

Hot mantle moves westward and drags N. America with it.   Hot mantle moves eastward and drags Europe with it.   Mantle

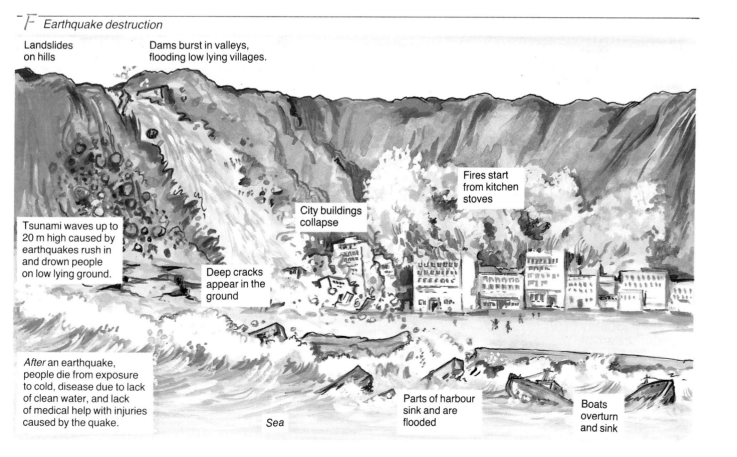

F | *Earthquake destruction*

Landslides on hills

Dams burst in valleys, flooding low lying villages.

Fires start from kitchen stoves

City buildings collapse

Tsunami waves up to 20 m high caused by earthquakes rush in and drown people on low lying ground.

Deep cracks appear in the ground

After an earthquake, people die from exposure to cold, disease due to lack of clean water, and lack of medical help with injuries caused by the quake.

Sea

Parts of harbour sink and are flooded

Boats overturn and sink

C   Volcanic destruction

ERUPTION

Lava and rock thrown
high into the air
e.g. Tambora Indonesia 1896.
150 km^3 of rock
thrown out

EXPLOSION

Krakatoa, Indonesia 1883
Island volcano explosion
heard over 10% of
Earth's surface.

Hot gases from
crater 100 km/hr
Mount Pelee
W. Indies 1902

Lava flows e.g.
Hawaii 1985

Snow melted by
volcanic lava
becomes mud flow.
Columbia 1984

Poisonous gas
from volcanic lake.
Cameroons, W. Africa
1986

Why do people live near volcanoes?

Lava weathers into
fertile soil which
allows farmers to
feed dense populations
on the lower slopes
of volcanoes

Volcanoes often
form wet highlands
in low dry areas.
Streams from the
highland rain attract
people to farm the
lower slopes.

1   What is the meaning of each of the following words or phrases? (3)

magma ....

Richter scale ....

plate ....

R U S V   `3 | | |`

2   Describe and explain the distribution of earthquakes and volcanoes shown on the map of the world in diagram A. (4)

....

....

....

....   `| 4 | |`

A World map showing earthquake activity and active volcanoes

Bezymianny

Fujiyama

Mt. Pelée

Krakatoa

Key

•   Active volcano

..... Earthquakes

◇   Major zones of earthquake activity

3   Read the accompanying newspaper article and study diagram B.

29th November Southern Italy has been struck by an earthquake of magnitude 6.8 on the Richter scale. The epicentre was near the village of Carello in Campania. There was almost complete destruction and a very high death toll in the surrounding parts of Campania and Basilicata. | The main tremor lasted for about 1 minute 20 seconds, and a minute after the main shock, the shock waves reached Foggia, Rome and Tuscany. There were many secondary shocks over the next three days. Over 3000 people are thought to be dead with over 180 000 made homeless.

B Southern Italy showing area of earthquake

TUSCANY

Rome

Foggia

CAMPANIA

Carello

Naples

BASILICATA

N

0   150 km

(i)   Why was South Italy prone to earthquakes? (1)

....   `| | 1 |`

(ii)   What is meant by the epicentre? (1)

....   `| 1 | |`

(iii)   Explain why the shock waves were felt later in Rome than in Carello. (3)

....

....

....   `1 | 2 | |`

(iv)   What may have caused the death of the 3000 people? (2)

....

....   `| 2 | |`

(v)   Suggest ways in which the number of deaths could have been reduced. (2)

....

....   `| 2 | |`

(vi)   Why will the effects of the earthquake be felt in the area for a long time? (3)   *R U S V*

....

....

....   `| 3 | |`

(vii)   What other forms of tectonic activity does South Italy suffer from? (2)

....

....   `| 2 | |`

4   Discuss the ways in which a volcanic eruption can be of value to an area.

....

....

....

....   `3 | | 1`

How people use the land can be affected by the **type** and **structure** of the underlying rocks.

Diagram A shows the differences between the three main types of rock.

Igneous rocks were once molten **magma** deep inside the Earth. They may have cooled inside the crust (**plutonic** rocks) or out on the surface of the Earth (**volcanic** rocks).

Sedimentary rocks were formed from mud, sand or shells which dropped down to the bottom of rivers, lakes and seas. Diagram B on the opposite page shows how the common sedimentary rocks were formed.

Metamorphic rocks have been changed from their original state by heat or pressure.

The **characteristics** of the different rock types affect how useful they are. One such characteristic is **hardness**. Another is **permeability** (how well the rock lets in water). A third is the **content of valuable minerals** like diamonds or sulphur.

Different types of rock can be used for different things. Clay is soft and can be moulded into shapes and baked to hardness to give pottery. Granite is much harder and can be used as it is for building stone.

Table C below shows the characteristics and usefulness of some common rock types.

A valuable type of rock may be under an area but it will not always be used. The people of that area may not know it is there, they may be too poor to quarry or mine it or the area may be too remote from a market for the valuable rock to make exploiting it worthwhile.

The pattern in which rocks are arranged in the Earth is called rock **structure**. Earth movements often bend (**fold**) or break (**fault**) rock layers to cause distinctive types of landscape.

Diagram D on the opposite page shows some of the ways in which rock structure affects scenery.

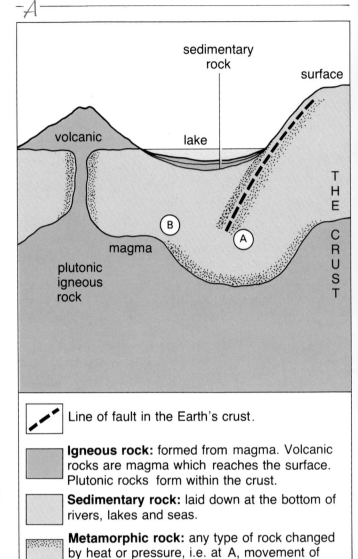

A

Line of fault in the Earth's crust.

Igneous rock: formed from magma. Volcanic rocks are magma which reaches the surface. Plutonic rocks form within the crust.

Sedimentary rock: laid down at the bottom of rivers, lakes and seas.

Metamorphic rock: any type of rock changed by heat or pressure, i.e. at A, movement of rock along a fault; at B, near magma in the crust.

C *Characteristics and usefulness of common rock types*

Rock type	Hardness	Permeability	Useful minerals	Use
Granite	Very hard	Little	None	Building stone
Slate	Hard	None	None	Roofing sheets
Sandstone	Hard	Some	None	Building stone
Limestone	Moderate	Very	Impure $CaCO_3$	Roadstone gravel
Chalk	Moderate	Very	Pure $CaCO_3$	Cement
Clay	Soft	None	None	Pottery
Coal	Moderate	Some	Carbon	Fuel

B Sedimentary rock types

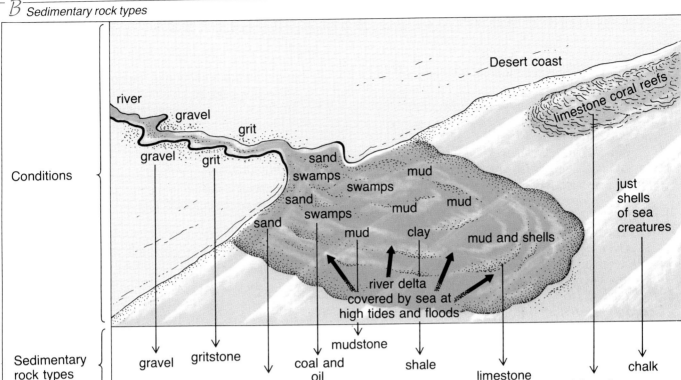

Desert coast

limestone coral reefs

river

gravel

grit

gravel   grit

sand

swamps

mud

swamps

sand

swamps   mud   mud

sand

mud   clay   mud and shells

just
shells
of sea
creatures

river delta
covered by sea at
high tides and floods

Conditions

Sedimentary rock types

mudstone

gravel   gritstone   coal and
oil   shale   limestone   chalk

sandstone   coral limestone

D Some ways in which rock structure affects scenery

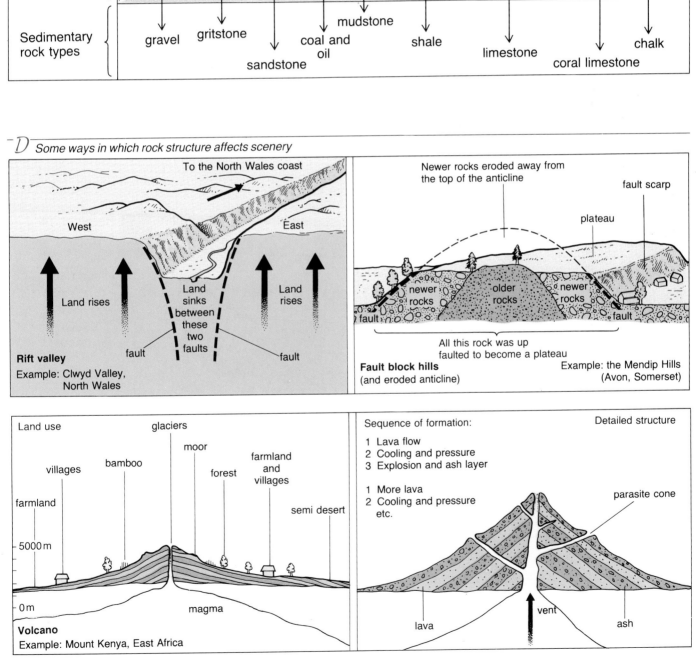

To the North Wales coast

West   East

Land rises

Land
sinks
between
these
two
faults

Land
rises

Rift valley
Example: Clwyd Valley,
North Wales

fault   fault

Newer rocks eroded away from
the top of the anticline

fault scarp

plateau

newer
rocks   older
rocks   newer
rocks

fault   fault

All this rock was up
faulted to become a plateau

Fault block hills
(and eroded anticline)

Example: the Mendip Hills
(Avon, Somerset)

Land use   glaciers

villages   bamboo   moor

forest   farmland
and
villages

farmland

semi desert

5000 m

0 m   magma

Volcano
Example: Mount Kenya, East Africa

Sequence of formation:

1 Lava flow
2 Cooling and pressure
3 Explosion and ash layer

1 More lava
2 Cooling and pressure
  etc.

Detailed structure

parasite cone

lava   vent   ash

1 Read the following descriptions of three   *RUSV*
   different rocks.
   Write down the name of the group of
   rocks to which each belongs.
   (i) The slates of the Blaenau Ffestiniog
        area of North Wales were formed
        by clays being crushed into layers
        by pressure. (1)

   ....

   (ii) The rock was formed from the
        remains of tiny animals and plants
        which dropped to the bottom of the
        sea and became impressed into
        rock. (1)

   ....

   (iii) The hexagonal columns of the
         Giants' Causeway in Northern
         Ireland were formed by molten
         material moving up from the
         interior of the Earth and solidifying
         on the surface. (1)

   .... | 3 | | |

2 Study the cross section of the South   *RUSV*
   Wales Coalfield, A.
   (i) Does it show folding, faulting or
        both? (1)

   .... | | 1 |

   (ii) Suggest why the early iron-working
        industry started in the northern
        part of the coalfield. (2)

   ....
   ....
   ....
   .... | 1 | | 1 |

   (iii) Explain how the rock types and
         structures would be responsible for
         features visible on the surface. (3)

   ....
   ....
   ....
   ....
   ....
   ....
   .... | | 3 | |

A Section of South Wales Coalfield

| Metres above sea level | | | | | | | Recent rocks (black) |
| Limestone Old Millstone Grit |
| Old Red Sandstone |
| Coal measures |
| Iron ore deposits |
| Ancient rocks |

South ... North
Brecon Beacons
Hirwaun
1000   Brecon
Bristol Channel   Maesteg   Rhondda
Vale of Glamorgan
0
0 —— km —— 50

3 Look at the two sketch maps B and C showing areas with different rock types.

(i) Describe the main features of the drainage shown on the maps. (4)

....
....
....
....
....
....
....

`[ | | 4 | ]`

(ii) Suggest reasons for the different patterns of drainage. (2)

....
....
....
....

`[ | 2 | | ]`

(iii) Suggest which rocks underlie these areas. (2)

....
....
....
....

`[ | 2 | | ]`

(iv) How might these areas be useful to people? (2)

....
....
....

`[ 1 | 1 | | ]`

4 Imagine you are conducting a public inquiry into a company's plan to commence a new mining operation. Describe the advantages and disadvantages of such a scheme to the people living in the area. Name an actual example of such a plan. (6)

....
....
....
....
....
....
....
....

`[ 1 | 3 | | 2 ]`
`[ 6 | 11 | 6 | 2 ]`

RUSV BC

B

PH □□□□
The Potters Arms

20
10

River Don

Clayton □□

10
20

Sandridge □□□□

Key for both maps

⌇⌇⌇ stream

0   1 km

⋯⋯⋯⋯ stream sometimes dries up

contour line in metres above sea level

C

10
20
30
40
50
60
70
80

White Down

91 ▲

White Horse Hill   • 86

90
105
80
70
60

tumulus ✿

80
70

80
70

Broad Chalke □□□□

ROCK STRUCTURE AND LANDSCAPE

It is fairly rare for rocks to be found in flat layers. Usually they are bent (**folded**) or broken (**faulted**).

Simple folding is shown in Diagram A. **Anticlines** are upfolds and **synclines** are downfolds. Diagram B shows how you can represent them by folding a piece of paper.

Oddly, the anticlines are not as resistant to erosion as the synclines, so they are usually eroded away first. When this happens the anticline is said to be 'unroofed'.

Much of the landscape of Britain and Europe has developed from unroofed anticlines. They are called **scarplands**. Block diagram C shows how people use the scarplands of south east England.

Faulting, too, shapes the landscape. Photograph D shows part of the Great East African Rift Valley. Diagram E and Map F show its formation and location. The important thing to notice is that there are two parallel faults in the Earth. The land to each side has been pushed upwards and the land in between has sunk down to form the rift valley. The steep valley sides are called **fault scarps**. With so much faulting, it is logical that there should be volcanic activity here. Africa's two highest mountains, Kilimanjaro and Mount Kenya, are both old volcanoes and lie close to the rift.

Block diagram G shows Britain's biggest rift valley, the Scottish Central Lowland. This lies between the Grampian Highlands and the Southern Uplands, and it, too, has volcanic hills within it, for example the Sidlaw Hills.

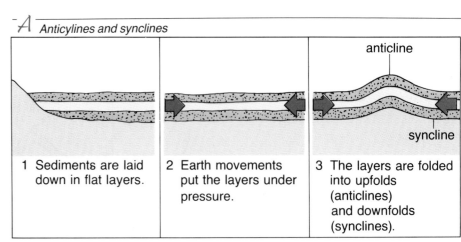

A Anticyclines and synclines

1 Sediments are laid down in flat layers.

2 Earth movements put the layers under pressure.

3 The layers are folded into upfolds (anticlines) and downfolds (synclines).

B

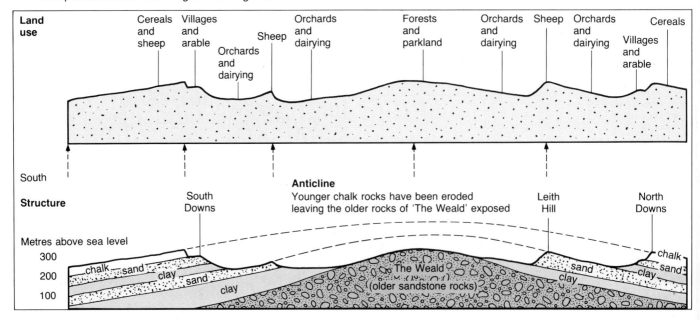

C Scarplands of south east England looking west

| Land use | Cereals and sheep | Villages and arable | Orchards and dairying | Sheep | Orchards and dairying | Forests and parkland | Orchards and dairying | Sheep | Orchards and dairying | Cereals / Villages and arable |

South

Structure

South Downs

Anticline Younger chalk rocks have been eroded leaving the older rocks of 'The Weald' exposed

Leith Hill

North Downs

Metres above sea level
300
200
100

chalk sand clay sand clay

The Weald (older sandstone rocks)

sand clay chalk sand

D *Part of the Great East African Rift Valley*

E

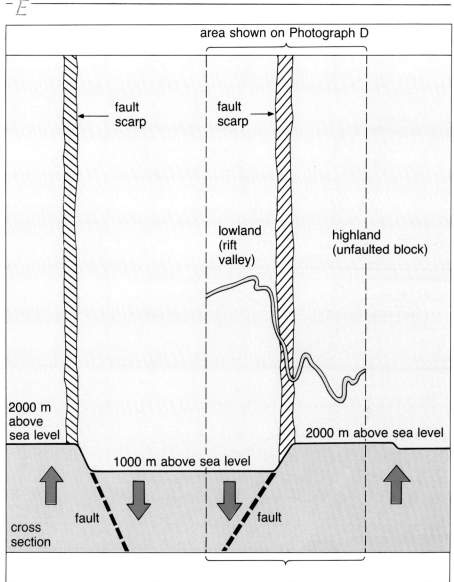

area shown on Photograph D

fault scarp

fault scarp

lowland (rift valley)

highland (unfaulted block)

2000 m above sea level

2000 m above sea level

1000 m above sea level

cross section

fault

fault

F

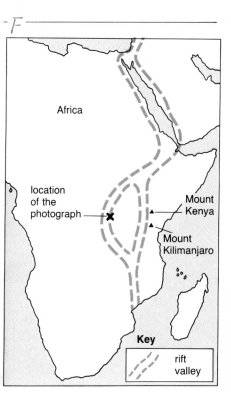

Africa

location of the photograph

Mount Kenya

Mount Kilimanjaro

Key

rift valley

G

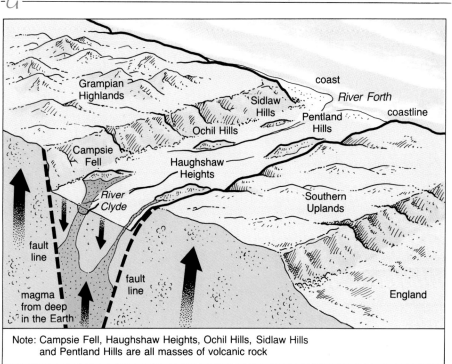

Grampian Highlands

coast

River Forth

Sidlaw Hills

coastline

Ochil Hills

Pentland Hills

Campsie Fell

Haughshaw Heights

River Clyde

Southern Uplands

fault line

fault line

England

magma from deep in the Earth

Note: Campsie Fell, Haughshaw Heights, Ochil Hills, Sidlaw Hills and Pentland Hills are all masses of volcanic rock

1   Name and locate an example of each of the following structures. (6)   *RUSV*

(i)

surface

Name .... Location ....

(ii)

surface

Name .... Location ....

(iii)

surface

Name .... Location ....

6 ☐ ☐ ☐

2   Suggest why anticlines are less resistant to erosion than synclines. (4)

....

....

....

....

4 ☐ ☐

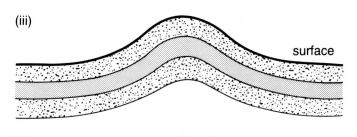

B The population of central Scotland

C Simplified geological map of Scotland

North West Highlands

Grampian Mountains

Old hard metamorphic and igneous rocks

F — rift valley sunk between two faults (F)

sedimentary rocks with some volcanic igneous rocks

F — Southern Uplands

sedimentary rocks with some igneous rocks

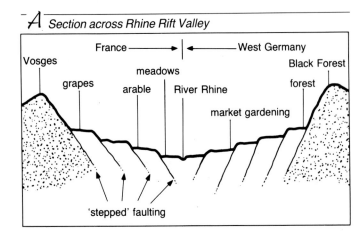

A Section across Rhine Rift Valley

France → | ← West Germany

Vosges

grapes

arable

meadows

River Rhine

Black Forest

forest

market gardening

'stepped' faulting

D Agriculture of central Scotland

Legend:

- **Nursery gardens and orchards**
- **Predominantly arable land (with much pasture in Ireland)**
- **Mixed arable and grassland**
- **Built-up areas**

E Industry in UK and Eire

- Textile factories (with 750 or more employees)
- Clothing and footware
- Leather products
- Hardware
- Tools and precision instruments
- Paper and paper products
- Printing and publishing
- Furniture and upholstery
- Sewing machines
- Refrigerators and washing machines

Aberdeen
Dundee
Glasgow
Edinburgh
Hawick
Newcastle
Leeds
Manchester
Liverpool
Sheffield
Stoke
Nottingham
Stafford
Norwich
Birmingham
Leicester
Northampton
Bristol
London
Cardiff
Yeovil
Dundalk
Drogheda
Dublin
Carrick
Cork

Main textile producing areas

RUSV

3 Study the cross section A of the valley of the River Rhine between Bingen and Bonn.

(i) Through what kind of structure does the River Rhine flow? (1)

....   [1]

(ii) This area is a good example of stepped faulting.
Explain how stepped faulting might occur. (2)

....
....
....   [2]

(iii) Explain how the rock type and structure has influenced the land use in this part of West Germany. (4)

....
....
....
....
....   [4]

(iv) What other factors may have influenced the use that has been made of the land? (3)

....
....
....
....   [2] [1]

[7] [12] [5] [1]

4 Study the atlas maps B to E.
Use the information to write a brief account of the geography of central Scotland. (5)

....
....
....
....
....
....
....
....
....
....
....
....   [5]

ROCK TYPES AND RESOURCE OPPORTUNITIES

Different rock types often give different kinds of scenery. Soft rocks, especially those which do not let water soak into them, are easily washed away by rivers and streams. The part that is left forms lowland valleys and plains. Clay is a soft rock of this type, and 'clay vales' are found in many parts of Britain and Europe.

In well watered areas, lowlands, such as clay vales, allow farmers and builders a range of opportunities for using the land. In hotter or drier lands, lowlands may be liable to drought, so farming is hazardous. It is usual for most people in a country to live in the lowlands, especially the central parts of plains and the gaps between hills, through which many people will pass. Sketch A shows some of the opportunities offered by a lowland rock type.

Hard rocks, or those which let water soak into them, are not easily eroded by rivers and streams. They are left standing high, as hills. Chalk is not very hard but water soaks into it, so the surface is not worn away by streams running over it. Chalk rocks often form gently sloping uplands. In England these are usually called 'downs'. It is a geographical riddle why our ancestors should have called uplands 'downs'.

If a rock mainly forms uplands, it tends to restrict the ways in which people can use it. Uplands are cooler, windier and wetter than surrounding lowlands. In high latitudes, like Britain, this is a disadvantage. High uplands are left as moors for sheep rearing or as deer runs for hunting. In dry, hot areas such as East Africa, highlands are often attractive to people as they have the water that the lowlands lack. Sketch B shows the sort of opportunities associated with highland rock types.

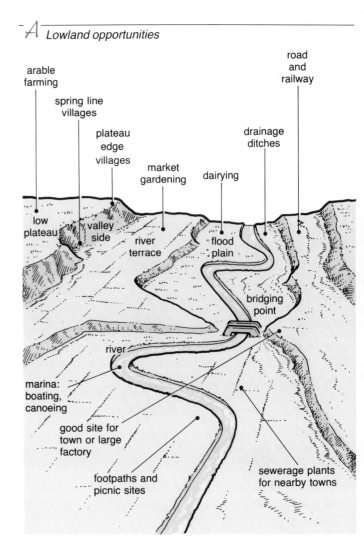

A Lowland opportunities

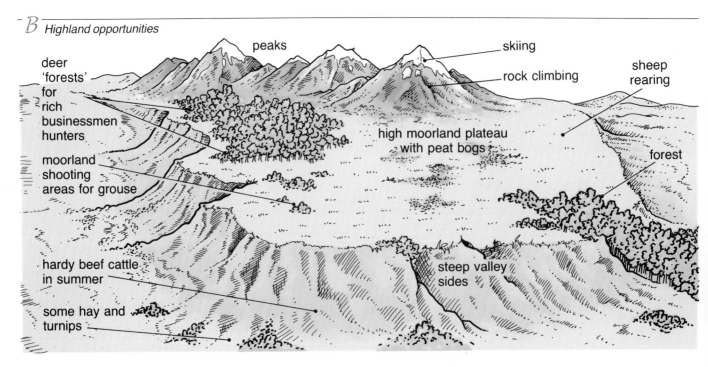

B Highland opportunities

Rocks are made of minerals, and these can offer opportunities to the people who live in the area. Rock formations associated with oil can attract people to live at great expense in the desert or in the North Sea!

Diagrams C, D, E and F show the typical landforms and land uses of four types of rock found in many parts of Britain.

C *Granite, for example, Dartmoor, Bodmin Moor*

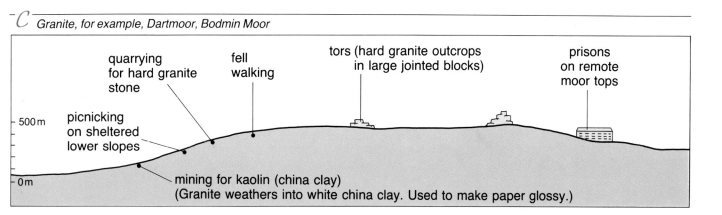

D *Sandstone, clay and yellow limestone escarpments, for example, South Yorkshire*

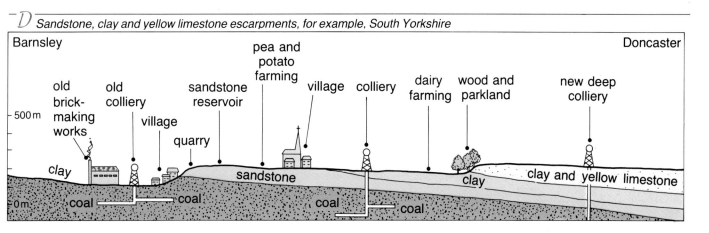

E *Chalk, for example, the Chiltern Hills*

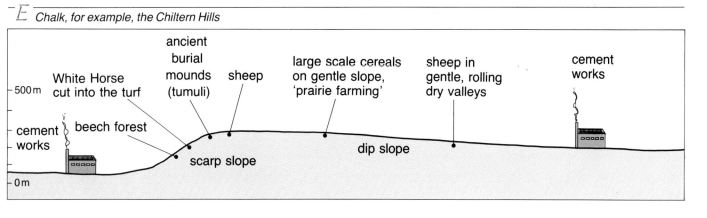

F *Carboniferous limestone, for example, Derbyshire White Peak (Peak District)*

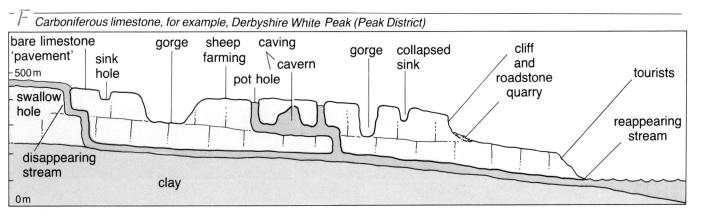

1 Which rocks outcrop in the following areas: (3)

RUSV

   (i) Dartmoor ....

   (ii) Chilterns ....

   (iii) Peak District ....
                        | 3 | | |

2 Study Photographs A and B showing the Cheddar Gorge area of Somerset.
   (i) List two physical attractions the area has for tourists (2).

.... | | 2 | |

....

   (ii) How is the rock type responsible for the attractive scenery of the Cheddar Gorge area? (4)

....

....

....

....

....

....

.... | 1 | 3 | |

(iii) What human facilities would be provided for the tourists? (3)

....

....

....

....

....

....

.... | | 3 | |

(iv) Apart from tourism, what other uses could the rock type found at Cheddar encourage? (2)

....

....

....

.... | 1 | 1 | |

A

B

3 Study Photograph C and the accompanying outline sketch D.

(i) Copy and complete the sketch and label it to show the main features of the photograph. (5)

| 5 | | |

(ii) Suggest a type of rock that might be quarried there. (1)

....

| 1 | | |

(iii) Name an area where the photograph might have been taken. (1)

....

| 1 | | |

(iv) What are the advantages and disadvantages of such a quarry to the people living in the area? (4)

....
....
....
....
....
....
....
....

| 2 | | 2 |

| 6 | 10 | 7 | 2 |

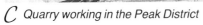

C Quarry working in the Peak District

D Sketch of quarry workings

Unit 4.1

WEATHERING AND ITS EFFECT ON LANDSCAPE

Diagram A shows how any rock near the Earth's surface is exposed to the forces of **weathering**. It is weathering which starts to change the Earth's surface by breaking solid rock into bits which can then be shifted by the forces of erosion.

Diagram B shows some of these weathering processes. Weathering affects any rock (or building) which is exposed. New faces of rock are exposed naturally on sea and mountain cliffs and by people in quarries and building work.

Weathering is rapid in two particular sets of conditions. Firstly, chemical and biological weathering cause rocks to break down quickly in hot and wet conditions. Secondly, freezing and thawing of water causes severe weathering in cold, wet areas where frosts are common.

Chemical weathering

Chemicals in the air and soil can quickly break up a rock surface, especially in hot, wet conditions. The most active chemicals are oxygen and water. They react with common elements in the rock, such as iron, to make softer iron compounds which powder away into dust.

Another type of weathering chemical is the weak carbonic acid formed when carbon dioxide from the air dissolves in rainwater. This acid dissolves limestone rock by a process called **carbonation**. It is through this process that streams wear away the rock to form tunnels in limestone areas. Sometimes the limestone is redeposited in weird forms. Stalactites (which hold *tight* to the roof of a tunnel) and stalagmites (which *might* grow up from the floor of a tunnel) are two such forms.

Acids made by lichens on the surface or by humus in the soil are also powerful chemical weathering agents.

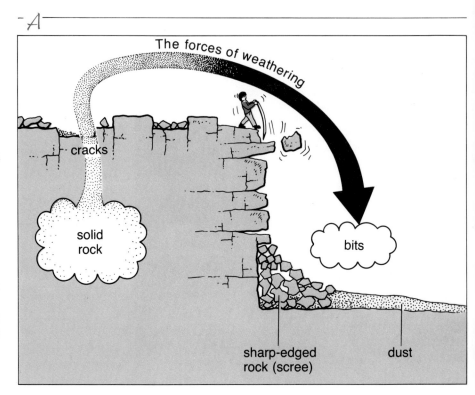

A — The forces of weathering

cracks

solid rock

bits

sharp-edged rock (scree)

dust

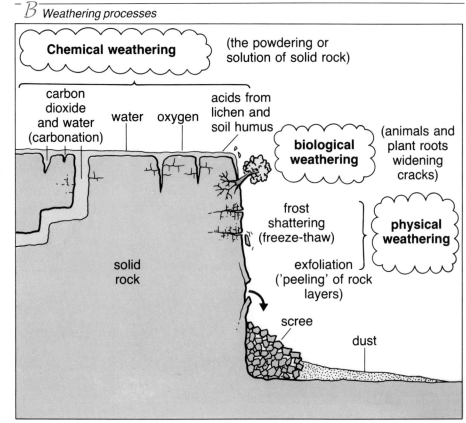

B Weathering processes

Chemical weathering (the powdering or solution of solid rock)

carbon dioxide and water (carbonation)

water   oxygen

acids from lichen and soil humus

biological weathering (animals and plant roots widening cracks)

frost shattering (freeze-thaw)

exfoliation ('peeling' of rock layers)

physical weathering

solid rock

scree

dust

Biological weathering

Animals and plants can get into cracks in rocks and widen them. Tree roots are especially important in this process. They can grow into rock faces or into the foundations of buildings, and, slowly but surely, they force the rock layers or blocks of masonry apart.

Freeze-thaw weathering

This can also be called 'frost shattering'. Freeze-thaw weathering is very important in wet places where the temperature falls below freezing point at night and rises above freezing during the day. At night the water freezes in cracks in the rock. As it freezes, it expands and takes up more space. This makes the crack in the rock wider. In the daytime the ice melts and the crack narrows again. This constant opening and closing of cracks causes the rock to break up and sharp bits of **scree** fall off.

Exfoliation

When a rock is exposed at the surface, it expands. Why is this? It is because it is not being compressed as it was when it had rock on top of it. This causes its surface to crack and peel off, like the outer skin of an onion. This process is called **exfoliation**. 'Ex' means outside, 'foliation' means peeling away like a leaf. (Think of foliage – leaves.)

Exfoliation is increased by the rock heating up and expanding in the sunshine by day, then cooling and contracting at night. The expansion and contraction causes existing cracks to widen and creates new ones.

Photograph C and Sketch D show how a cliff is weathered in a semi-desert part of Arizona, in the south west of the USA.

C Weathering in Arizona, USA

D Sketch of Photograph C

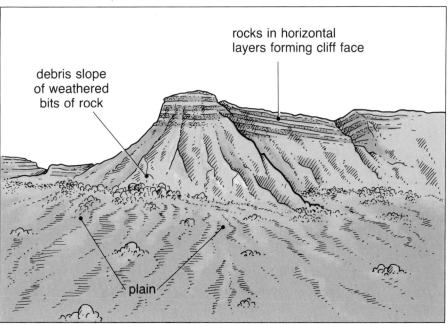

rocks in horizontal layers forming cliff face

debris slope of weathered bits of rock

plain

1 Define precisely the word 'weathering'. (2)

RUSV

....
.... | 2 | | |

2 (i) Name these weathering processes:

(a) living things moving into cracks in solid rock and widening them

.... | 1 | | |

(b) shattering of solid rock by frost

.... | 1 | | |

(c) carbon dioxide in rainwater dissolving limestone rock (3)

.... | 1 | | |

(ii) For each of these processes give a location where it is taking place. (3)

(a)
....

(b)
....

(c) | 3 | | |
....

3 Explain the weathering processes which cause:

(i) rocks to be heard to crack with a noise like a rifle shot in the desert (2)

....
....
....
....

(ii) piles of sharp-edged rocks to accumulate at the base of a mountain slope in very cold areas. (2)

....
....
....
.... | 4 | | |

4 Study Photograph A.

RUSV

(i) Draw a simple sketch of the photograph in the space provided. (2)

| | 2 | |

(ii) Add labels to show the following:
valley sides
pile of debris at bottom of slopes
glacier   (4)

| | 4 | |

(iii) With reference to the photograph and any examples you have studied, suggest why it is often stated that without weathering there would be little change to the Earth's surface. (4)

....
....
....
....
....
....
....
.... | 2 | | 2 |

5 With reference to specific examples, explain how weathering can affect man-made objects. (3)

....
....
....
....
....
.... | 3 | | |

| 8 | 9 | 6 | 2 |

A

LANDFORMS CREATED BY RIVERS

Diagrams A, B and C show the landforms found in a typical river valley, from source to mouth, and the uses which people usually make of them.

Near the source, upland river valley landforms include interlocking spurs, waterfalls and a rocky river bed. The river cuts down into its bed (**vertical corrasion**) when the loose rocks it picks up knock against the solid bedrock and break it up.

If the source lies above 300 metres, in Britain the surrounding area is likely to be too cold and too exposed to strong winds for crops to grow. The valley sides are left as moor, and sheep grazing is the most likely land use. At this height, trees will be stunted because of the cold, but slightly lower down plantations of conifers are common on otherwise unused valley sides.

The landforms found in the middle stages of a river's course usually include a narrow flood plain, a river terrace and steep valley sides. The river meanders may cause a river cliff if they cut into the valley sides at the edge of the flood plain.

Flood plains are used for grazing dairy cattle in the UK because the water table is near the surface. The wet soil makes it difficult to use farm machinery but encourages the growth of the thick grass, which is suitable for dairy cattle. River terraces are drier and are used for arable farming, communications and settlement. The valley sides may be cultivated. Deciduous plantations, such as beech, are often found on the steeper slopes where ploughing is awkward.

In the lower part of a river's course, the flood plain is wider, cut off lakes are common and river banks are built up by flooding to form raised 'levees'. Tributaries cannot easily get to the main river and have to follow it downstream before they can get through the levee. Land use tends to be pasture, but on coastal sites the cheap, marshy land may be drained and large industrial works built.

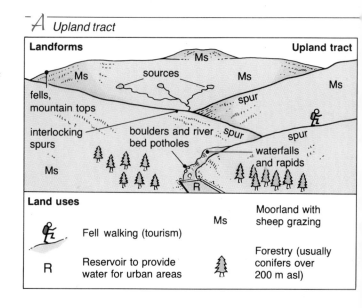

A Upland tract

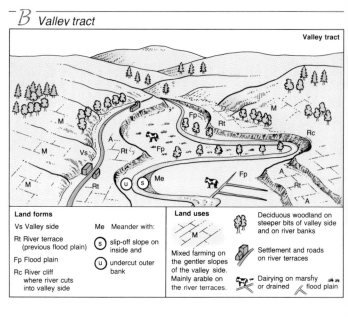

B Valley tract

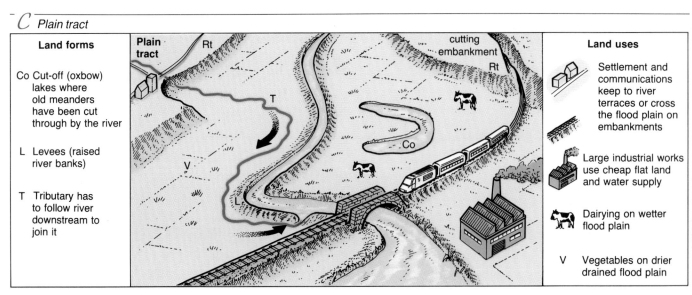

C Plain tract

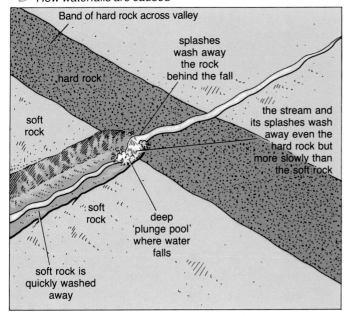

D How waterfalls are caused

Band of hard rock across valley

hard rock

splashes wash away the rock behind the fall

soft rock

the stream and its splashes wash away even the hard rock but more slowly than the soft rock

soft rock

deep 'plunge pool' where water falls

soft rock is quickly washed away

E

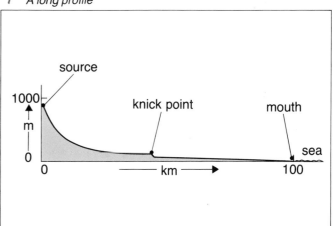

Rejuvenation (getting young again)

Sea level falls (or the land rises)

rapids or a waterfall form where the river meets the sea

At first

once formed, the plunge pool splashes wear back the rock behind the waterfall

old coastline = **raised beach**

sea

'old' plain tract river

river is 'young' again

Later

gorge

the waterfall has worn itself back to form a gorge

The future

waterfall (knick point)

In **rejuvenation** the waterfall end of the gorge is called a 'knick' point

Waterfalls and gorges are often found in the upper and middle parts of a river's course and sometimes in the lower parts. A waterfall may be caused by a band of hard rock or by **rejuvenation**. This is where the sea level drops and rapids or a waterfall are formed at the coast. Once a waterfall has formed, it wears its way back upstream, leaving a gorge where it has been (Diagrams. D and E).

A section *along* a river's course from source to mouth is called a **long profile** (as in Diagram F) . It is useful in showing the steepness of each part of the river's course.

A section *across* any part of the river's valley is called a **cross profile**. It shows the steepness of valley sides, terraces and the flood plain at just one location. Cross profile G is an example.

After rain, rivers are full, but after dry spells they are much lower. In semi-arid areas they may dry up completely for part of the year. Graph H shows how the size of a river varies throughout the year. This is called the river's **regime**. This graph would be typical of a river like the Tiber near Rome. Rome has hot, dry summers and warm, wet winters.

F A long profile

source

1000 m

knick point

mouth

sea

0

km

100

G A river valley cross profile

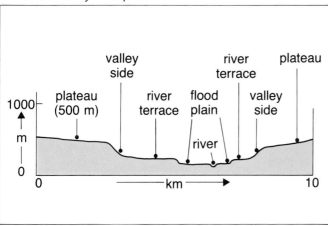

valley side

river terrace

plateau

plateau (500 m)

river terrace

flood plain

valley side

1000 m

river

0

km

10

H A river regime

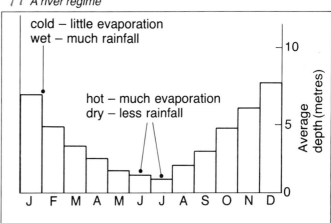

cold – little evaporation
wet – much rainfall

hot – much evaporation
dry – less rainfall

10

5

Average depth (metres)

J F M A M J J A S O N D

0

1   Explain the meaning of the following
    terms: (3)

    levee ....

    ....

    rejuvenation ....

    ....

    river regime ....

    ....   `3` □ □

2   Study Graph A which shows the
    discharge of a river following a short
    period of heavy rain.
    (i)   What was the total amount of rain
          that fell? (1)

    ....   □ □ `1` □

    (ii) For how long did it rain? (1)

    ....   □ □ `1` □

    (iii) What was the maximum discharge
          of the river? (1)

    ....   □ □ `1` □

    (iv) Why was there a time lag between
          the period of rainfall and the
          maximum discharge? (2)

    ....
    ....
    ....
    ....   □ `2` □ □

    (v)   Explain why the river would
          become a more effective agent of
          erosion following the period of
          heavy rain. (3)

    ....
    ....
    ....
    ....
    ....
    ....   □ `3` □ □

RUSV   ¬A A river's discharge following a period of heavy rain

A river's discharge following a period of heavy rain

$\widetilde{B}$ Section through Niagara Falls

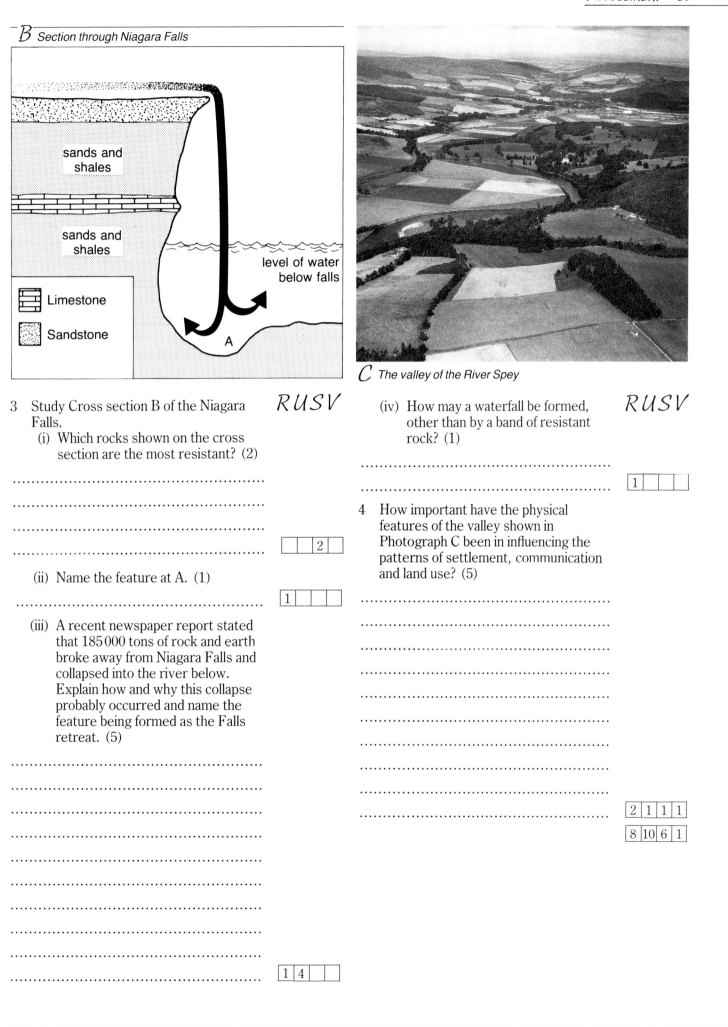

sands and
shales

sands and
shales

level of water
below falls

Limestone

Sandstone

A

$\mathcal{C}$ The valley of the River Spey

3   Study Cross section B of the Niagara   *RUSV*
    Falls.
    (i) Which rocks shown on the cross
         section are the most resistant? (2)

....

....

....

.... | | |2| |

    (ii) Name the feature at A. (1)

.... |1| | | |

    (iii) A recent newspaper report stated
          that 185 000 tons of rock and earth
          broke away from Niagara Falls and
          collapsed into the river below.
          Explain how and why this collapse
          probably occurred and name the
          feature being formed as the Falls
          retreat. (5)

....

....

....

....

....

....

....

....

....

.... |1|4| | |

    (iv) How may a waterfall be formed,   *RUSV*
          other than by a band of resistant
          rock? (1)

....

.... |1| | | |

4   How important have the physical
    features of the valley shown in
    Photograph C been in influencing the
    patterns of settlement, communication
    and land use? (5)

....

....

....

....

....

....

....

....

....

.... |2|1|1|1|
                                                      |8|10|6|1|

If the climate of a place changes so that snow falls instead of rain, great changes to the land occur. Falling snow compresses underlying snow to form ice. The ice moves slowly downhill and wears away the bottom of any valleys that were there before. Moving ice is a very powerful eroding force, so valleys are deepened and steepened.

On its edges, the ice melts by day and freezes again at night. As water freezes it expands. This **freeze-thaw** process widens cracks in the rock until it breaks up into sharp-edged bits. The bits collect at the foot of slopes and are called **scree**. Diagram A shows this process.

Mountain scenery which is the result of ice action is called **glaciated scenery**. Diagram B shows how such a landscape may have been formed and gives some names for its landforms.

B How highland glaciation works

1 Before: a mountain valley

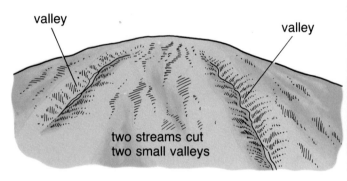

2 Snow and ice at work

3 The snow and ice melt, leaving corries, aretes and peaks

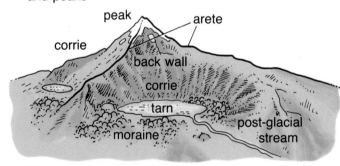

4 After the snow and ice have gone, rainwater cuts gullies into the corrie back walls and deposits fans of debris

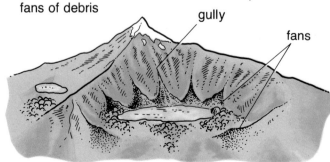

A

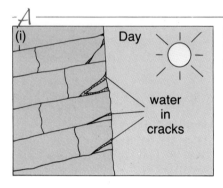

Meltwater runs into cracks in the solid cliff

Meltwater freezes, expands and forces crack to widen

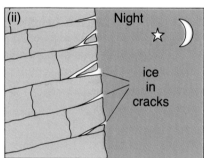

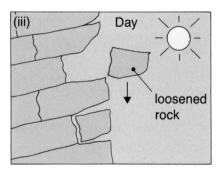

Ice melts again. Loosened blocks fall as scree. Water fills the new crack.

Pile of scree forms below the cliff

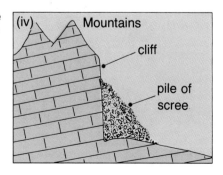

In Britain this sort of scenery can be seen in the North West Highlands and the Grampians in Scotland, the Lake District in England, Snowdonia, Cader Idris and the Brecons in Wales, and the Macgillycuddy Reeks in Ireland. It is usually at heights over 800 metres above sea level that such scenery is found.

Diagram C shows some of the landforms you might see in a glaciated valley and how they may be formed.

Some of the opportunities offered by these landscapes are shown in the last part of Diagram C. Tourists may come to walk and climb in the mountains or canoe or sail on the deep ribbon lakes in the valleys, or they may picnic and just sit and look. They may want car parks, places to eat and to buy souvenirs. Electricity may be generated from hydro-electric power stations on large streams in narrow, dammable valleys. Though there are few suitable places in Britain, mountainous countries like Norway and Sweden make most of their electricity in this way. Farmers may tend sheep on the moors and have beef cattle, oats and fodder crops on the lower valley slopes. The Forestry Commission plants conifers on unused valley sides to provide an income from sales of softwood.

Lowland plains which were glaciated by ice sheets may display some of the features shown in Diagram D. Much of northern Europe is like this.

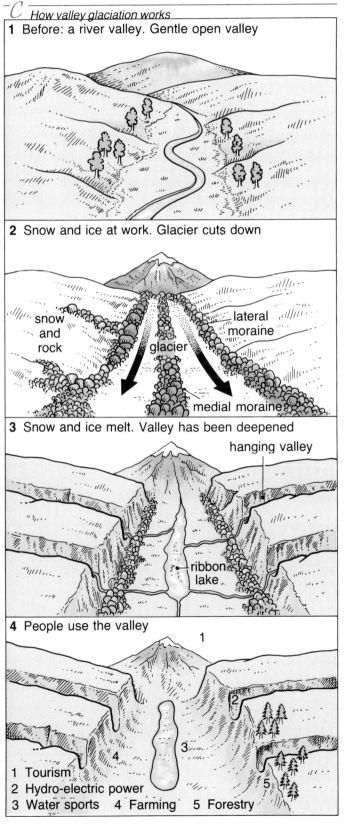

C How valley glaciation works

1 Before: a river valley. Gentle open valley

2 Snow and ice at work. Glacier cuts down

snow and rock

glacier

lateral moraine

medial moraine

3 Snow and ice melt. Valley has been deepened

hanging valley

ribbon lake

4 People use the valley

1 Tourism   2 Hydro-electric power
3 Water sports   4 Farming   5 Forestry

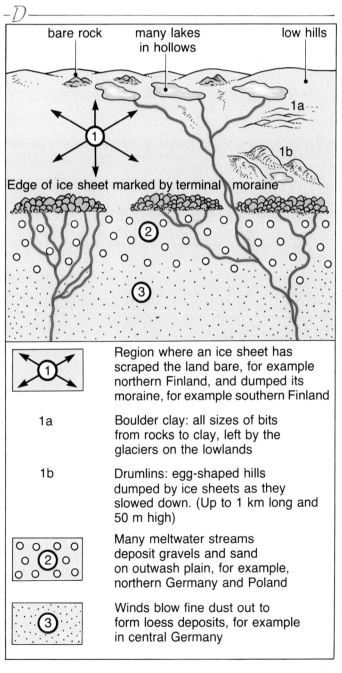

D

bare rock   many lakes in hollows   low hills

1a

1b

Edge of ice sheet marked by terminal moraine

	Region where an ice sheet has scraped the land bare, for example northern Finland, and dumped its moraine, for example southern Finland
1a	Boulder clay: all sizes of bits from rocks to clay, left by the glaciers on the lowlands
1b	Drumlins: egg-shaped hills dumped by ice sheets as they slowed down. (Up to 1 km long and 50 m high)
②	Many meltwater streams deposit gravels and sand on outwash plain, for example, northern Germany and Poland
③	Winds blow fine dust out to form loess deposits, for example in central Germany

Diagram E shows how people use the landforms which have resulted from lowland glaciation.

E

Where ice has been:

1 Summer holiday cabins and watersports on lakes
2 Winter skiing on the low hills
3 Forests and farming on boulder clay
4 Forests on terminal moraines
5 Pasture on drumlins

outside the glaciated areas where meltwater streams laid down deposits:

6 Gravel pits (gravel for concrete)
7 Vegetables on gravel
8 Sandpits for building or glass
9 Heathland or cereals on sandy soils
10 Cereals and market gardening on fertile, wind-blown loess

Assessment ICE CREATING LANDSCAPE OPPORTUNITIES

1 Explain the meaning of the following: (3)

freeze-thaw process ....

....

arête ....

....

terminal moraine .... ☐3☐☐☐

....

2 Study Sketch A which shows a glaciated highland area.

(i) Sketch a cross section across Cader Idris from Llyn-y-gadair to Llyn Cau and mark in the location of each of the following: (4) peak, corrie, tarn. ☐☐4☐

(ii) Explain the formation of Tal-y-Llyn lake. (4)

....

....

....

.... ☐4☐

RUSV

A A glaciated highland area

Llyn Y Gadair

600

700

800 ●893

700 Cader Idris

600

Llyn Cau

Craig Lwyd

700

600

Cwm Amarch

600

400

200

Tal-Y-Llyn Lake

200

300

400

☐ water ── roads

⌒ rock crags

km
0 1 2

(iii) Why have scree slopes developed at the base of Craig-Llwyd? (3)

....

....

....

....

....

....

`[2][1][ ][ ]`

3 Study the sketch map of Denmark (B) which shows the main soil types.
   (i) State the direction from which the ice advanced. (1)

....

`[ ][ ][1][ ]`

   (ii) Give two pieces of evidence to support this. (2)

....

....

`[ ][ ][2][ ]`

   (iii) How may Denmark have been affected by the deposits left by the ice? (3)

....

....

....

....

....

....

`[ ][3][ ][ ]`

4 With reference to specific examples, examine the value of glaciated landscapes for human use. (5)

....

....

....

....

....

....

....

....

....

....

`[2][1][ ][2]`

`[7][9][7][2]`

RUSV

B Soil types in Denmark

Sweden

Baltic Sea

0   100
     km

N

■ Western Jutland, sand dune coast

▤ Central Jutland, low morainic hills

▦ Eastern Jutland and the islands, chalky boulder clay

COASTAL LANDFORMS AND LAND USES

Coasts are shaped by moving sea water, rivers, movements of slopes and ground and changes in sea level.

Moving sea water at the coast breaks down rocks and washes parts of them away. The debris is smoothed by the action of the sea and is set down as mud, sand, shingle, pebbles or cobbles on other shores.

Shores where there is erosion are marked by cliffs, where the sea has cut into the land, and platforms of flat rock offshore (wave-cut platforms) where the incoming waves smooth the rock. The cliffs will usually have caves, blow holes and arches, which are evidence of attack by the sea at weak parts of the cliff. Resistant towers of solid rock stand out of the sea offshore

(**stacks**). These show where the headland used to be.

Shores where there is deposition will have sand bars and spits, with sand dunes on the shore and marshy lagoons where rivers deposit silt in sea water enclosed by the spits. The spit in Diagram A points in the direction of the **longshore drift**.

Both types of coast are used by holidaymakers. Settlements are especially common where one type of coastline meets the other. Low sand dunes make excellent golf courses and raised beaches provide light soils for arable farming.

Sketch B shows an example of a coast where both types are present.

A Longshore drift and its landforms

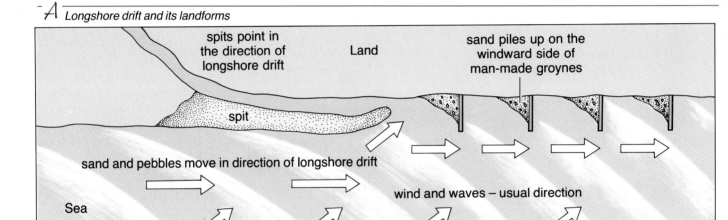

spits point in the direction of longshore drift

Land

sand piles up on the windward side of man-made groynes

spit

sand and pebbles move in direction of longshore drift

wind and waves – usual direction

Sea

B Landscape formed by moving sea water

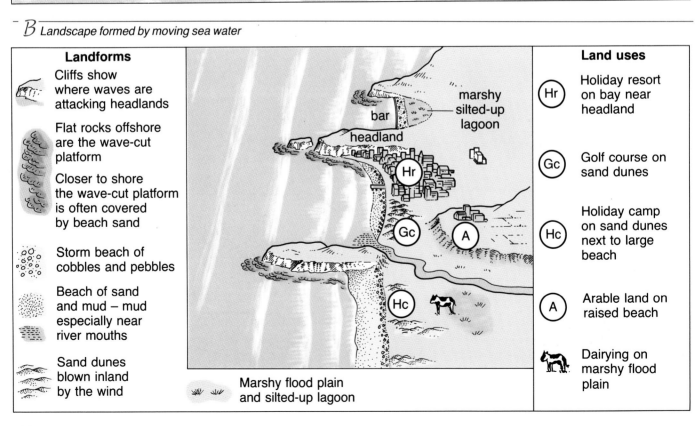

Landforms

Cliffs show where waves are attacking headlands

Flat rocks offshore are the wave-cut platform

Closer to shore the wave-cut platform is often covered by beach sand

Storm beach of cobbles and pebbles

Beach of sand and mud – mud especially near river mouths

Sand dunes blown inland by the wind

marshy silted-up lagoon

bar

headland

Marshy flood plain and silted-up lagoon

Land uses

Hr Holiday resort on bay near headland

Gc Golf course on sand dunes

Hc Holiday camp on sand dunes next to large beach

A Arable land on raised beach

Dairying on marshy flood plain

C Cliff shapes

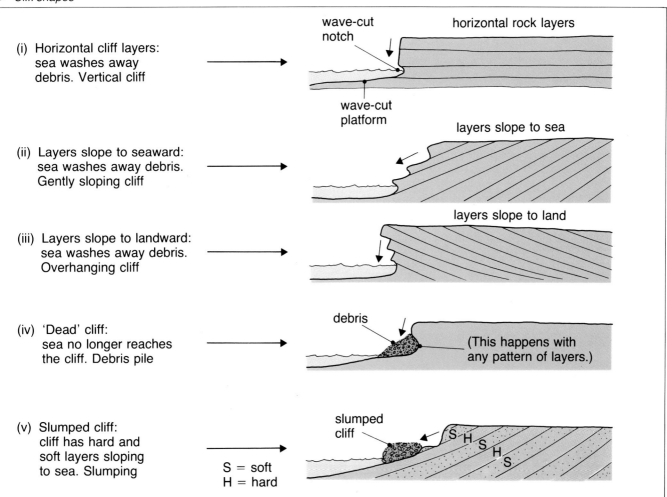

(i) Horizontal cliff layers: sea washes away debris. Vertical cliff

wave-cut notch
horizontal rock layers
wave-cut platform

(ii) Layers slope to seaward: sea washes away debris. Gently sloping cliff

layers slope to sea

(iii) Layers slope to landward: sea washes away debris. Overhanging cliff

layers slope to land

(iv) 'Dead' cliff: sea no longer reaches the cliff. Debris pile

debris
(This happens with any pattern of layers.)

(v) Slumped cliff: cliff has hard and soft layers sloping to sea. Slumping

S = soft
H = hard

slumped cliff
S H S H S

Once a steep slope is formed, its top parts tend to weather away and slip down to the bottom of the slope. This happens with sea cliffs and dunes. If the sea still washes up to the cliff, it will carry this debris away. If not, piles of scree will form at the cliff base. If the cliff contains soft, slippery rocks like clay, landslides or slumping occur. After a lot of rain, the rock above the clay slips down and forms mounds at the bottom of the slope. A new bare cliff of soft clay is left behind. This is shown in Diagram C. Places like those in (i) and (v) are the most dangerous for people.

Rivers entering the sea bring mud with them. If there is a strong tide at the river mouth, the mud is washed out to sea and the river mouth remains open. If there is little or no tide, as in the Mediterranean Sea, the mud is deposited at the river mouth as a **delta**. Map D shows the delta of the river Nile.

D A delta

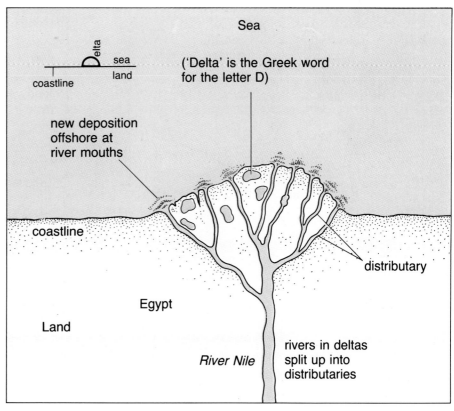

Sea

Delta
sea
land
coastline

('Delta' is the Greek word for the letter D)

new deposition offshore at river mouths

coastline

Egypt

Land

River Nile

distributary

rivers in deltas split up into distributaries

The level where the sea meets the land is called the **base level**. It often rises or falls (quite apart from the daily rise and fall of the tide). Diagram E shows the landforms resulting from a positive base level change (rise in sea level). Diagram F shows this for a negative base level change (fall in sea level).

E *Drowned coastline (positive base level change)*

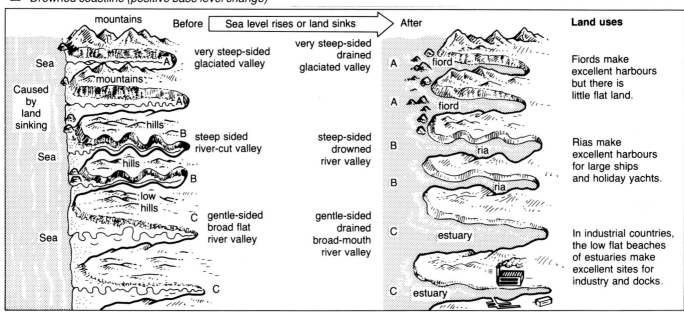

F *Raised coastline (negative base level change)*

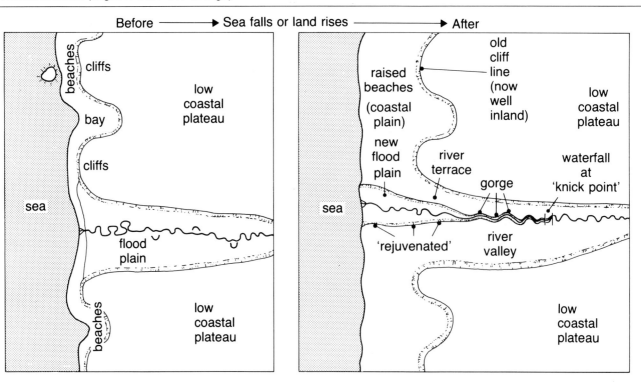

Raised beaches and river terraces are well-drained and fertile.
They make first-class arable or market gardening farmland
if they are close to city markets.
Gorges and waterfalls are hazards but can be tourist attractions.

1 Explain the meaning of the
   following: (3)

   RUSV

   longshore drift ....

   ....

   stack ....

   ....

   fjord ....

   .... `3` ` ` ` `

2 Study the photograph of Great
   Yarmouth (A).

A Great Yarmouth, Norfolk

   (i) What coastal feature is
        illustrated? (1)

   .... ` ` ` ` `1`

   (ii) Explain the formation of this feature
        as illustrated. (5)

   ....

   ....

   ....

   ....

   ....

   ....

   ....

   ....

   ....

   .... ` ` `5` ` `

   (iii) Describe the man-made features
         that have been built along the
         beach. Suggest reasons for their
         construction. (4)

   RUSV

   ....

   ....

   ....

   ....

   ....

   ....

   .... ` ` `2` `2`

   (iv) How has the human use of the
        coast been influenced by the
        physical features? (3)

   ....

   ....

   ....

   ....

   .... ` ` ` ` `3`

3 With reference to specific examples,
   examine how effective the various
   attempts to reduce erosion around
   Britain's coast have been. (3)

   ....

   ....

   ....

   ....

   ....

   .... `1` `1` ` ` `1`

4 Explain how a river's delta can influence
   the lives and activities of the people
   living there. (6)

   ....

   ....

   ....

   ....

   ....

   ....

   .... `3` `3` ` ` ` `
   .... `7` `11` `6` `1`

5. Physical environment and people: Weather processes

ELEMENTS OF THE WEATHER

There is a saying, to be 'at the mercy of the elements'. It means to be out in the open, on the sea or on a mountain, exposed to the full range of the weather. Diagram A shows what these elements are.

$\mathcal{A}$ The elements of the weather

Basic Definitions

Temperature: a measure of how warm or cold the air is.
Pressure: a measure of the force exerted by the air.
Humidity: how much water there is in the air.
Precipitation: things which fall out of the air, e.g. rain.
Wind: moving air.
Sunshine: when the sun is visible from the ground.
Cloud cover: the amount of the sky covered by cloud, measured in eighths.
Cloud type: whether cloud is flat like a blanket (stratus cloud) or towering upwards (cumulus cloud) or a combination of the two.

Predicting what the weather conditions will be like in the future is big business. Farmers, the Electricity Board, local councils, airports and airlines and agencies of travel and tourism pay hundreds of millions of pounds per year, worldwide, for such information. The information is provided by organisations such as the Meteorological Office, based at Bracknell, near London.

Elements of the weather are carefully measured, either by meteorologists (weather scientists) or by automatic machines set up in remote parts of the world's oceans and deserts. The information is sent via telephone, radio or sometimes satellite to huge computers, such as the one at Bracknell. They are programmed to do complex mathematical calculations. They then output information on current weather and possible future weather as figures or maps.

Cold weather will encourage people to turn up their house heating. Power stations need to know beforehand, so they are ready to increase the electricity output. Local councils need to know if heavy frost and snow are predicted so they can grit dangerous accident spots. Airlines need to be warned of strong winds, fog, frost and snow. All of these are known as **weather hazards**. They are shown in Diagram B.

Calm weather hazards

If air pressure is high, wet air from the sea can form fogs and dew when it cools down at night. In winter the dew will freeze to form frost.

Fog makes travelling dangerous. A mixture of smoke and fog (smog) is thicker, more dangerous to travel through, and makes lung diseases much worse.

Frost kills delicate plants, shatters concrete and stone, and makes roads and runways treacherous.

Drought   Calm weather is usually free of rain. If no rain falls, crops die and reservoirs empty, and there is said to be a drought.

Storm weather hazards

When air pressure falls really low, wind force increases. Rain and sea surges may cause flooding.

Winds   Hurricanes give winds of 200 km per hour over huge areas of ocean. If they hit a coast, they die down, but cause great damage first. Tornadoes are much smaller but can give even stronger winds. On water, waterspouts are a form of tornado.

Sea surges   Hurricanes can suck up the ocean surface to a level several metres higher than normal. Much of the damage to coasts during a hurricane is caused by sea surge flooding.

Rain   Too much rain can cause flooding, which damages farmland and stops traffic on roads and railways.

B   Weather hazards

Calm (high pressure) hazards

Fog   Motorway accidents

Frost   Heaves and shatters stonework

Drought   Lack of rain – no crops or grass for animals

Storm (low pressure) hazards

Winds

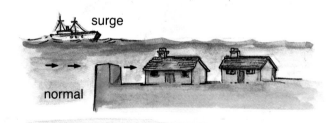
Sea surge floods
surge
normal

Rain water floods
rivers flood

1   Name five elements of the weather. (5)   *RUSV*

....

....

....

....

.... | 5 | | |

2   Explain the meaning of the following
    meteorological terms:
    relative humidity, precipitation,
    pressure, stratus. (4)

....

....

....

....

....

.... | | 4 | |

3   Study Photograph A and Maps B, C and
    D, which are concerned with the floods
    in York in 1982.
    (i) What two weather hazards were
         responsible for the heavy floods in
         York? (2)

....

....

.... | | 2 | |

    (ii) Between 40 and 50 mm of rain fell
         in Ripon between the 1st and 6th of
         January 1982. How much fell in
         York during the same period? (1)

.... | | 1 | |

(iii) Why was the city of York
      particularly prone to flooding? (4)   *RUSV*

....

....

....

....

....

.... | | 2 | 2 |

(iv) What kinds of problem would result
     from the flood, as shown in
     Photograph A? (4)

....

....

....

.... | | 4 | |

4   By reference to specific examples,
    explain how accurate weather
    forecasting can reduce the effects of
    some weather hazards. (5)

....

....

....

....

....

....

....

.... | 2 | 2 | | 1 |
                                                      | 7 | 12 | 5 | 1 |

A Flood damage in York, 1982

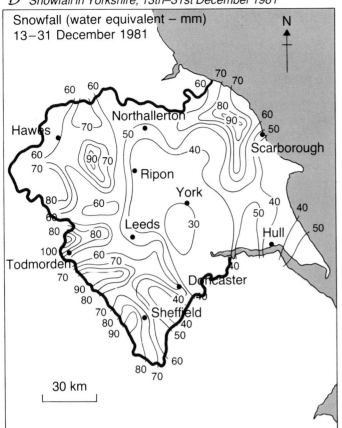

B *Snowfall in Yorkshire, 13th–31st December 1981*

Snowfall (water equivalent – mm)
13–31 December 1981

N

30 km

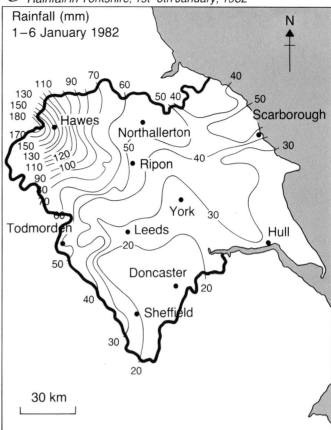

C *Rainfall in Yorkshire, 1st–6th January, 1982*

Rainfall (mm)
1–6 January 1982

N

30 km

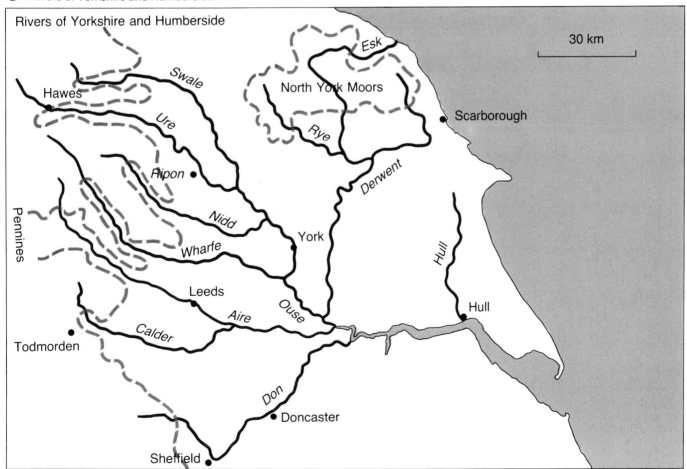

D *Rivers of Yorkshire and Humberside*

Rivers of Yorkshire and Humberside

30 km

MEASURING THE WEATHER

It makes sense if the data sent out from every weather station is measured in the same way. To make this possible, most land measurements are taken from instruments stored in a **Stevenson's screen**. This is just a white painted box, which has slatted walls to allow air to flow gently around the instruments inside, as shown in Diagram A. The instruments are read at regular intervals, usually every six hours. They measure:

A Stevenson's screen

1 Painted white to reflect sunlight
2 Louvred (slatted) sides to allow free air flow but no wind on to the instruments
3 One metre above the ground
4 Gives the same conditions in all weather stations
5 Placed on grass away from buildings

Stevenson screen

sloping roof

front door on hinge

louvred sides

instruments

1 metre high

Temperature

(How warm or cold the air is)
This is measured by a maximum and minimum thermometer, as shown in Diagram B. At night, the mercury contracts up the left hand tube, pushing the pin upwards. By day, it expands up the right hand tube, pushing the right hand pin with it. The positions of the two pin heads show the minimum (lowest) and maximum (highest) temperatures since the pins were last reset (by a magnet) to the top of the mercury.

B Maximum and minimum thermometer

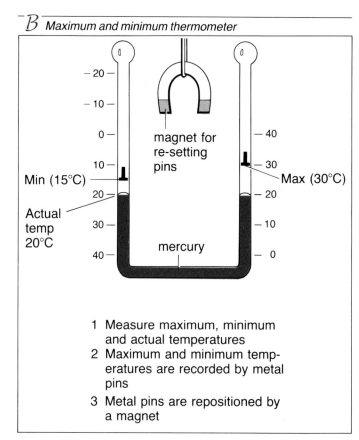

magnet for re-setting pins

Min (15°C)

Actual temp 20°C

Max (30°C)

mercury

1 Measure maximum, minimum and actual temperatures
2 Maximum and minimum temperatures are recorded by metal pins
3 Metal pins are repositioned by a magnet

Humidity

(How 'wet' the air is)
Humidity is important as it gives an indication of whether rain is likely. **Relative humidity** (RH) is the actual value that is measured. Relative humidity can be measured using a **hygrometer** (worked by a human hair which stretches in wet conditions!) or by a wet and dry bulb thermometer, as shown in Diagram C. The wet bulb temperature gives the dew point temperature (at which dew would form on cold surfaces like classroom windows). It is usually lower than the dry bulb temperature. The greater the difference between the two temperatures, the drier the air is and the lower the RH will be. RH is given as a percentage. 50 per cent is very dry air. 100 per cent is very wet, in fact it is the wettest the air can be and it is said to be 'saturated'.

C Wet and dry bulb thermometer

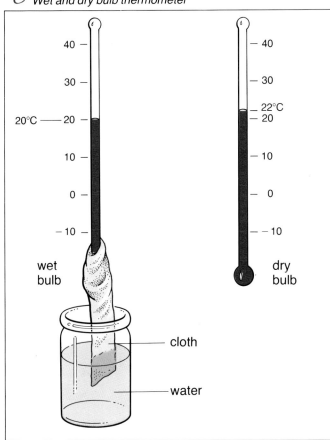

wet bulb — cloth — water

dry bulb

1 Wet bulb has wet muslin cloth round it
2 Dry bulb measures actual temperature
3 Wet bulb measures dew point temperature
4 Dry bulb and difference are used on tables to find the relative humidity

		Difference (dry bulb − wet bulb) °C					
		0	1	2	3	4	5
Dry bulb temperatures in °C	25	100	92	84	76	68	61
	24	100	91	83	75	68	60
	23	100	91	83	75	67	59
	22	100	91	82	74	66	58
	21	100	91	82	73	65	57
	20	100	91	81	73	64	56

| Dry bulb 22° |
| Wet bulb 20° |
| Difference 2° |

22° and 2°
RH = 82%
This air holds 82% of its possible water vapour.

Wind

Diagram D shows the equipment used for measuring winds. The strength of the wind is measured accurately using an **anemometer**, or it can be estimated using the Beaufort scale and observing the environment. Wind direction can be found by looking at a wind vane, by watching the movement of clouds, by watching smoke or by inventing your own test (for example, seeing the direction of small draughts inside a room, or sprinkling a light powder such as baby powder and watching it drift. This is also useful outside on calm days.)

D Anemometer and wind vane

(a) Arrow points to where wind comes *from*. What direction is it?
(b) Cups. 10 metres above the ground, whirl round and measure wind in metres per second

Sunshine

Sunshine recorders use a glass ball to focus sunlight so it makes a small burn in a piece of graph paper. They are expensive and are usually only found in professional weather stations and universities. Diagram E shows how a sunshine recorder works.

E Sunshine recorder

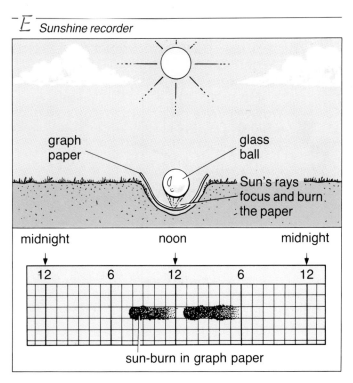

graph paper   glass ball
Sun's rays focus and burn the paper

midnight   noon   midnight
12   6   12   6   12

sun-burn in graph paper

Pressure

(The force exerted by the air)
Pressure is measured by a barometer (Diagram F) which is graded in millibars (mb). Average pressure at sea level is 1016 mb. 1030 mb would be high pressure, 990 mb would be low pressure.

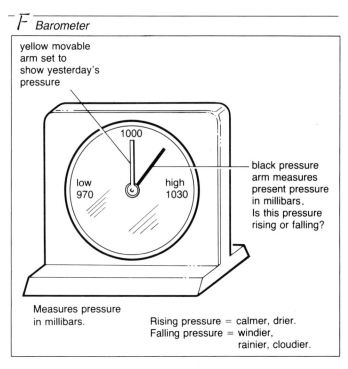

F Barometer

yellow movable arm set to show yesterday's pressure

1000

low 970

high 1030

black pressure arm measures present pressure in millibars. Is this pressure rising or falling?

Measures pressure in millibars.

Rising pressure = calmer, drier.
Falling pressure = windier, rainier, cloudier.

Precipitation

(Things which fall out of the air)
This is usually rain, but also includes snow, sleet and hail. Rainfall is measured in a rain gauge such as the one shown in Diagram G.

G Rain gauge

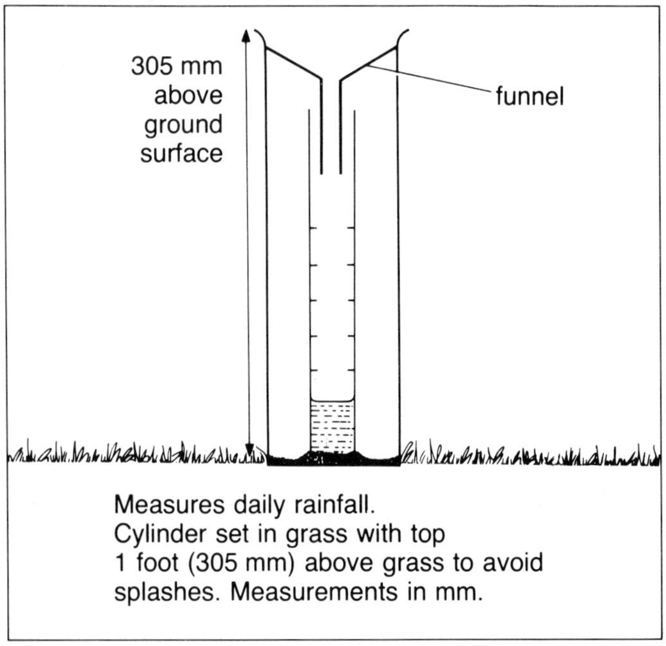

305 mm above ground surface

funnel

Measures daily rainfall.
Cylinder set in grass with top 1 foot (305 mm) above grass to avoid splashes. Measurements in mm.

Cloud cover

This is estimated by eye. It is usually measured in eighths. 8/8ths cover means that the sky is overcast. 4/8ths cover means that there is half cloud and half blue sky. 0/8ths means a clear sky. If there is fog or mist and you cannot see the sky, the sky is said to be 'obscured'.

Cloud type

This is also estimated by eye and described using these terms:
stratus (flat), cumulus (towering), cirrus (high and icy), alto (middle height), nimbus (rain). For example, a flat blanket of cloud giving rain would be called stratus-nimbus (usually made easier to say as nimbo-stratus).

Symbols used for wind speed, cloud cover and weather conditions are shown on Diagram H. A typical weather diagram for a weather station is shown in Diagram I.

H Weather symbols

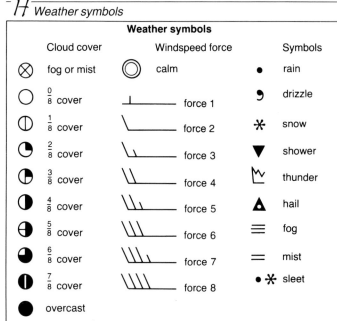

Weather symbols

Cloud cover	Windspeed force	Symbols
⊗ fog or mist	◎ calm	• rain
○ $\frac{0}{8}$ cover	force 1	� drizzle
◑ $\frac{1}{8}$ cover	force 2	✳ snow
◕ $\frac{2}{8}$ cover	force 3	▼ shower
◕ $\frac{3}{8}$ cover	force 4	ᙍ thunder
◐ $\frac{4}{8}$ cover	force 5	▲ hail
◐ $\frac{5}{8}$ cover	force 6	= fog
◐ $\frac{6}{8}$ cover	force 7	= mist
◑ $\frac{7}{8}$ cover	force 8	•✳ sleet
● overcast		

I Weather diagram

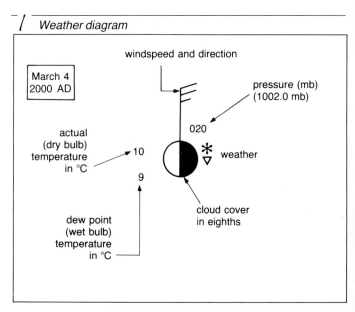

March 4
2000 AD

windspeed and direction

pressure (mb)
(1002.0 mb)

020

actual (dry bulb) temperature in °C

10

✳
▽ weather

9

dew point (wet bulb) temperature in °C

cloud cover in eighths

1 (i) Which weather element is
          measured with: (2)   *RUSV*

     a barometer? ....

     an anemometer? .... | 2 | | |

   (ii) State four features of the weather
          at the following station. (4)

....
....
....
.... | 4 | | |

A

2 Study Sketch A showing the position of
   a school's rain gauge.
   (i) Draw a labelled sketch of the rain
         gauge. (4) | 2 | | 2 |

   (ii) Why is this a poor position for the
          rain gauge? (3)

B Graph of hygrometric readings

.... *RUSV*
....
.... | 2 | 1 |

3 Explain:
   (i) Why wet muslin is wrapped around
         the bulb of one of the
         thermometers in a hygrometer. (2)

....
.... | | | 2 | |

   (ii) How you could work out the
          relative humidity with a
          hygrometer. (2)

....
.... | | | 2 | |

   (iii) Study Graph B which shows
           hygrometric readings.
           On which day was the air
           saturated?

....
           On which day was the relative
           humidity at its lowest? (2)

.... | | | 2 | |

4 (i) Describe the weather at a UK
         weather station where the readings
         in Table C were taken. (4)

....
....
....
....
.... | 4 | | |

   (ii) Suggest the time of the year when
          these reading were taken. (1)

.... | 1 | | |

   (iii) What type of weather system was
           the area experiencing? (1)

.... | 1 | | |
                                          | 8 | 12 | 4 | 1 |

C

| Visibility (km) | Sunshine (hrs) | Cloud | | Rainfall (mm) | Wind | | Temperature | | | | | Humidity % |
		Amount	Type		Direction	Force	Dry	Wet	Maximum	Minimum	Grass minimum	
10	5	0/8	–	Nil	NE	1	1	5	6	−2	−4	75

AIR MASSES AND HIGH AND LOW PRESSURE SYSTEMS

British weather is imported. We get dry **continental** weather from Europe and wet **maritime** weather from the Atlantic Ocean. Weather from the **polar** north tends to be cold, while weather from the **tropical** south is warm. This weather is shaped by the conditions in these places and is brought to us on great winds called **air masses**. They are named by **where they come from**.

Map A shows the names of the main British air masses and the weather they bring. If you find the direction of the clouds now, you may be able to make out which air mass is over you at present. Notice that Pmr starts off as Pm but then swings round and 'returns' to Britain from the west or south west. It is our most common air mass.

Sometimes this pattern of weather is altered by high and low pressure systems. High pressure systems are called **anticyclones**. Map B shows the sort of weather found in an anticyclone. Ridges of high pressure are bits of anticyclones which poke out into lower pressure areas. They bring high pressure weather but pass over more quickly than a full anticyclone.

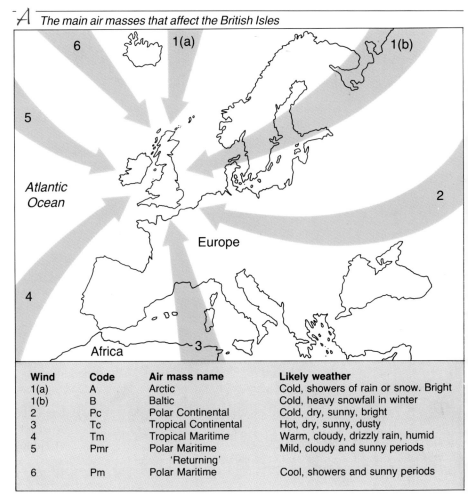

A The main air masses that affect the British Isles

Wind	Code	Air mass name	Likely weather
1(a)	A	Arctic	Cold, showers of rain or snow. Bright
1(b)	B	Baltic	Cold, heavy snowfall in winter
2	Pc	Polar Continental	Cold, dry, sunny, bright
3	Tc	Tropical Continental	Hot, dry, sunny, dusty
4	Tm	Tropical Maritime	Warm, cloudy, drizzly rain, humid
5	Pmr	Polar Maritime 'Returning'	Mild, cloudy and sunny periods
6	Pm	Polar Maritime	Cool, showers and sunny periods

B High pressure systems – anticyclones

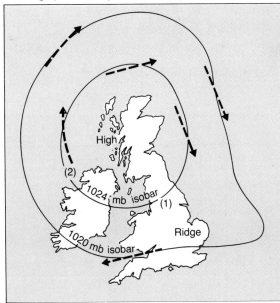

Average sea level air pressure is about 1016 mb. Over this, air pressure is said to be 'high'. High air pressure is linked with calm or gentle breezes and dry weather. Summer and winter anticyclones give different sorts of weather conditions, as shown below.

Summer anticyclone, e.g. July 4

1 Cool misty mornings
2 Hot sunny afternoons
3 Usually clear sky
4 No low cloud
5 Dry
6 Light and variable wind

Winter anticyclone, e.g. January 6

1 Freezing, foggy mornings
2 Cold afternoons
3 Clear or high 'blanket' cloud
4 No low cloud
5 Dry
6 Light and variable wind

(1) Note that the ridge of high pressure will bring a period of calm, dry weather to the place it lies over.

(2) Note that the winds usually blow clockwise along the isobars and slightly out of the high pressure.

Low pressure systems over Britain are called **depressions**. They happen when polar and tropical air masses get caught up with each other over the Atlantic Ocean. The whole lot comes swirling in over Britain from the west, passes over us, and dies out somewhere in Europe. Map C shows what a depression looks like on a weather map. The **fronts** are lines of thick cloud and rain, where the air masses meet. They are called fronts because they remind people of battlefronts where one army meets another.

Diagram D shows the pattern of weather which a depression can bring as it passes over Britain.

So, if the weather forecast is for high pressure, you can expect calm weather conditions, often with morning fog and afternoon sun. If the forecast is for low pressure, on the other hand, expect stormy winds, cloud and rain.

C *Low pressure systems – depressions and fronts*

Low pressure indicates wind, cloud and rain. Depressions are huge swirls of low pressure, 1000 km across, which move across Britain from the Atlantic. Fronts are rain belts where warm air masses are being forced up over cold air. There are warm fronts (drizzly rain), cold fronts (heavy rain, hail and maybe thunder) and occluded fronts (a warm front followed straight away by a cold front). A depression with fronts is shown on the weather map below.

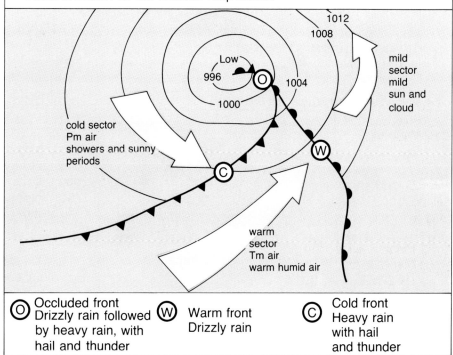

◎ Occluded front Drizzly rain followed by heavy rain, with hail and thunder	Ⓦ Warm front Drizzly rain	Ⓒ Cold front Heavy rain with hail and thunder

D *A depression passing over Cardiff*

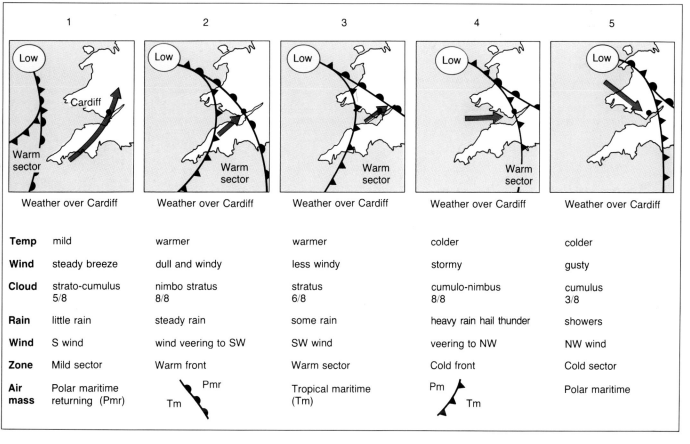

	1	2	3	4	5
	Weather over Cardiff	Weather over Cardiff	Weather over Cardiff	Weather over Cardiff	Weather over Cardiff
Temp	mild	warmer	warmer	colder	colder
Wind	steady breeze	dull and windy	less windy	stormy	gusty
Cloud	strato-cumulus 5/8	nimbo stratus 8/8	stratus 6/8	cumulo-nimbus 8/8	cumulus 3/8
Rain	little rain	steady rain	some rain	heavy rain hail thunder	showers
Wind	S wind	wind veering to SW	SW wind	veering to NW	NW wind
Zone	Mild sector	Warm front	Warm sector	Cold front	Cold sector
Air mass	Polar maritime returning (Pmr)	Pmr / Tm	Tropical maritime (Tm)	Pm / Tm	Polar maritime

1   What is an air mass? (1)   *RUSV*

....

....   [1][ ][ ][ ]

2   Diagram A summarises the main air masses which can affect the weather of the British Isles.

A *Main air masses that affect the British Isles*

Polar Maritime
Arctic
Polar Continental
Polar Maritime Returning
Tropical
Tropical Maritime
Tropical Continental

(i) Which air mass is likely to give: *RUSV*

     warm wet conditions? ....

     cold dry conditions? .... (2)   [2][ ][ ][ ]

(ii) For each, explain why. (4)

....

....

....

....   [2][2][ ][ ]

3   Study Map B which shows the weather conditions over Wales at three different times of the year.

    (i) Which map shows the warm front? (1)

....   [ ][ ][1][ ]

    (ii) What name is given to the numbered lines on the maps? (1)

....   [1][ ][ ][ ]

    (iii) In which direction would the winds have blown over Wales in March? (1)

....   [ ][1][ ][ ]

    (iv) Describe the weather conditions that Wales experienced in May? (3)

....

....

....   [2][1][ ][ ]

B *Weather conditions over Wales during three different months of the year*

Low
980 mb
984
988
992
A September

High
1036 mb
1032
B May

Low
976
980 mb
984
988
992
C March

(v) State two ways in which the weather in south and west Wales in September would have differed from that in north and east Wales? (2)

RUSV

....

....

.... | | 2 | | |

(vi) Name a month when a depression and a month when an anticyclone was influencing the weather conditions over Wales. (2)

....

....

.... | | 2 | | |

4 Study the satellite picture (C) of a depression passing over western Europe.
Place tracing paper on the outline map of western Europe (D). Mark and label the position of the following:
  (i) the centre of the depression
  (ii) the warm front
  (iii) the cold front
  (iv) warm and cold sectors
  (v) rain belts. (6)

| | 3 | 3 | |

C Depression passing over Western Europe

5 Why have satellite photographs become so important in present day weather forecasting? (2)

RUSV

....

....

.... | | | | 2 |

| 8 | 11 | 4 | 2 |

D Outline map of Western Europe

CLIMATE AND LOCATION

Different parts of the world have different climates.

There is a difference between weather and climate. Weather is what happens in the atmosphere day by day. Climate is the weather taken on average over a period of thirty years. For example:

The *weather* for Myplace, London, at noon on March 1, 1970 was 5°C, NE wind force 5, 8/8 cloud, 98% RH, 1.4 hours sunshine, with 11.6 mm rain in the last 12 hours.

The *climate* for Myplace, London, for March 1, 1955–1985 was 10°C, SW wind force 4, 5/8 cloud, 82% RH, 4.1 hours sunshine, with 1.1 mm rain in the last 12 hours.

The climate for Yourplace Cornwall, for March 1 1955–85 was 12°C, SW wind force 5, 6/8 cloud, 93% RH, 3.7 hours sunshine, with 1.6mm rain in the last 12 hours.

Yourplace's climate is warmer, wetter and windier than Myplace's. Map A shows some of the main reasons for differences in British weather and climate, from place to place.

Map B describes some of the main features of European climate. The climate affects where people live, how they farm and travel, and their leisure. This sort of knowledge is also of interest to travel agents and holidaymakers. However, we really want much greater detail to be able to choose where to go at different times of the year.

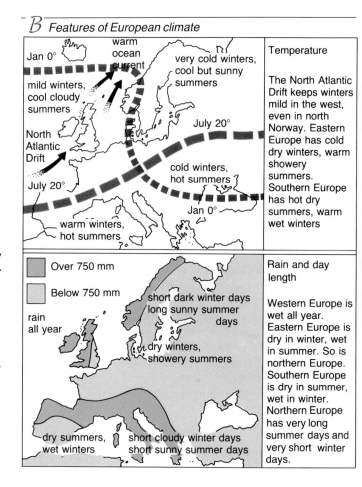

B Features of European climate

Temperature

The North Atlantic Drift keeps winters mild in the west, even in north Norway. Eastern Europe has cold dry winters, warm showery summers. Southern Europe has hot dry summers, warm wet winters

Rain and day length

Western Europe is wet all year. Eastern Europe is dry in winter, wet in summer. So is northern Europe. Southern Europe is dry in summer, wet in winter. Northern Europe has very long summer days and very short winter days.

A British climatic facts

Temperature	Rainfall	Sun and fog
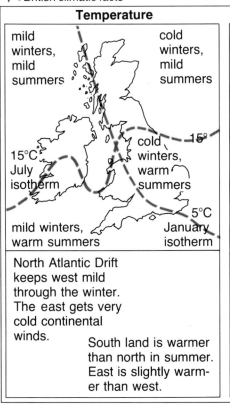	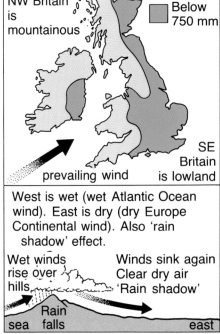	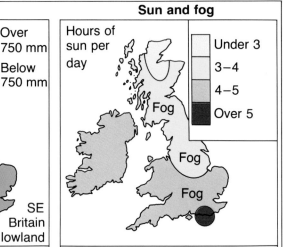
North Atlantic Drift keeps west mild through the winter. The east gets very cold continental winds. South land is warmer than north in summer. East is slightly warmer than west.	West is wet (wet Atlantic Ocean wind). East is dry (dry Europe Continental wind). Also 'rain shadow' effect.	North and west is cloudy because of wet winds and mountains. South and east are sunny because of lowland, dry continental air and 'rain shadow' effect. Fog in inland lowland areas especially where industry pollutes the air.

Here are some of the factors affecting climate.

The seasons

Weather (and therefore climate) is caused by the sun's energy, which drives air masses and ocean currents from hotter, tropical areas to colder, polar ones. The Northern Hemisphere tilts more towards the sun from March 21 to September 23 each year, so this is the warmer season (summer). It tilts away from the sun in the other half of the year, so this is the colder season (winter). Because the Earth (especially areas of water) holds the summer sun's heat for a while, autumn is warmer than spring.

Air masses

Air masses take the weather of the place they start from to the places they move over. Air masses which start in polar areas are cold, whereas those from tropical areas are warm. Those from oceans (maritime) are cloudy and bring rain, and those from the centres of continents are dry.

Ocean currents

Warm ocean currents like the North Atlantic Drift warm up coastal places, even in high latitudes. Cold currents like the Labrador Current cool the coast down, cause fogs, and cause the coast to be drier than warm currents.

Continentality

The nearer a place is to the centre of a continent, the colder it is in winter, and the warmer it is in summer. Coastal places usually have wet, mild weather throughout the year. Inland places usually have dry winters and showery summers.

Latitude

The higher the latitude (the nearer the North or South Pole), the colder it is likely to be. (But see the section on ocean currents above.)

Altitude

The greater the altitude (the further the place is above sea level), the colder, windier and wetter it is likely to be.

Aspect

South and west facing slopes are likely to be sunnier and warmer than north and east facing slopes.

People can create their own weather by heating and air conditioning their houses. They can also affect the weather outside their houses by cloud seeding, windbreaks, frost burners, deforestation and desertification. This is shown in Diagram C.

C How people can change their own weather and climate

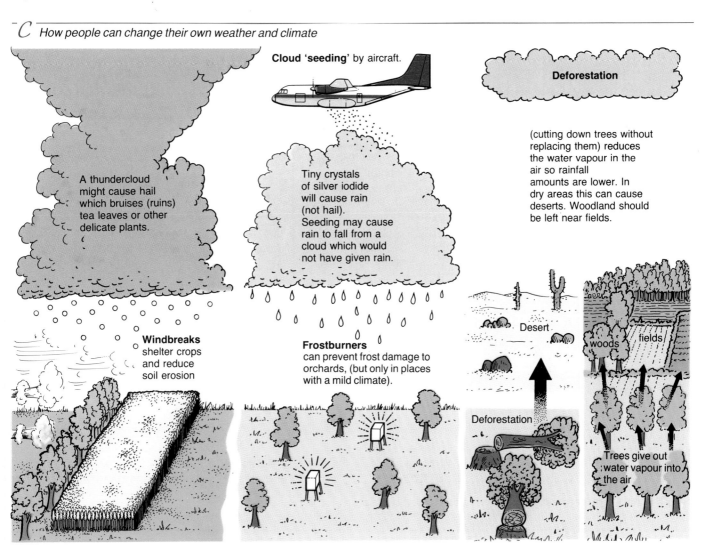

Cloud 'seeding' by aircraft.

Deforestation

A thundercloud might cause hail which bruises (ruins) tea leaves or other delicate plants.

Tiny crystals of silver iodide will cause rain (not hail). Seeding may cause rain to fall from a cloud which would not have given rain.

(cutting down trees without replacing them) reduces the water vapour in the air so rainfall amounts are lower. In dry areas this can cause deserts. Woodland should be left near fields.

Windbreaks shelter crops and reduce soil erosion

Frostburners can prevent frost damage to orchards, (but only in places with a mild climate).

Desert

Deforestation

woods / fields

Trees give out water vapour into the air

1 Explain the difference between climate and weather. (2)   *RUSV*

....
....
....
....   2 ☐ ☐ ☐

2 List four factors influencing the climate of a particular place. (4)

....
....
....
....   4 ☐ ☐ ☐

3 Study the climate graph (A) for Winnipeg in central Canada.

A Climate graph for Winnipeg

(i) What is the temperature of the warmest month? (1)

....   ☐ ☐ 1 ☐

(ii) What is the temperature of the coldest month? (1)

....   ☐ ☐ 1 ☐

(iii) What is the temperature range? (1)

....   ☐ ☐ 1 ☐

(iv) Explain why the temperature range is so large in an area like Canada. (3)   *RUSV*

....
....
....
....
....
....   3 ☐ ☐ ☐

B Prevailing winds and ocean currents in Chile

4 Study the labelled map of Chile (B), which
  shows the prevailing winds and ocean
  currents, and Photographs C, D and E
  showing three different locations in the
  country.

RUSV

(i) With the aid of a diagram, explain
    why northern Chile is warmer than
    southern Chile. (4)

....
....
....
....
....
....
....
....

`[ | 4 | ]`

(ii) State two causes of the low rainfall in
     northern Chile. (2)

....
....

`[ | 2 | ]`

(iii) In which season will the majority of
      the rain fall in central Chile? (1)

....

`[ | 1 | ]`

(iv) State one advantage and one
     disadvantage of the climate of central
     Chile to local farmers. (2)

....
....
....
....

`[ | | 2 ]`

(v) Why are parts of the Andes snow-
    covered? (1)

....
....

`[ 1 | | ]`

(vi) Why will south facing slopes of the
     Andean valleys have a longer period
     of snow cover than north facing
     slopes? (3)

....
....
....
....
....
....

`[ | 3 | ]`
`[ 7 | 13 | 3 | 2 ]`

C Atacama Desert in northern Chile

D Mediterranean climate in central Chile

E Densely forested slopes in southern Chile

6. Population

POPULATION DENSITY, DISTRIBUTION AND ENVIRONMENTAL OPPORTUNITIES

Is your part of the world crowded or empty? Table A shows the terms used to describe **population density**.

Population density is the number of people in an area. For example, population density in Switzerland in 1980 was 125 people per square kilometre. It was worked out by dividing the total population by the total area like this:

$$\text{Population density} = \frac{\text{Swiss population}}{\text{Area of Switzerland}} = \frac{6\,000\,000 \text{ people}}{40\,000 \text{ sq km}}$$

$$= \frac{600}{4} \text{ people per sq km} = 125 \text{ people per sq km}$$

A formula which helps you work this out is $D = \dfrac{P}{A}$

where D = population density, P = population and A = area

Similarly, $A = \dfrac{P}{D}$ and $P = D \times A$

Areas of high population density are obviously crowded. Those of low population density are said to be sparsely populated. Map B shows the crowded and sparsely populated areas of the world. Highly populated areas of the world include the north eastern USA, Western Europe, the Nile Valley and lowland areas of South East Asia, China and Japan. The sparsely populated areas include the mountainous areas of North and South America and Asia, the tropical rainforests of the Amazon and Zaire basins, and the desert areas of the Sahara, Atacama, Kalahari and central Asia.

The chief factors influencing the world distribution of population include the following:

Relief

Lowland areas have gentle slopes and are the most attractive areas for settlement since they provide opportunities for farming, building and travel. Mountain areas are too steep for people to grow crops, build or travel. However, some lowland areas are empty as people do not settle on plains which are flooded or in river basins, like that of the river Amazon, where there is still dense forest which is difficult to penetrate.

Climate and vegetation

Very cold and very dry areas do not favour settlement. 99 per cent of the world's population lives in places with average monthly temperatures between 0°C and 25°C and an annual rainfall of between 250 and 2000 mm.

Resources

Mineral wealth, like oil and iron ore, can encourage dense populations, even in otherwise inhospitable areas. The presence of coal which provides power, encourages dense populations near exposed coalfields. A reliable water supply allows farmers to grow crops, even in deserts. This explains the dense population in the lower Nile Valley, which lies in the Egyptian part of the Sahara Desert. The prospect of more than one harvest of rice per year explains why more than 25 per cent of the world's population live on the fertile land of the great river plains of SE Asia.

A Terms used to describe population density

	crowded	almost empty
Everyday term	crowded	almost empty
Essay language	densely populated	sparsely populated
Technical term	high population density	low population density

B *Simple map of world population densities*

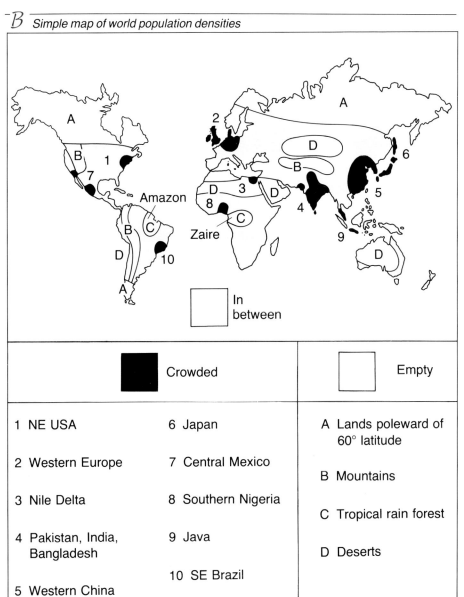

	Crowded			Empty

1 NE USA	6 Japan	A Lands poleward of 60° latitude
2 Western Europe	7 Central Mexico	B Mountains
3 Nile Delta	8 Southern Nigeria	C Tropical rain forest
4 Pakistan, India, Bangladesh	9 Java	D Deserts
5 Western China	10 SE Brazil	

Employment opportunities

People want to live where they can earn money by working. In poor countries, jobs are found on the land or near sources of raw materials or power. In rich countries, modern industry is not so tied to these sources. National grids supply electricity to most parts of such countries. Modern firms are usually small and use few bulky raw materials. As a result, they can have premises in planned trading estates on main routeways near major cities. They may choose to develop in the richer parts of the country, like north western Italy or south eastern England, or they may choose to locate in small, rural market towns, where rents are low.

Accessibility

This means being 'easy to get to'. People like to live in places near the centre of things, where life seems to be most interesting. These places usually have the best network of roads and railways, have good airports, and are easy to get to. In Europe, the triangle formed by London, Paris and Cologne is a major centre and has a high population density. Places like northern Scotland and southern Italy are remote from here and their population densities are lower.

C *Reasons for population densities in the UK (simplified)*

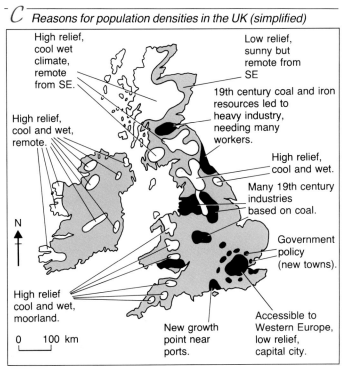

Government policy

A country's government may decide that it does not want all its new firms to set up in the richest part of the country. People would come into that area, wanting homes and increasing traffic on the existing roads. The area would become congested. So the government uses its powers to encourage people to live elsewhere and to populate a less accessible place. In Australia, Brazil, Pakistan, Nigeria and many other countries, governments have moved their capital cities for this reason.

After the Second World War, the centre of many British cities needed repair after bomb damage. Many local authorities took this opportunity to move people out of the crowded city centres into less crowded housing estates on the outskirts of the cities. In London, the authorities decided that this would make the city outskirts grow too much. So, people were encouraged to move into eight new towns, five expanded towns and one new city, as shown on Map C.

Map C shows how the population distribution of the UK has been influenced by all of these factors.

Assessment POPULATION DENSITY, DISTRIBUTION AND ENVIRONMENTAL OPPORTUNITIES

RUSV

1 Explain the meaning of 'population density'. (1)

....

.... 1

2 Complete the following table. The numbers have been simplified. (4)

Country	Area (thousands km²)	Population (thousands)	Population density (people/km²)
Norway	300	3900	
Bangladesh		90 000	600
Australia	7500		2
Singapore		2500	5000

4

3 Study Map A which shows the most densely and sparsely populated areas in the world.

(i) Against each of the letters P, Q and R write down the correct hostile environment chosen from the following list:
mountain; equatorial; rain forest; arctic; hot desert.

P ....

Q ....

R .... (3) 3

RUSV

(ii) (a) Describe the features of hot desert environments that help to explain their low population density. (3)
(b) Describe one way in which they can be improved so that they can support more people. (2)

....

....

....

....

....

....

....

.... 4 1

(iii) Explain why some hostile environments are able to support pockets of dense population. (3)

....

....

....

....

....

.... 1 2

A *Map of densely and sparsely populated areas*

Population density
R
R
Q
Q
P
P
Over 100 people per sq km
Less than one person per sq km
P, Q and R are three types of hostile environment.

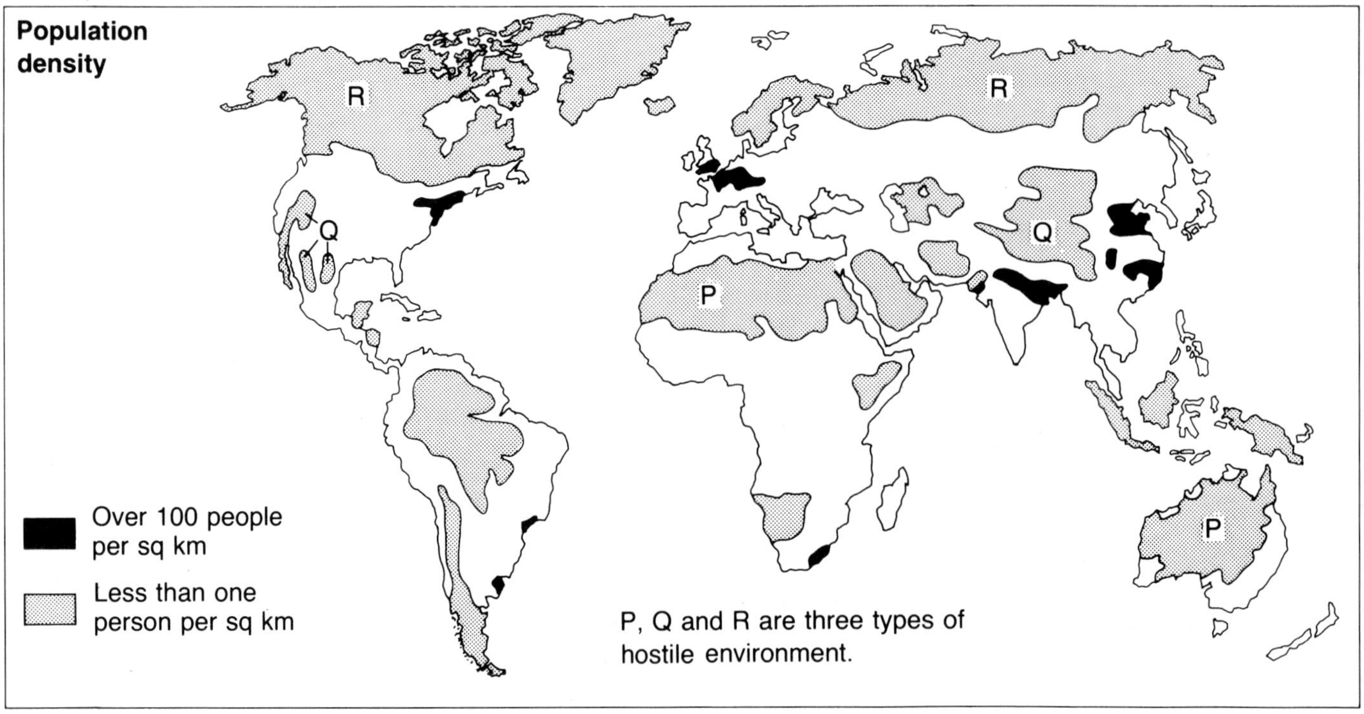

4 Study Maps B and C of Ghana.

(i) With the aid of the maps explain the pattern of population density in Ghana. (4)

		4	

(ii) In what ways can this distribution of population be considered a disadvantage to the economy of a country like Ghana? (5)

1	3		1
7	12	4	2

RUSV

B Population density of Ghana

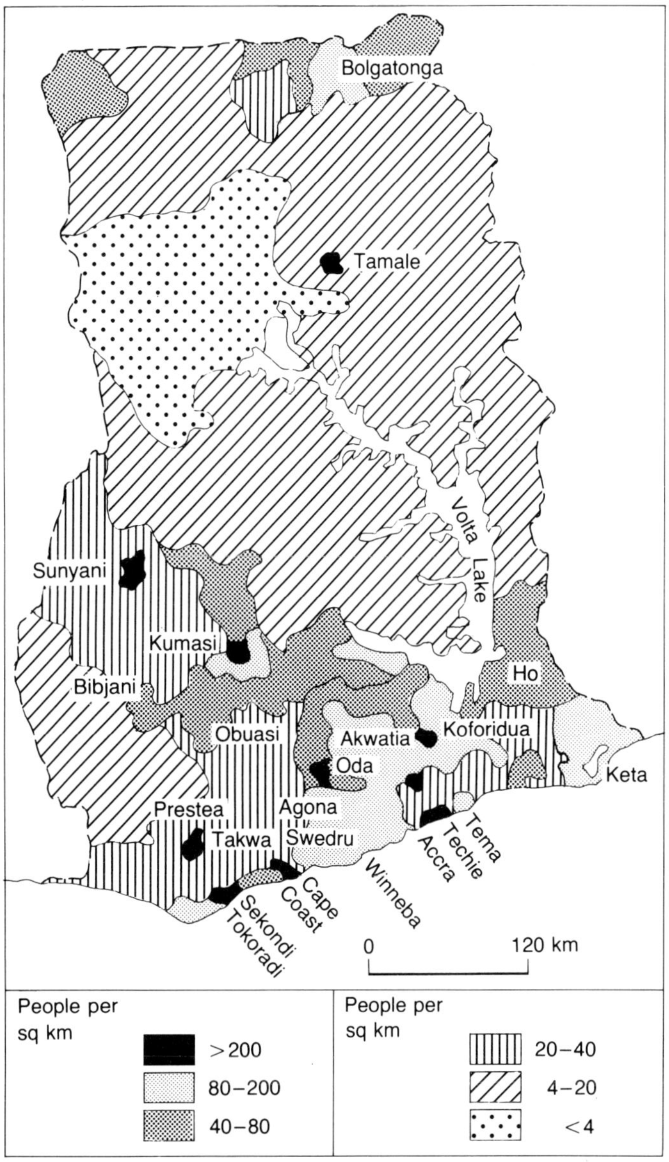

Bolgatonga
Tamale
Volta Lake
Sunyani
Kumasi
Bibjani
Ho
Obuasi
Akwatia
Koforidua
Oda
Keta
Prestea
Agona
Takwa
Swedru
Tema
Techie
Accra
Winneba
Cape Coast
Sekondi Tokoradi
0
120 km
People per sq km
>200
80–200
40–80
People per sq km
20–40
4–20
<4

C Distribution maps for Ghana

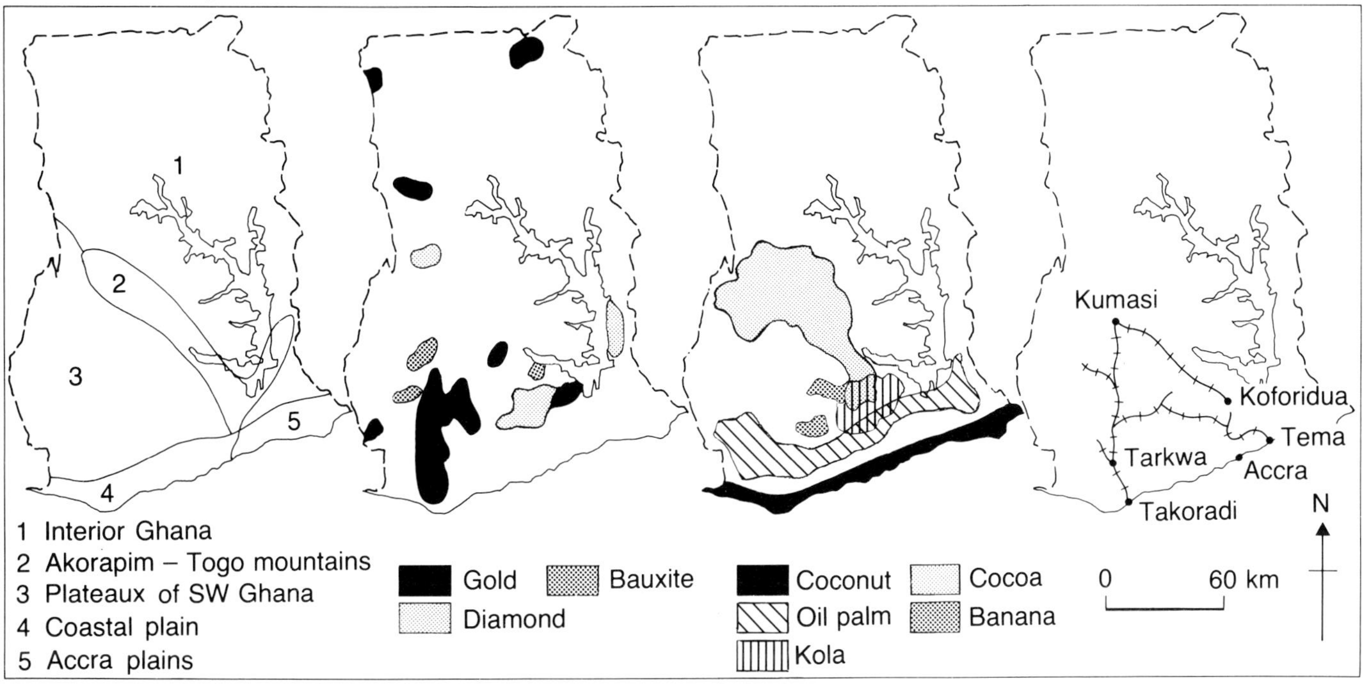

1
2
3
4
5
1 Interior Ghana
2 Akorapim – Togo mountains
3 Plateaux of SW Ghana
4 Coastal plain
5 Accra plains
Gold
Bauxite
Diamond
Coconut
Cocoa
Oil palm
Banana
Kola
Kumasi
Koforidua
Tema
Tarkwa
Accra
Takoradi
N
0
60 km

NATURAL INCREASE: CAUSES AND EFFECTS

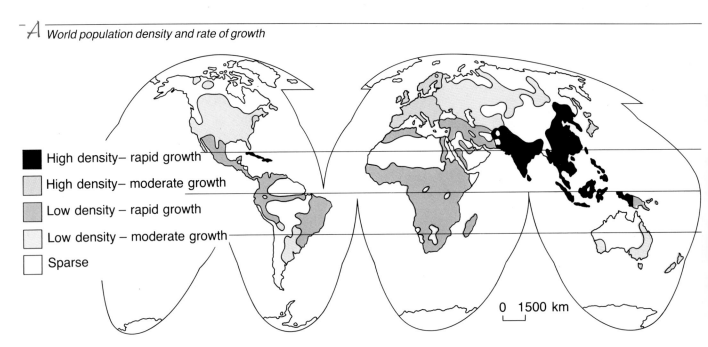

A World population density and rate of growth

High density– rapid growth

High density– moderate growth

Low density – rapid growth

Low density – moderate growth

Sparse

0 1500 km

The number of people in the world has doubled to 4000 million since 1950. It will double again by 2100 AD, but as Map A shows, this increase is not spread evenly. In some countries the population is growing rapidly, in others slowly, and in some numbers are falling. This is because of differences in the **natural increase of population** and **migration** of people from one area to another.

Diagram B shows what is meant by the natural increase of population. It is the difference between the number of people born and the number of people who die. It may cause a growth in population, or a decline. The natural increase of population in an area depends on the **crude birth rate** and the **crude death rate**.

The crude birth rate is the number of births per 1000 people. The crude death rate is the number of deaths per 1000 people. The natural increase is birth rate minus death rate.

There are a number of factors which influence birth and death rates and so influence the rate of natural increase. Five important ones are given here.

Population structure

The age and sex ratios in the population, as shown on a population pyramid, are important. The birth rate will reflect the number of potential parents, in particular the number of women of child-bearing age. The high birth rate in many parts of the developing world means a very youthful population. The birth rate is likely to remain high in the future (Diagram C).

The low birth rate in the UK means an ageing population. The birth rate is likely to stay low (Diagram D).

Improving living standards

If the people in an area get a clean water supply, and can buy soap, disinfectant and simple medical drugs, their death rate drops rapidly. As the birth rate stays high, the natural increase is very high. More children survive infancy. There are many more potential parents. As people get richer, however, they may decide to limit their birth rate by family planning.

B Natural increase of population

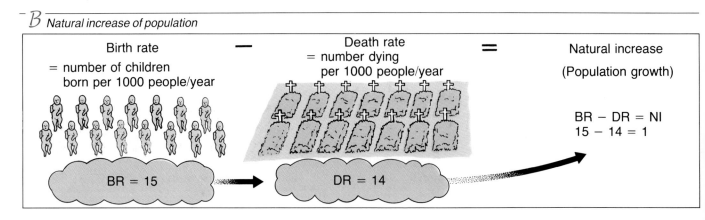

Birth rate	—	Death rate	=	Natural increase
= number of children born per 1000 people/year		= number dying per 1000 people/year		(Population growth)
BR = 15		DR = 14		BR − DR = NI 15 − 14 = 1

Social attitudes

In many parts of the developing world a large family is a sign of prestige. It also provides labour for work in the fields and acting as a kind of insurance for a person's old age. In richer countries it is now acceptable for people to use contraceptives. Couples can choose whether or not to have children. Usually they choose to have small families. The birth rate drops rapidly as this happens. The governments of some poorer countries try to keep the birth rate down by trying to persuade parents that one or two children is quite enough for a family and having more is selfish.

Religious attitudes

Some religious authorities (for example, Roman Catholic and Hindu) discourage the use of contraception. Their arguments are based on a belief in the importance of children to family life and that parental love should bring children into the world naturally.

Population stages

Some authorities have recognised four population stages marked by differing birth and death rates (Diagram E). The developed world is at Stage 4 but the bulk of the developing world is still in the rapid growth period of Stage 2.

C Population pyramid for India

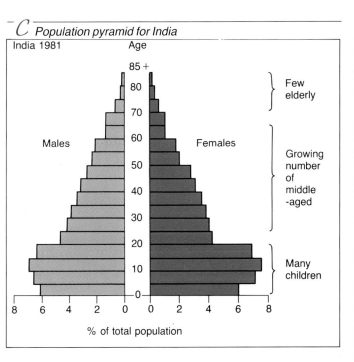

D Population pyramid for the UK

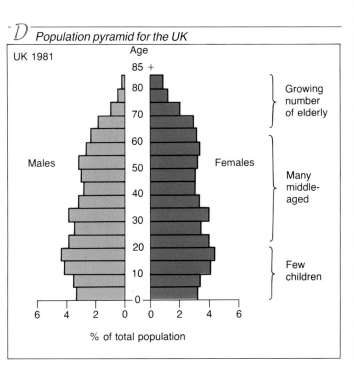

E Stages in world population growth

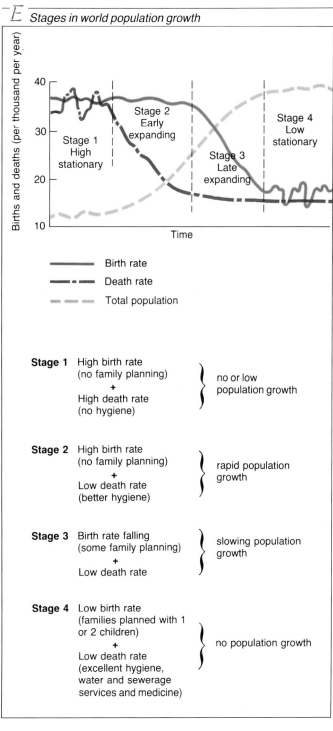

1   Study the following graph (A):

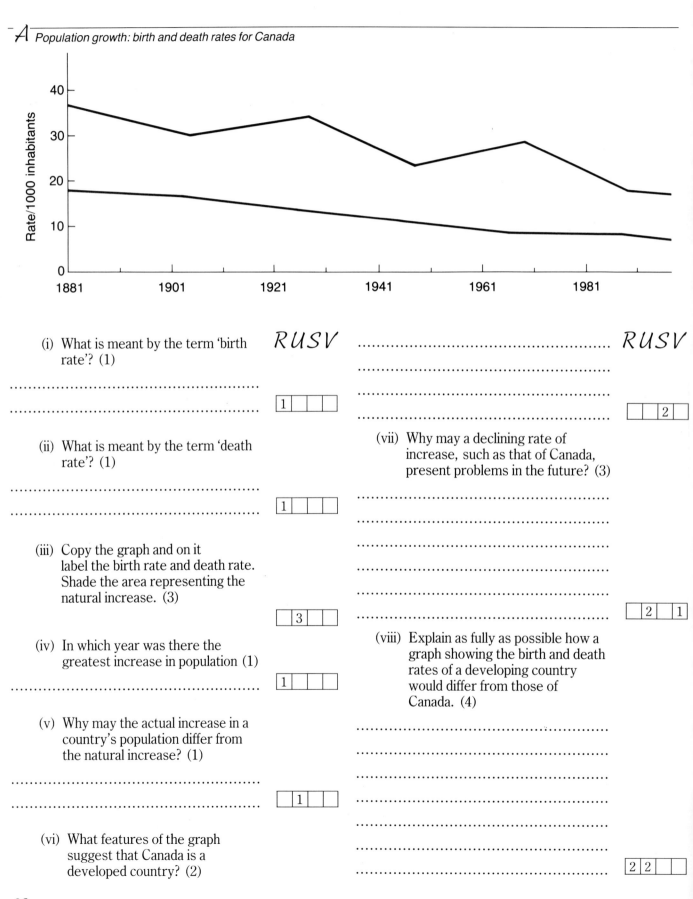

A Population growth: birth and death rates for Canada

(i)   What is meant by the term 'birth rate'? (1)

RUSV

....

....

[1][ ][ ][ ]

(ii)   What is meant by the term 'death rate'? (1)

....

....

[1][ ][ ][ ]

(iii)   Copy the graph and on it label the birth rate and death rate. Shade the area representing the natural increase. (3)

[ ][3][ ][ ]

(iv)   In which year was there the greatest increase in population (1)

....

[1][ ][ ][ ]

(v)   Why may the actual increase in a country's population differ from the natural increase? (1)

....

....

[ ][1][ ][ ]

(vi)   What features of the graph suggest that Canada is a developed country? (2)

RUSV

....

....

....

....

[ ][ ][2][ ]

(vii)   Why may a declining rate of increase, such as that of Canada, present problems in the future? (3)

....

....

....

....

....

....

[ ][2][ ][1]

(viii)   Explain as fully as possible how a graph showing the birth and death rates of a developing country would differ from those of Canada. (4)

....

....

....

....

....

....

....

[2][2][ ][ ]

2 Study Diagram B.

   (i) What kind of diagram is it? (1)

.... `1` ` ` ` ` ` `

   (ii) What percentage of the population is aged between 20 and 24? (1)

.... ` ` ` ` `1` ` `

   (iii) Is this diagram representative of a developed or a developing country? Give two reasons for your answer. (3)

....

....

....

....

....

.... ` ` `3` ` ` ` `

   (iv) In which of these population stages is the country with the pattern shown on the diagram? (See Table C.) (1)

.... ` ` `1` ` ` ` `

C Population growth stages

Stage	Death rate	Birth rate
1	High	High
2	Low	High
3	Low	Falling
4	Low	Low

   (v) Draw a simple diagram like the one in B to show the population structure of a country in Stage 4 of population growth. (3)

` ` ` ` `3` ` `
`6` `12` `6` `1`

RUSV B

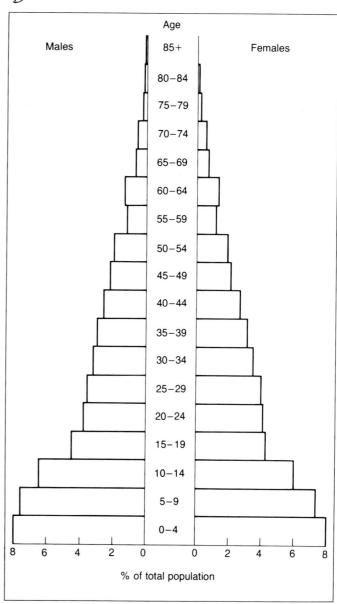

THE POPULATION EXPLOSION AND AVAILABLE RESOURCES

Diagram A shows that the population of the world is increasing more rapidly than ever. This is because many parents are having large families and, at the same time, improving medical help is allowing people to live longer. This can be shown by a simple equation:

$$\text{Birth rate} > \text{Death rate} = \text{Natural increase}$$

(If the birth rate is much greater than the death rate then there is a high natural increase.)

Our planet is likely to have seven thousand million inhabitants by 2000 AD. It is almost certain to rise to eleven thousand million eventually. The question is, can we feed, clothe, shelter, care for and educate all these people? The answer is Yes! All these people *can* be looked after. It will need the following actions, each of which brings its own problems.

Better use of existing land

1 Irrigation (putting water on to farm land) but too little can cause salt pollution.
2 High yielding seeds, which may exhaust the soil.
3 Increased use of fertilisers, which are expensive.
4 Ley farming (rotating legumes such as clover with cereals), which is more expensive at first.
5 Contour banking and ploughing (reduce soil erosion), which need skill and care. (See Diagram B.)

More new farm land

1 Low polders, reclaimed from the sea, which cost a lot to create and maintain.
2 Reclaimed heathland, by applying expensive fertilisers year after year.
3 Cleared rain forests, but the soil is soon exhausted when farmed. (See Diagram C).

A World population, 1600–2000 AD

- 7000 million
- 1000 million
- 500 million
- 300 million
- 400 million

1600   1700   1800   1900   2000

B How to improve the use of existing land

Irrigation
river
channels lead water on to fields
High yield seeds
Super-phosphate fertiliser

Ley farming
Wheat yields (tonnes per hectare) in South Australia
ley farming improves yields
fertilisers
soil exhausted

1.5
1.0
0.5
0

1860   1900   1940   1980

plough furrows
higher land
lower land
earth bank

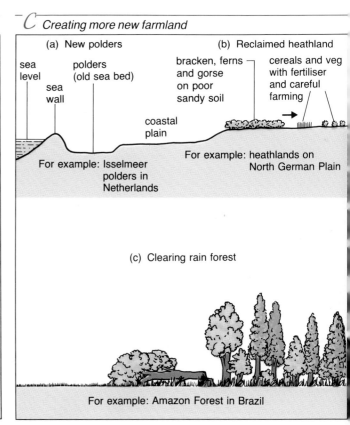

C Creating more new farmland

(a) New polders
sea level
sea wall
polders (old sea bed)
coastal plain
For example: Isselmeer polders in Netherlands

(b) Reclaimed heathland
bracken, ferns and gorse on poor sandy soil
cereals and veg with fertiliser and careful farming
For example: heathlands on North German Plain

(c) Clearing rain forest
For example: Amazon Forest in Brazil

Produce more 'factory food'

1 Beans: cheap but not always to the people's taste and custom.
2 Yeast: cheap but not always to the people's taste and custom.
3 Factory animals: suit the people's taste (in non-vegetarian societies) but *very* expensive on resources. (See Diagram D.)

Increased search for non-renewable resources

(Non-renewable means you can only use them once, for example, coal)
1 Fossil fuels (for example, oil, coal, gas).
2 Metal ores (for example, iron ore).
3 Natural chemicals (for example, salt, potash). (See Diagram E.)

Alternative sources of energy

1 Solar. ⎫ All of these are very
2 Wind. ⎬ expensive to develop at
3 Tidal. ⎭ present. (See Diagram F.)

Graphs G and H show what might happen. Family planning could dampen down the population increase and give scientists and engineers a chance to put the above into practice. But many people feel that family planning should not be the answer. What do you think?

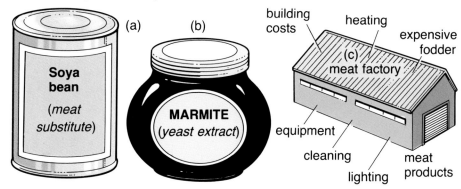

D Producing more 'factory food'

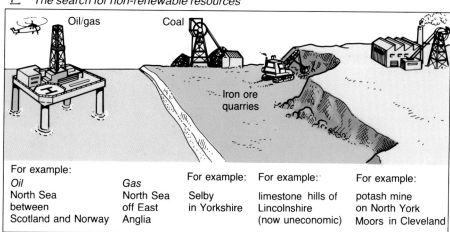

E The search for non-renewable resources

For example:
Oil
North Sea between Scotland and Norway

Gas
North Sea off East Anglia

For example: Selby in Yorkshire

For example: limestone hills of Lincolnshire (now uneconomic)

For example: potash mine on North York Moors in Cleveland

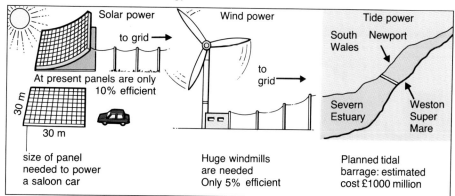

F Alternative sources of energy

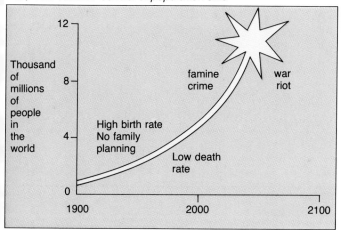

G The 'natural' control of population size

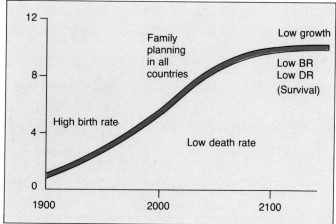

H How family planning can control population without disasters

1 Explain the term 'natural increase of a population'. (2)   *RUSV*

....

....

....

.... 2 ☐ ☐ ☐

2 Study Map A showing the natural increase of a population.
  (i) Name the two continents showing the greatest natural increase in population. (2)

....

.... ☐ ☐ 2 ☐

(ii) Name the continent showing the smallest natural increase in population. (1)   *RUSV*

.... ☐ ☐ 1 ☐

(iii) What factors influence the rate of natural increase in a particular part of the world? (4)

....

....

....

....

.... ☐ 4 ☐

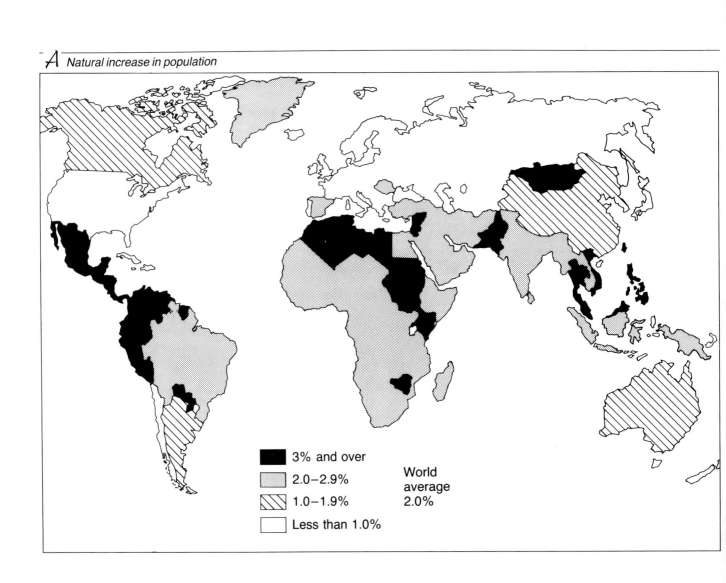

A Natural increase in population

■ 3% and over

▦ 2.0–2.9%

▨ 1.0–1.9%

□ Less than 1.0%

World average 2.0%

3   Study Poster B.   *RUSV*
    (i) How may a government encourage family planning? (3)

....
....
....
....
....   `1 2 ☐ ☐`

    (ii) Name two countries where there have been family planning campaigns. (2)

....
....   `2 ☐ ☐`

    (iii) Why has family planning often taken a long time to be accepted in developing countries? (3)

....
....
....
....
....
....   `☐ 2 ☐ 1`

B Poster to encourage family planning from Papua New Guinea

(Poster text)
Famili plan i helpim mama na pikinini long kamap strong na hepi

Famili plan

Strong na hepi

    (iv) In what other ways, apart from family planning campaigns, may a government attempt to cope with population growth? (3)   *RUSV*

....
....
....
....
....
....   `2 1 ☐ ☐`

4   Read the following quotations:

> Chairman Mao (1949): 'It is a very good thing that China has a big population. Even if China's population multiplies many times, she is fully capable of finding a solution; the solution is production.'

> Shao Li-tsu, a deputy to China's First National People's Congress (1954): 'It is a good thing to have a large population but in an environment beset with difficulties, it appears that there should be a limit set.'

Explain what these two leaders meant and why they suggest different solutions to China's population problem. (5)

....
....
....
....
....
....
....
....
....
....   `☐ 5 ☐ ☐`
`7 14 3 1`

A What is meant by migration

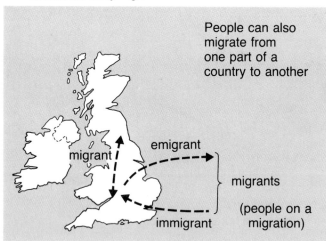

People can also migrate from one part of a country to another

migrant

emigrant

immigrant

migrants

(people on a migration)

Diagram A shows what is meant by **migration**.

An **immigrant** is someone who has been allowed to enter a country with the intention of living there. When people leave their own countries, they are called **emigrants**. During their journey, and as statistics, they are called **migrants**.

Map B shows some of the great migrations of the last one hundred years.

People migrate for two groups of reasons, often called 'push' and 'pull' factors. Firstly, they may wish to get away from what they feel are unpleasant or dangerous circumstances at home. These are the 'push' factors, as they tend to push people away from their native land. Secondly, people are attracted by what they hope are better opportunities in a different place. These are the 'pull' factors, as they pull people to the new country (Diagram C).

B Major world migration flows in the last 100 years

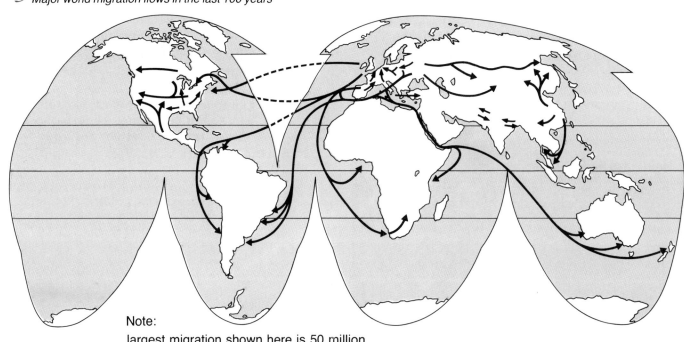

Note:

largest migration shown here is 50 million people from Europe to North America

C 'Push' and 'pull' factors

Push factors

Religious fears

Famine

Economic fears

War

Racial oppression

Political fears

Pull factors

More chance to use talents

Government assistance

Chance of a higher standard of living

D West Germany: foreign labour inflows

1972

km
0   400

200
100
0

migrants × 1000

< 1000

E

1981

People who move because of push factors tend to be the rich or the very poor. Rich people tend to move when a government favouring them is replaced by one which is likely to take away their wealth. They usually move to rich countries or to rich parts of countries. Very poor people tend to move in fear of their lives. They tend to move from one very poor country to nearby poor countries, because of war or famine.

The sort of people who emigrate because of pull factors are usually those who are neither poor nor rich. They can afford to move and feel their lives will be better elsewhere. The very poor cannot afford to move and the very rich are comfortable enough anyway. In poor countries, women often move to become house servants, for example, from Sri Lanka to Saudi Arabia. Men often move to mining areas, from Botswana to the 'Rand' in South Africa, for instance. Usually these movements are from villages to towns and cities.

In Western Europe, the 1950s and 60s were a period of mass migration, as workers from countries with high unemployment were encouraged by governments to move to countries such as West Germany, the UK and France, where there were not enough workers for growing businesses and services. Since 1973, when the soaring oil prices put lots of firms out of business, this migration has almost stopped, save for wives and children moving to be with the original migrant. Maps D and E show the change in migration to West Germany.

Migrants have to face obstacles between leaving their home and getting to their destination. The usual ones are cost and distance. Some others include government immigration controls (for example, Pakistan to USA) and pirates (for example, the 'boat people' migrating from South East Asia across the South China Sea).

When migrants get to their new country, they often find difficulty in settling down. Unless they have a lot of money to start with, they tend to settle in immigrant camps or in poorer city areas. Jobs are hard to find and local people can appear unfriendly. Not being fluent in the local language is a barrier to finding jobs and making friends. Diagram F illustrates what can happen.

F Problems which migrants might have to face

Difficulties in housing

'Sorry, Madam, this flat has just been let.'

Living in ghettos

'Don't go down there, Shiela they're all British!'

Discrimination against immigrants in jobs

'Sorry, Madam, no vacancies.'

Language barriers

'Why don't you learn to speak our language?'

Just plain homesickness!

1 Explain the terms 'push factor' and 'pull factor' with reference to the migration of people. (2) *RUSV*

....

....

....

.... 2 ☐ ☐ ☐

2 Study the following list:
   A Western European emigrants travelling to Australia on a £10 assisted passage.
   B The 'brain drain' of scientists to the USA where there are many colleges able to offer research facilities and good employment prospects.
   C Turks moving to West Germany in the 1970s where they could earn wages ten times higher than at home, with prices only five times as high.
   D Retired people moving to south west England where the winters are not as severe as in the rest of the UK.
   E Afghans fleeing from the Russian invasion of Afghanistan.
   F Moslems fleeing from Hindu India in the 1940s.
   Separate the list into two groups, one under the heading 'push factors', the other under the heading 'pull factors', using the letters to distinguish them. (6)

....

....

....

.... 3 3 ☐ ☐

3 Study the population pyramid of migrants into Calcutta (A). *RUSV*
   (i) Where is Calcutta situated? (1)

....

.... 1 ☐ ☐ ☐

   (ii) What percentage of men aged 30 to 34 migrated into Calcutta? (1)

....

.... ☐ ☐ 1 ☐

   (iii) How many people between 15 and 19 years old migrated into Calcutta? (1)

....

.... ☐ ☐ 1 ☐

   (iv) What does the diagram tell you about the migrants who move into Calcutta? (3)

....

....

....

....

....

.... ☐ ☐ 3 ☐

A Population pyramid of migrants into Calcutta

Age groups: over 60, 55–59, 50–54, 45–49, 40–44, 35–39, 30–34, 25–29, 20–24, 15–19, 10–14, 5–9, 0–4

Male   Female

14 12 10 8 6 4 2 0 2 4

%

B Main routes of migrations to and from West Africa

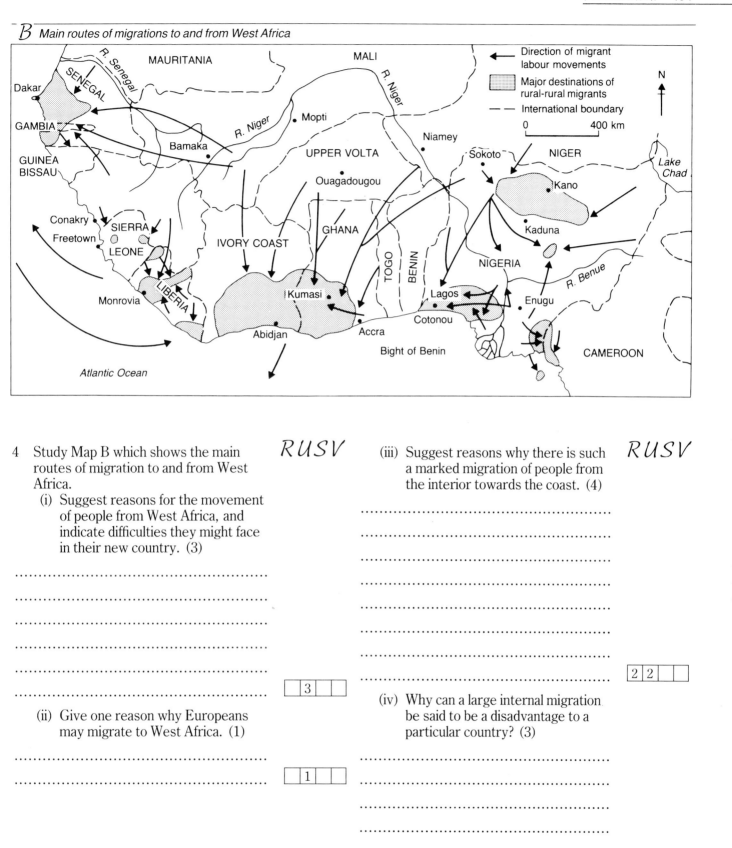

4 Study Map B which shows the main routes of migration to and from West Africa.

RUSV

(i) Suggest reasons for the movement of people from West Africa, and indicate difficulties they might face in their new country. (3)

....
....
....
....
....
....

☐3☐☐

(ii) Give one reason why Europeans may migrate to West Africa. (1)

....
....

☐1☐☐

(iii) Suggest reasons why there is such a marked migration of people from the interior towards the coast. (4)

RUSV

....
....
....
....
....
....
....
....

2 2 ☐☐

(iv) Why can a large internal migration be said to be a disadvantage to a particular country? (3)

....
....
....
....
....
....

2 ☐ 1

8 11 5 1

7. Settlement

Unit 7.1

FACTORS AFFECTING SITE, SITUATION AND LAYOUT OF SETTLEMENTS

A settlement is a place where people live. It may be a farm, miles away from the next building, or a city with millions of people. All settlements have a site, situation, function and layout.

The **site** of a settlement is the actual landform on which it is built. Obviously, a site is concerned with physical factors, such as those shown on Photograph A. The advantages of a good site usually last for as long as the settlement exists. All new housing developments in rich countries have careful surveys by site engineers to make sure that the site is right.

A supply of water without the danger of flooding was vital before piped water was available in developed countries. It is still a most important factor of site location in poorer countries. Some settlements are **wet sites** (near water) in dry areas, for example, desert oases. Others are **dry sites** (away from flooding) in wet places such as river plains.

In the past, defence was important in areas of conflict, such as the English/Scottish borders, southern Italy and south west Nigeria. A site inside a bend in a river or on a hill top is easy to defend, so these were favourite places for villages in these war zones.

A — The site of Looe, Cornwall

Relief
Bottom of a steep sided valley

Drainage
On the banks of a small stream

farmland

woodland in shadow

sea

Rock types
Seaward rocks look resistant to erosion. Possible building materials

Other
River mouth sheltered from sea winds, makes a good harbour site

Aspect
Mainly in sunny part of the valley

Exposure
Sheltered from strong sea winds

Altitude
Almost at sea level

Defence
Poor defensive site in valley (but out of sight of sea raiders in Viking times)

The **situation** of a settlement is how it is placed in relation to nearby landforms, such as hills and rivers, and land uses, such as roads, industries and other settlements. Map B shows the situation of some important places in northern France.

The **function** of a settlement is the main work that goes on there. In south Yorkshire it may be coal mining. On the Cornish coast it may be fishing or tourism. On the rim of the Paris Basin it may be growing grapes to make champagne.

The situation of a place determines how successful its function will be. Economic factors decide whether the situation is favourable or not. The most important economic factor is how easy it is to get to from other places. A settlement in the centre of an area which has good transport systems will be easier to get to and from than a place on the edge of the area. Businesses will want to set up in the centre, which can be reached from where most people live and work. So, central places are usually bigger and richer than more remote settlements.

Another important economic factor is the development of nearby resources. Aberdeen, in north east Scotland, became prosperous when deposits of oil under the North Sea were exploited. In times of low oil prices its prosperity declines.

As the economic factors of a situation change, so do the functions of the settlements. A new motorway or the opening of a holiday camp may bring prosperity. The closing down of old industries may bring unemployment and decline.

The **layout** of a settlement is the pattern of its built-up areas. Social factors are a very important influence on the layout of rural villages in developing countries, as Map C shows. In western countries the layout of a place reflects its history and the stages of its growth. Each stage has its own pattern.

B Situation of cities in northern France

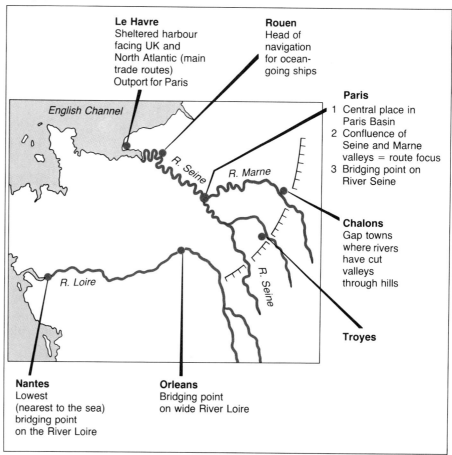

C Typical Zulu 'kraal', in Natal, South Africa

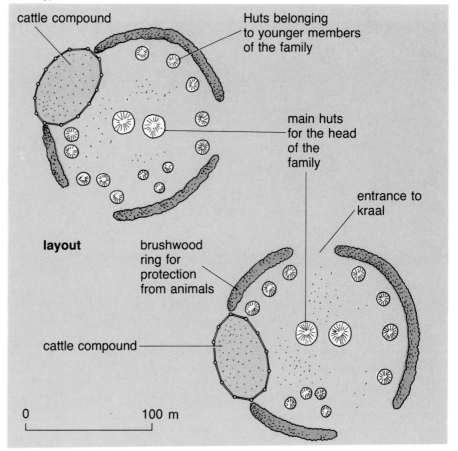

Assessment FACTORS AFFECTING SITE, SITUATION AND LAYOUT OF SETTLEMENTS

RUSV

1 Write down four advantages which the early settlers would have considered important in choosing the site for a village. (4)

....
....
....
....
....
....
....
....

4			

2 Study Photograph A of a town in northern England.

(i) Draw a labelled sketch to show the main features of the city's site. (3)

		3	

(ii) Suggest why the early settlers chose this site for a settlement. (4)

....
....
....
....
....
....
....
....

RUSV

	2	2	

(iii) Why will the site probably prove difficult for modern developments? (2)

....
....
....
....

	1		1

3 Explain the difference between the 'site' and the 'situation' of a settlement. (4)

....
....
....
....
....
....
....
....

	4		

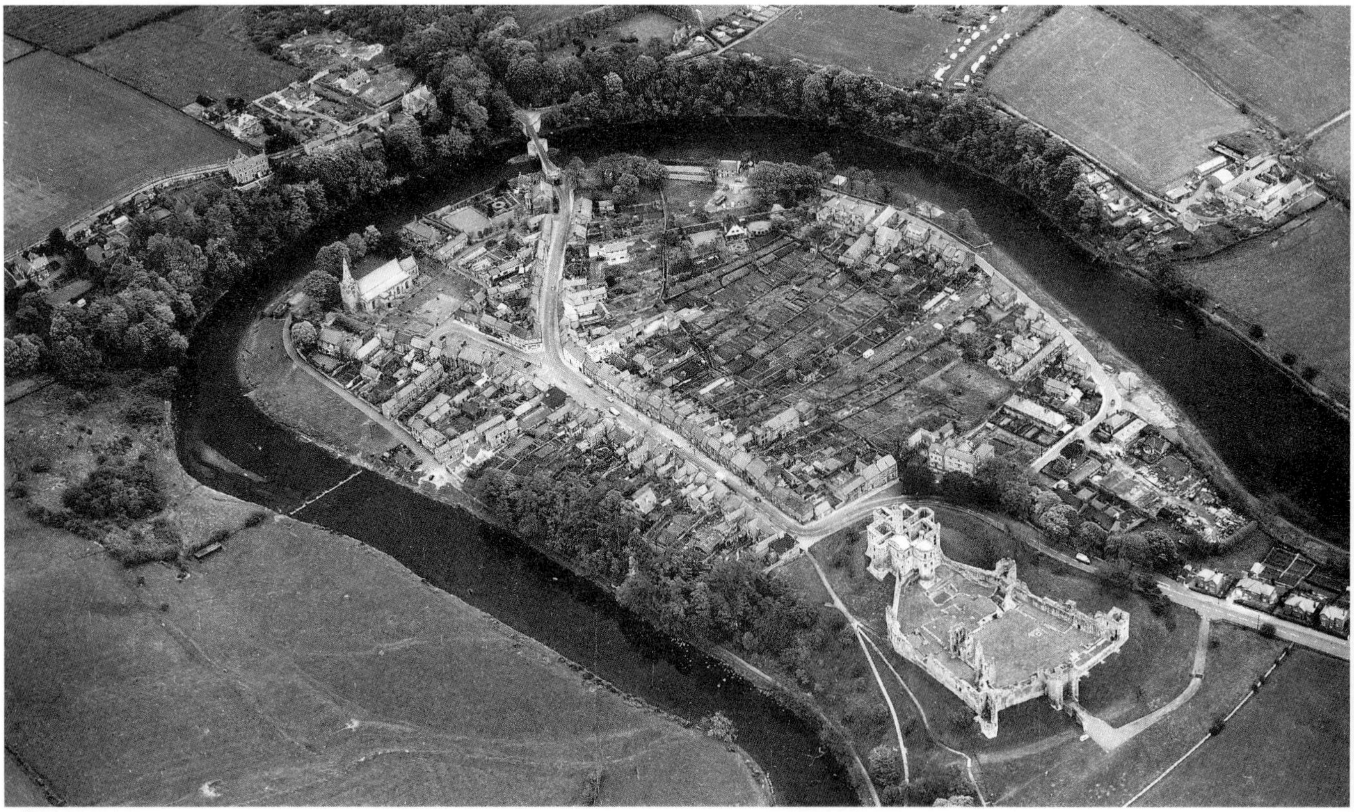

A

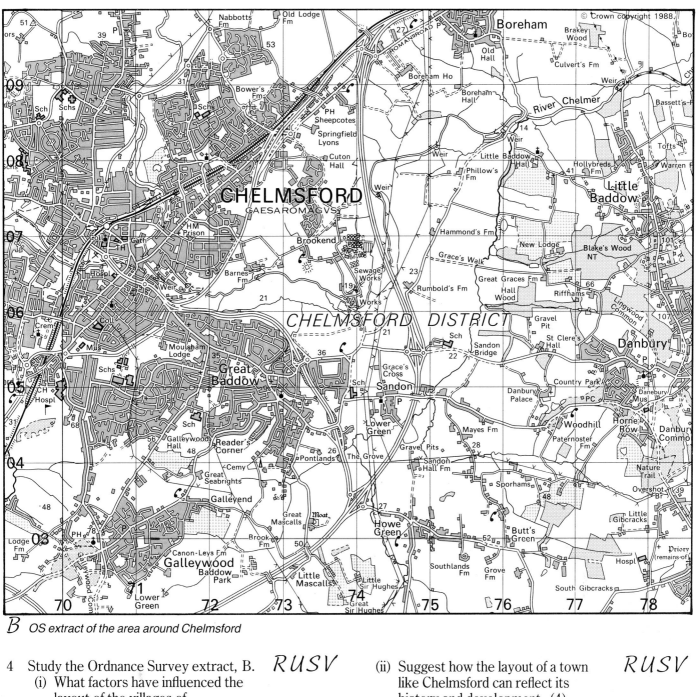

B OS extract of the area around Chelmsford

4 Study the Ordnance Survey extract, B.   *RUSV*
   (i) What factors have influenced the
        layout of the villages of
        Little Baddow (7707) and
        Galleywood (7102)? (4)

   ....
   ....
   ....
   ....
   ....
   ....
   ....
   ....

   | 2 | 2 | |

   (ii) Suggest how the layout of a town   *RUSV*
         like Chelmsford can reflect its
         history and development. (4)

   ....
   ....
   ....
   ....
   ....
   ....
   ....
   ....

   | 4 | | |

   | 5 | 13 | 7 | 1 |

SETTLEMENT PATTERNS AND PROCESSES

Map A shows the pattern of settlement in East Anglia. It has villages, small towns, large towns and cities. There are a lot of villages, few towns and only three cities. This is sometimes called a **settlement hierarchy**. The hierarchy for the area shown on Map A is given in Table B. It shows that the larger the population of a settlement, the fewer there are of them.

A The pattern of settlement in East Anglia

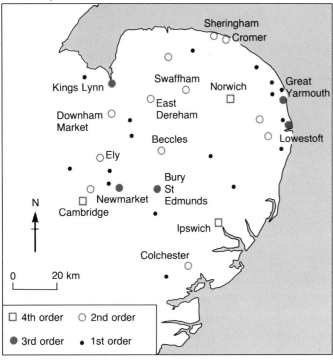

B The pattern of settlement in East Anglia

Fourth order (cities)	3
Third order (large towns)	5
Second order (small towns)	12
First order (large villages)	20

The settlement pattern shows that the three cities are far apart and are surrounded by towns and villages. Villages have few services. There may be a village shop, a garage, a pub, a post office and a church. A village is sometimes called a **first order settlement** because it has few services. Small towns will have more than one of some of the services which villages have, plus others such as banks, supermarkets and building societies. They can be called **second order settlements**.

Large towns may have hospitals, fire services and hypermarkets. They can be called **third order settlements**. Cities may have all of these plus universities and cathedrals. They can be called **fourth order settlements**. Usually, the bigger the place is, the more services it has, and the higher order it is said to be.

Table C shows the typical number of outlets of different services in four settlements of different order.

C Services and settlement order

Service	Order			
	4	3	2	1
Supermarket	14	4	1	0
Grocer	35	9	4	1
Newsagent/tobacconist	47	17	3	1
Clothes shop	36	10	4	0
Chemist	24	14	1	0
Furniture shop	18	8	1	0
Department store	6	1	0	0
Bank	37	12	3	0
Estate agent	27	11	2	0
Hairdresser	23	8	2	0

Shops in first order settlements will sell **convenience goods** like bread and newspapers. These are cheap but are purchased regularly. A fourth order settlement will have these too, but will also have very specialised shops selling goods such as jewellery and suites of furniture. Shoppers do not often buy these expensive goods and are prepared to travel long distances to compare their prices. So they are called **comparison goods**.

The **range** of a product or service (such as hairdressing) is the maximum distance people will travel to buy it. Convenience goods have a short range. Comparison goods and services have longer ranges. The **threshold** of a product or service is the minimum number of sales needed to make a profit. In an evenly populated region, the threshold can be drawn on a map as a circle centred on the city where the product is sold. Range and threshold form the maximum and minimum areas of sales (**market areas**) of goods and services, as Diagram D shows.

D Range and threshold

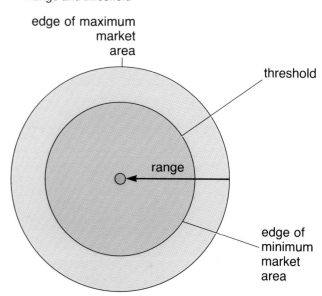

Because high order goods and services need large market areas, high order settlements have to be a long way apart. A city like Ipswich will pull shoppers into it from nearby villages and towns like Beccles and Bury St Edmunds. These settlements are said to be in Ipswich's 'sphere of influence'. Villages around East Dereham and Swaffham are in Norwich's 'sphere of influence'.

This pattern of villages clustered around towns, with towns surrounding cities, is clearest in a large lowland area like East Anglia. The hills and valleys in other areas like South Wales cause different patterns. There are still high and low order settlements but they are strung out along valleys, rather than forming circles round each other. Map E shows this.

E The settlement pattern of South Wales

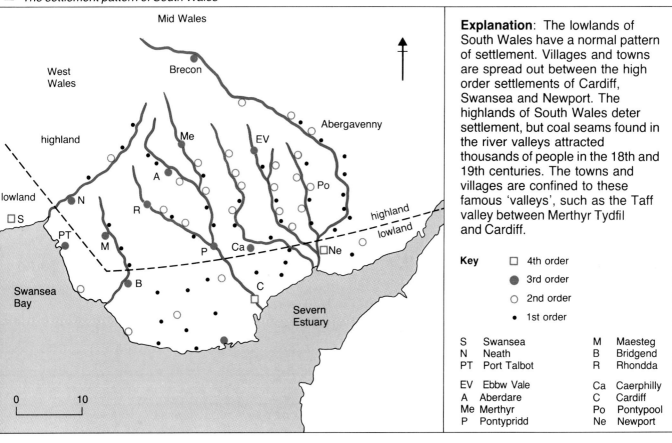

Explanation: The lowlands of South Wales have a normal pattern of settlement. Villages and towns are spread out between the high order settlements of Cardiff, Swansea and Newport. The highlands of South Wales deter settlement, but coal seams found in the river valleys attracted thousands of people in the 18th and 19th centuries. The towns and villages are confined to these famous 'valleys', such as the Taff valley between Merthyr Tydfil and Cardiff.

Key

- □ 4th order
- ● 3rd order
- ○ 2nd order
- • 1st order

S	Swansea	M	Maesteg
N	Neath	B	Bridgend
PT	Port Talbot	R	Rhondda
EV	Ebbw Vale	Ca	Caerphilly
A	Aberdare	C	Cardiff
Me	Merthyr	Po	Pontypool
P	Pontypridd	Ne	Newport

A Number of shops and population

1   Study Graph A which shows the relationship between the number of shops and the population of some settlements.   *RUSV*

(i)   How many shops are there in settlement A? (1)

....   ☐ ☐ 1 ☐ ☐

(ii) What is the population of settlement B? (1)

....   ☐ ☐ 1 ☐ ☐

(iii) Briefly describe the relationship between the number of shops and the population size as shown on the graph. (2)

....
....
....
....   ☐ 1 1 ☐ ☐

(iv) Explain what is meant by the term 'urban hierarchy', using examples from the graph. (3)

....
....
....
....
....
....   3 ☐ ☐ ☐

(v)   Why may the number of shops not necessarily be a good indicator of a settlement's importance? (3)   *RUSV*

....
....
....
....
....
....   ☐ 1 ☐ 2 ☐

2   (i)   List two kinds of shops or services you would expect to find in a low order settlement. (2)

....
....
....   2 ☐ ☐ ☐

(ii) Why are high order settlements further apart than low order settlements? (3)

....
....
....
....
....
....   1 2 ☐ ☐

(iii) Suggest what differences you would find in the shopping facilities of town settlements A and B. (4)

RUSV

....
....
....
....
....
....
....
....

| 4 | | |

3 (i) Study Photograph B. What order do you think this settlement is in an urban hierarchy (1st, 2nd, 3rd or 4th)? (1)

....
....
....
....

| 1 | | |

(ii) Explain how you could investigate the size of the sphere of influence of the town shown in Photograph B. (5)

RUSV

....
....
....
....
....
....
....
....
....

| 5 | |
| 7 | 13 | 3 | 2 |

B

URBAN SETTLEMENTS: PROCESSES AND PATTERNS

Towns and cities are called **urban** settlements, as opposed to **rural** settlements like farms, hamlets and villages. Urban settlements have patterns within them. All cities are different, yet most have the same sort of internal pattern. Maps A, B, C and D are models of cities. (Models are not real, they just show what might be the case.) They show the sort of patterns which may exist in cities in developed countries. Each model contains the four zones described below.

C

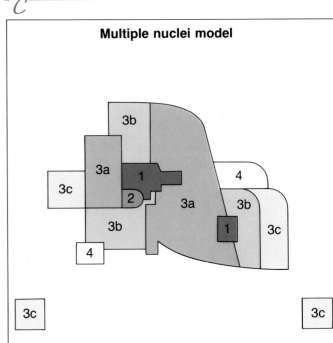

Multiple nuclei model

A

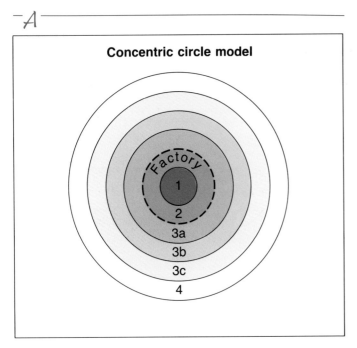

Concentric circle model

B

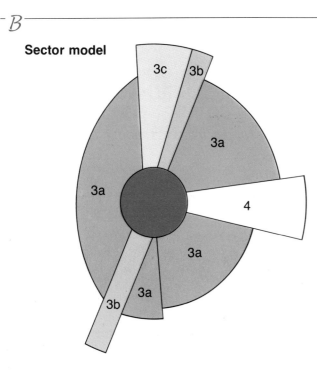

Sector model

D

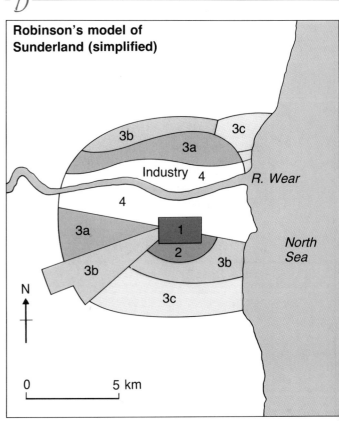

Robinson's model of Sunderland (simplified)

Central business district

The central business district (CBD) is the heart of the urban area, where department stores, cinemas, offices, banks and high class shops are found. These have to be highly accessible to all customers. The centres of towns are highly accessible. In other words, all the people from the city can get to them easily, by bus, car or on foot. They are therefore the most sought-after places in the city and their rents are the highest. To offset this cost, architects design high-rise blocks of offices and shops. This allows more square metres of usable space on this expensive land.

The inner city

Around the central business district there is usually an area of tightly-packed housing, where workers lived in the 19th century to be within walking distance of their work in the city centre. Nowadays, some parts of the inner city are in decline. The buildings are in a state of disrepair, as they come to the end of their natural life. Inner cities are sometimes called **twilight zones**. They have low rents and, as well as the original inhabitants, often house students and relatively poor people who cannot afford high rents or mortgage payments. Other parts of the inner city may be more fashionable. Young people with high wages decide to live here and improve the cheap houses (on expensive land) which are so close to the facilities of the centre.

Residential areas

These are divided into different types of housing such as:
(a) pre-1945 houses with gently curving avenues and straight streets, often forming inner suburbs,
(b) post-1945 houses with curving crescents and cul-de-sacs often forming the outer suburbs of the town,
(c) 1960s tower block developments near the twilight zone.

Industrial areas

Some old, established industry may remain near the centre, but the cost of land is high and is increasing. Many firms sell or rent this expensive land and move to cheaper sites on industrial estates. These are areas of mainly light industry which are found near main roads on the city outskirts. Lorries can easily bring goods to them without causing congestion in the town.

Originally, towns in the UK had a single central nucleus and the zones radiated from this in circles or sectors. Modern cities have several nuclei where they have grown outwards to surround villages and even nearby towns. Manchester has grown around Stockport and Salford, for instance, so it does not have one central business district but several.

The rate of city growth in the Third World is now rapid. Land use patterns are often unclear because growth has been haphazard. Many people are attracted to these cities and the authorities are not able to provide proper houses or services. Newcomers build houses out of scrap materials. These form 'shanty towns'. Between the central business district and the outer zone of shanty towns there is usually a complex pattern of industry, housing and shops.

Map E shows the land use zones of Ibadan in Nigeria.

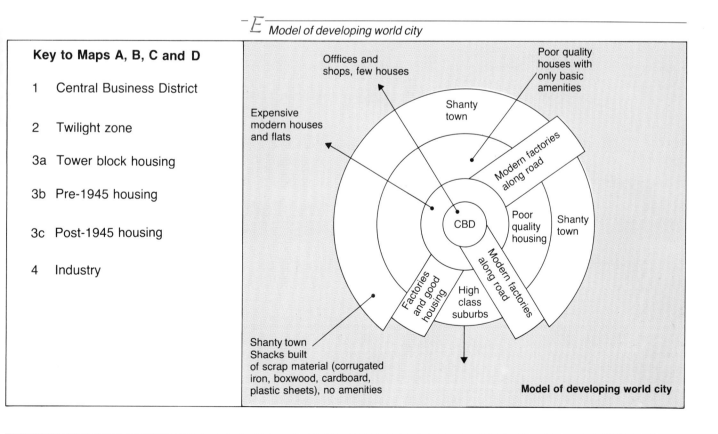

E Model of developing world city

Key to Maps A, B, C and D

1 Central Business District

2 Twilight zone

3a Tower block housing

3b Pre-1945 housing

3c Post-1945 housing

4 Industry

Model of developing world city

1 Study the 1:2500 Ordnance Survey map extract A showing the Aston Newtown area of Birmingham before redevelopment.   *RUSV*

(i) Write down four features that typify the part of Birmingham shown on the map. (4)

....

....

....

....

....

....

☐ ☐ 4 ☐ ☐

(ii) Is this an inner city or a suburban area? (1)

....

☐ 1 ☐ ☐

(iii) When was the area likely to have been built? (1)

....

1 ☐ ☐ ☐

(iv) Describe the problems you would expect in an area like Aston Newtown. (3)   *RUSV*

....

....

....

....

....

....

☐ 3 ☐ ☐

(v) What is urban redevelopment? (1)

....

1 ☐ ☐ ☐

(vi) Why is urban redevelopment preferred to slum clearance as a solution to the problems of an area like Aston Newtown? (2)

....

....

....

1 ☐ ☐ 1

A OS extract 1:2500 of the Aston Newtown area of Birmingham

© Crown copyright 1988.

2 Study Map B of the Paris region and Table C showing the population figures for the region.

(i) Which departement showed the greatest population change? (1)

....

(ii) What is the meaning of the word 'suburban'? (1)

....

....

(iii) Why has the total region showed an increase in population? (2)

....

....

(iv) Why is it possible that Paris City will become the 'dead heart' of the region? (2)

....

....

....

....

(v) Explain why the outer suburbs of a city like Paris show the greatest population growth. (2)

....

....

....

....

3 How far can the land use of Calgary (Map D) be explained in terms of land use models? (5)

....

....

....

....

....

....

....

....

....

....

RUSV

B Paris region

C Population figures for the Paris region

	Approx. population (millions)	Percentage change
Paris City	2.3	−11.2
Inner suburban departements		
Hauts-de-Seine	1.4	−1.6
Seine St Denis	1.3	+5.8
Val de Marne	1.2	+8.4
Outer suburban developments		
Essonne	0.9	−37.1
Val d'Oise	0.8	+21.3
Seine-et-Marne	0.7	+25.1
Yvelines	1.0	+26.7
Total region	9.8	+6.8

D Land use of Calgary

Key
1 Administration offices
2 Light industrial estates
3 Low value residential areas
4 Medium value residential areas
5 High value residential areas

PROBLEMS CAUSED BY TOO MANY PEOPLE LIVING IN CITIES

A

B *Growth in the number of large cities, 1920s–1980s*

Numbers of large cities			
Decade	Millionaire	Super	Mega
1980s	198	34	5
1960s	113	23	0
1940s	41	11	0
1920s	24	4	0

Millionaire city – over one million people
Super city – 3 to 10 million people
Mega city – over 10 million people

C *Population of cities in Egypt, showing Cairo as the primate city*

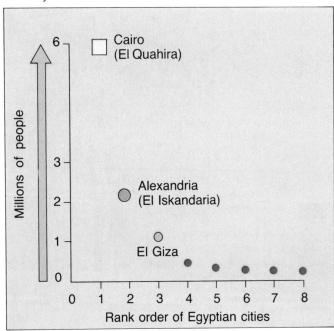

Photograph A shows a traffic jam in Calcutta, India. Calcutta has over 10 million inhabitants now and is expected to have 17 million by the year 2000.

Table B, Graph C and Table D show some interesting and important facts about the growth of cities and some opinions about what is likely to happen.

Urbanisation (the movement of people into cities) is increasing in the developing world. People move away from villages and farms to what they see as better prospects for jobs, education and social life in the cities. The rapid rate of urbanisation means that, in the future, most of the largest cities will be in the developing countries of the Third World. However, large numbers of people cause problems for city authorities in the following ways:

Lack of work

The cities are the main centres of industry in developing countries but there are not enough jobs for all the hopefuls. Most city jobs are low paid service jobs, such as cooks and cleaners.

Shanty towns

The authorities cannot house all the people who move into the cities. The people coming in have to build their own shacks out of scrap material on unused land on the edge of cities. In this way shanty towns grow up.

Lack of public facilities

There is inadequate provision of clean water, sewers, roads, street lighting, fire, ambulance and police services. This is especially true of the shanty towns but is also the case in parts of the cities themselves.

Social problems, health and crime

People living in poor conditions, often without jobs, and away from their family and home community, become depressed and ill. Those in work can be easily sacked. Crime and prostitution are common in these desperate situations.

D *Shanty town populations*

Estimates of shanty towns as a percentage of city population		
City	City population (millions)	Percentage in shanty towns
Mexico City	14	50
Lima	5	40
Calcutta	10	33
Djakarta	5	25
São Paulo	10	20

Primate city problems

Often, one city dominates all the others in a country and attracts more than its fair share of newcomers. This is true of Cairo in Egypt, and of Mexico City. The primate city tends to get more than its fair share of government grants, new industry, new roads and so on. The rest of the country is drained of its best talent and resources in favour of this top-dog city. The city itself gets congested, crime-ridden and ungovernable, while the rest of the country resents the priority it is given and has not enough farm workers to provide food for its inhabitants.

In the developed world the main urban problems are different. Some are given here.

Housing

Many inner-city properties lack facilities like bathrooms and indoor toilets. People with good jobs and enough money will not live there, so they become slum properties. The poorest people cannot even afford to live in these houses and roam around the city, homeless. Agencies like Shelter try to inform us of problems like this.

Inadequacy of services

Many inner-city areas lack services such as centres for sport or leisure. The problem is made worse by people moving away, so the cities are left with a 'dead heart'. Few residents are left, so there is no pressure to do anything about the litter, crime and vandalism which may take place.

Traffic congestion

This occurs in city centre areas at the rush hours in the morning and evening when people are travelling to and from work. Exhaust fume pollution is unpleasant and can cause illness.

Urban sprawl

This is the growth of built-up areas into the surrounding countryside. It is a serious problem in a small country like the UK where all the farmland is needed to feed the people living there.

Solutions to these problems need to be at national and local levels. Suggested remedies have included:

1 Moving overspill population to new towns such as those shown on Map E (new towns near London) and Map F (new towns near Paris).
2 Green belts to reduce further expansion.
3 Urban motorways, traffic lanes and bypasses to reduce traffic congestion. Examples include London's M25 'orbital' motorway and the Peripherique around Paris.
4 At local level, slum clearance or urban development with the use of urban renewal grants.

Nowadays, people are moving out of the cities in developed countries to live in smaller, less congested towns, so many of these problems are easing.

E London overspill settlements

(Map showing London overspill settlements, with 50 km scale bar and North arrow. Settlements labelled: Peterborough, Kings Lynn, Wellingborough, Thetford, Daventry, Huntingdon, Bury St Edmunds, Northampton, Bletchley, Milton Keynes, Stevenage, Aylesbury, Welwyn Garden City, Hemel Hempstead, Hatfield, Witham, Swindon, Harlow, Bracknell, Andover, Ashford, Basingstoke, Crawley, Hastings.)

Key:
○ New town
Greater London Green belt
● Expanded town
□ New city

To stop London's built-up area growing outwards, a 'green belt' was set up. No farmland was to be sold for houses or factories within it. Instead these could be built in the new towns which were started in 1946. Later, old towns like Swindon and a new city, Milton Keynes, were used to house the people who moved out from overcrowded London.

F Paris's new towns

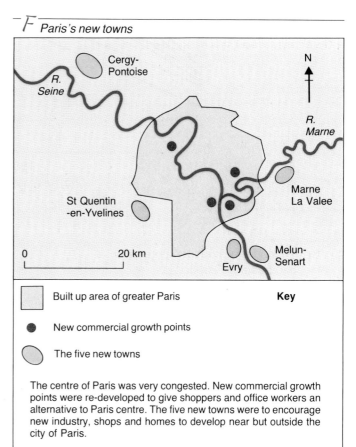

Key
▢ Built up area of greater Paris
● New commercial growth points
⬭ The five new towns

The centre of Paris was very congested. New commercial growth points were re-developed to give shoppers and office workers an alternative to Paris centre. The five new towns were to encourage new industry, shops and homes to develop near but outside the city of Paris.

1   Study Graph A which shows the growth
of the world's largest cities.

A Growth of selected world cities

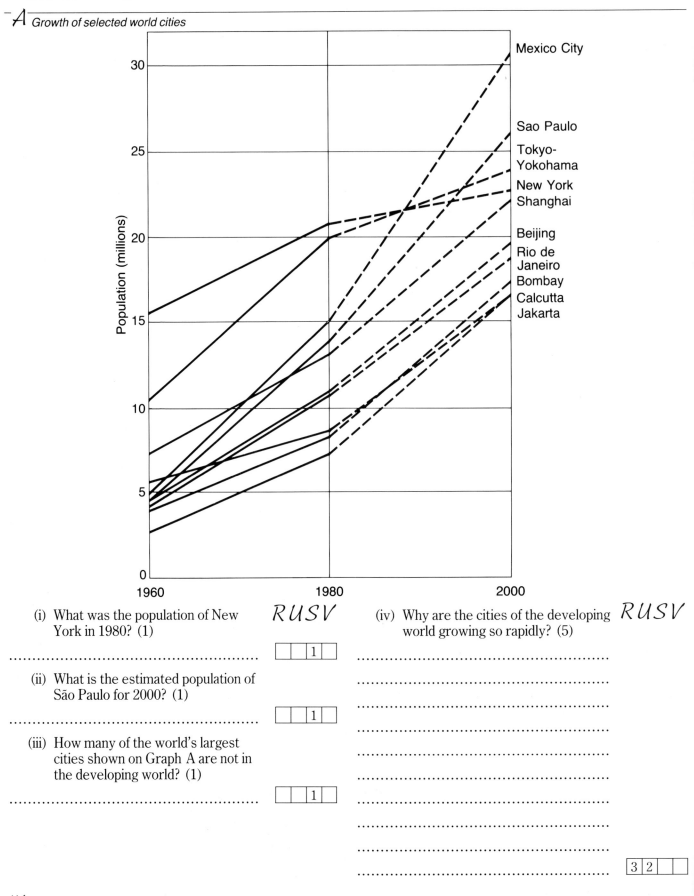

(i)   What was the population of New
York in 1980? (1)

RUSV

....   ▢▢1▢

(ii) What is the estimated population of
São Paulo for 2000? (1)

....   ▢▢1▢

(iii) How many of the world's largest
cities shown on Graph A are not in
the developing world? (1)

....   ▢▢1▢

(iv) Why are the cities of the developing
world growing so rapidly? (5)

RUSV

....

....

....

....

....

....

....

....

....

....

3 2 ▢▢

2 (i) What is a shanty town? (1)   *RUSV*

....

....   `1 □ □`

   (ii) In which part of a developing world
         city would you find shanty
         towns? (1)

....

....   `1 □ □`

   (iii) Describe the problems associated
          with the growth of shanty towns,
          such as the one shown in
          Photograph B. (6)

....

....

....

....

....

....

....

....

....

....

....   `3 3 □`

   (iv) Do you think the drift to the towns   *RUSV*
         is a good or bad thing?
         Give reasons to justify your
         answer. (4)

....

....

....

....

....

....

....   `□ 2 □ 2`

3   With reference to a specific New
      Town, explain how the planners have
      attempted to provide a pleasant
      environment for people to live in. (5)

....

....

....

....

....

....

....

....

....

....   `□ 5 □`

                                                `8 12 3 2`

B Shanty town in Santo Domingo, Dominican Republic

8. Agriculture

ENVIRONMENTAL AND HUMAN FACTORS WHICH INFLUENCE LAND CAPACITY

Photograph A shows a date palm oasis in Algeria. It might produce fifty tons of dates per year, plus enough grain and vegetables to feed the one hundred or so people who live there. The maximum farming **output** from this oasis is called its **land capacity**.

The labels around Photograph A show some of the more important factors which influence land capacity. They can be divided into **environmental** factors and **human** factors. The environmental factors are described here.

Relief

The steeper the land, the lower the land capacity is likely to be. The most favourable relief for most types of farming is a gentle slope, which lets water drain away slowly and allows all types of machinery to be used.

Climate and microclimate

Ideally the climate should be close to the optimum (best) rainfall and temperature conditions for the plants or animals being farmed. It is important that the rainfall is predictable. When farmers do not get the rain they expect there is a **drought**, which can have disastrous effects on the crops.

Microclimate (local climate) is mainly determined by whether the land faces the sun (aspect), the wind conditions (exposure) and how the land is affected by frost. The more sun, the less wind and the less frost there is, the greater the land capacity is likely to be.

Soils

An ideal soil is one which contains a variety of minerals and has a high humus (organic matter) content. It should have a firm but spongy structure, so plants can be supported and air and rain water can get to the roots.

If a farmer tries to produce the maximum output every year, he or she may exhaust the soil. Output would then drop in future years. True land capacity is one which can be sustained year after year, not for a few years only.

It is not just the tonnage of output that is important in a modern farm. It is the **profit** which a farmer makes. Profit can be thought of as *cash income minus costs*. A farmer must decide how much of the profit to keep for personal use and how much to invest in the farm for future years.

Farmers have difficult choices to make. They can aim for maximum output or for maximum profit. For instance, a farmer might be able to produce more tons of wheat than oil seed rape from a field. But if the oil seed rape needs less looking after and sells for a greater price per tonne, it may be more profitable. So land capacity is often thought of in terms of profit as well as output. Farmers need to consider these **human factors** which influence land capacity.

The list below shows some of the human factors which influence land capacity and what a farmer will grow. The more of these factors, the greater the potential land capacity.

Capital

The amount of money available to the farmer for investment in such things as seeds, young animals, buildings and machinery. The more capital, the greater the potential land capacity of the farm.

Machinery

The more appropriate the machinery to the terrain and skills of the farmer, the better the chance of success.

Water supply and conservation

Irrigation and the use of dry farming techniques give plants and animals the right amount of water and can greatly improve land capacity.

Labour supply and skills

People with the ability to get the best out of the land are always needed. A wide range of traditional and modern skills will improve the chances of success in new ventures. Effective management is a key skill.

Accessibility to markets

Being near the customer, both in terms of distance and time, can be vital, especially for fresh food. If the farm is too remote, it may not be possible to grow certain profitable crops. Good road and rail links to cities improve the market for remote areas.

Quality of seeds and livestock (animals)

Better seeds will give a greater yield per hectare. Good quality livestock will yield a high profit per head, as they provide what the customer wants.

A — Desert oasis in Algeria showing low land capacity

Bare rocky hills, steep slopes, much erosion after rainstorms. No shelter from winds.

Dry desert climate.

Thin, exposed soil. Dry, sandy desert basin.

Remote. No routeways, no market.

Scrub vegetation on bed and banks of stream.

Date palms near water hole. Little awareness of landscape value.

Bare gravel on gently sloping desert plain. Bare soil and boulders on moderately sloping valley sides.

Farmers know little about outside markets. Traditional farming skills and methods. Only traditional machinery.

Little capital.

No government encouragement.

No chemical input.

Chemical inputs

Fertilisers and pesticides will improve output if applied correctly. However, there are growing concerns about the effect they have on the environment and on the food produced.

Government policy

Governments can make farming more or less profitable by adjusting taxes and grants to farmers. For example, if a government decides to give a grant to farmers who grow wheat, the land capacity in terms of profit will be affected: the farmer may be able to produce more barley than wheat on the land, but if wheat yields more profit, it will probably be grown.

The farmer's perception of opportunities

If a farmer is aware of all the options available, he or she will have more chance of making the maximum profit from the land. Knowledge of farming and information about prices and new methods affect land capacity.

The community's evaluation of landscape

A farm may be productive but ugly. The local community may be prepared to support a farmer to use a method of farming which makes the countryside more pleasant.

Sketch B shows how the oasis could be developed to give a higher farming output (higher land capacity).

B — Alternative scene showing higher land capacity

Soil thicker and richer with humus and chemical input

Wetter climate after planting and care of trees

Dry conditions: ranching on grassed desert basin

Oasis dwellers aware and proud of their landscape, fully aware of its value

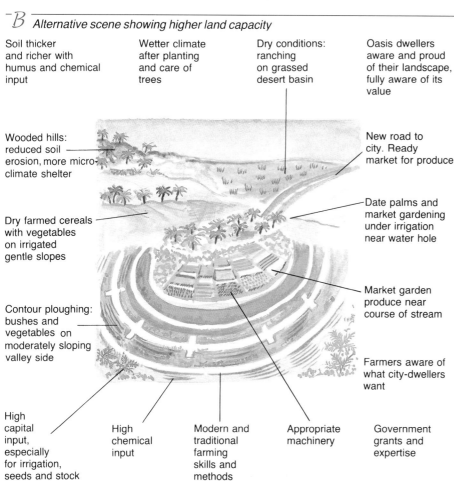

Wooded hills: reduced soil erosion, more micro-climate shelter

New road to city. Ready market for produce

Dry farmed cereals with vegetables on irrigated gentle slopes

Date palms and market gardening under irrigation near water hole

Contour ploughing: bushes and vegetables on moderately sloping valley side

Market garden produce near course of stream

Farmers aware of what city-dwellers want

High capital input, especially for irrigation, seeds and stock

High chemical input

Modern and traditional farming skills and methods

Appropriate machinery

Government grants and expertise

1 Name two physical controls and two human constraints on the agricultural capacity of a particular piece of land. (4)

RUSV

....

....

....

....

....

....

....

.... | 4 | | | |

A   *Part of coastal Wales*

2 Study Photograph A which shows part of Wales.

   (i) Study the areas labelled I and III. Pick out from the list below four environmental disadvantages to farming in these areas. (4)

Acid soil	Frost danger
Waterlogging	Thick woodland
Too far from market	Hummocky relief
	Too little capital
Sandy soils blow away	Not enough fertiliser
Climate too dry	Taxes too high
Steep slopes	Sea air adds salt to soil

....

....

....

....

....

....

.... | 2 | 2 | |

   (ii) What physical and human factors have encouraged the development of agriculture in area II? (4)

....

....

....

....

....

....

....

.... | 2 | 2 | |

3 Study Map B which shows an African irrigation scheme.

(i) What is meant by irrigation? (1)

....

....

`1 | | |`

(ii) Describe how the irrigation scheme has made use of the physical geography of the area. (3)

....

....

....

....

....

....

`| 2 | 1 | |`

(iii) Despite the availability of irrigation in an area like that in the map, many African farmers face considerable problems. What human factors would work against these farmers getting the most out of their land. (4)

....

....

....

....

....

....

`| 4 | |`

4 Why is government policy so important in modern farming?
Illustrate your answer with examples. (5)

....

....

....

....

....

....

....

....

....

....

`| 2 | 1 | | 2 |`

`| 7 | 11 | 5 | 2 |`

RUSV

B *Gezira irrigation scheme in Sudan, Africa*

Khartoum

Jebel Aulya Dam

White Nile

Blue Nile

canals

400

Kosti

450

Sennar Dam

N

Irrigated land

--- Contours (m)   0   50 km

FARM SYSTEMS AND DECISION MAKING

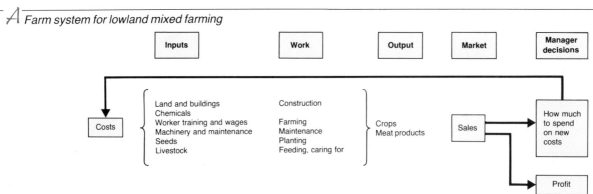

A Farm system for lowland mixed farming

The work of any farmer is very complex but, like all jobs, it can be represented in a simple way. Diagram A shows a system which fits all types of work.

The system shown in Diagram A is for one of the common British types of farming. This and four other common British farming types are described below.

British farming types

Arable farming (field crops)
● light, well drained soil such as river terrace gravel or chalk
● dry sunny climate, with most rain in summer just before the harvest.

Dairy farming (rearing cattle for milk production)
● clay or river flood plain soils which produce thick grass
● wet, mild climate which allows grass to grow and animals to stay outdoors for most of the year
● near towns and cities to reduce transport costs.

Market gardening (growing salad vegetables and flowers)
● light, sandy or gravel soils rather than heavy clays
● mild, moist climate with a long growing season and early harvest
● closeness to cities so that produce arrives fresh and unbruised
● glasshouses and cloches (transparent plastic sheeting) on sunny slopes allow crops like tomatoes to ripen quickly.

Upland farming (rearing sheep on moorland, with beef or dairy cattle and some fodder crops near farms in upland valleys)
● high altitude means short growing season, allowing only hay and other fodder crops to grow; strong winds and heavy rain mean few plants or animals can survive
● high relief means that the ground is too steep for ploughing
● sheep are the only farm animals which can survive on the moors and hillsides; they are herded into the valleys for lambing
● often remote from towns and cities

Lowland mixed farming (crops, with dairying and beef or sheep fattening for slaughter)
● on heavy clay soils in the sunny parts of eastern Britain
● sheltered lowlands are suitable for outdoor animals
● dairy cattle must have calves each year to keep their milk flowing; the calves replace old dairy cows or are sold for beef
● local surpluses of wheat, barley and sugar beet can be fed to the animals in winter and can be added to their diet in summer to fatten animals for market.

Farming elsewhere in the world is very varied. There are twelve major categories of farming types. Here are their main characteristics.

Major world farming types

Shifting subsistence farming (farming to feed a family)
● cut down the forest or bush; seeds are the only input; some hens and pigs; very low output per hectare
● plant crops for food until soil is exhausted, then move on
● find new area to clear; old fields are left to become forest.

Settled subsistence farming (farming to feed a family)
● plant crops for food; hens and pigs root for their own food
● inputs might be animal manure and burned weeds and grass
● more care taken of the soil, as farmer has to stay on it.

Intensive subsistence farming (farming to feed the village)
● plough and weed ground with great care; plant seeds singly
● many people at work; soil enriched with animal and human manure
● high output per hectare; many people working so low output per head
● land stays productive for centuries (as in eastern Asia).

B Farm system for intensive subsistence gardening

| INTENSIVE SUBSISTENCE | For example: rice, beans |

Small plots of land
Many workers
Little capital
or machinery
Poor seeds/stock → Dawn till dusk in the fields with great care → High output per hectare, low per worker → Most of food eaten by farmers' families

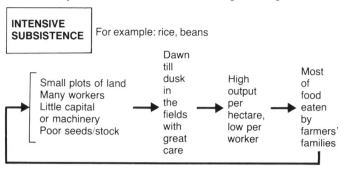

E

C

F

Mixed subsistence and cash crop farming (surplus produce sold)

- as above for settled and intensive subsistence farming but a surplus is sold at market
- moderate output per head and per hectare
- this is the most common type of farming in the world.

Plantation farming (one crop grown for cash in tropical area)

- farm carefully planned; much capital input; good infrastructure
- planting, weeding, irrigating, fertilising, harvesting all done by paid labour; moderate output per hectare, low output per head
- produce sold for export.

Market gardening (intensive farming of salad vegetables)

- near rich cities; salad fruits and vegetables (tomatoes, lettuce, etc.) for the city's inhabitants
- much capital input (glasshouses, lighting, heating, chemicals)
- very high output per hectare.

Extensive field crop farming (food such as peas and potatoes or industrial crops like cotton and jute)

- much input of capital for machinery and buildings for storage
- moderate output per hectare; high output per head.

Extensive animal ranch farming

- huge ranches, few workers, much machinery
- low output per hectare, high output per head
- farm often owned by business (for example, Fray Bentos corned beef).

G Farm system for extensive animal ranching

| EXTENSIVE RANCHING | For example: beef cattle for canned meat and leather, sheep for mutton and wool |

Huge (100 km²) ranches
Few (10) workers
Much capital
for fences
and land and
veterinary help
High quality
livestock → Little work to do except monitor and dip herd when necessary and maintain fences → Very low output per hectare
Very high output per person → All produce for sale at high industrial prices

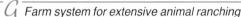

D Farm system for intensive market gardening

| INTENSIVE MARKET GARDENING | For example: tomatoes, lettuce, cress, flowers (chrysanthemums, carnations) |

Small plot of land
Many workers
Much capital
for buildings,
heat, light,
equipment
Highest quality
seeds → Great care taken to get growing conditions just right → Very high output per hectare and per worker → All produce is for sale at high urban prices

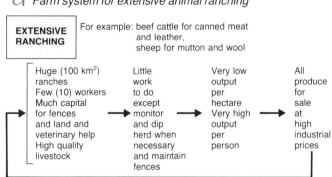

H

Dairy farming
- high capital input for milking machinery and buildings
- milk is usually sold to a marketing board for a regular price
- good access by road to city suburb dairies for house rounds.

Modern mixed farming
- the most common type of farming in richer countries
- crops used to feed animals in winter; animals manure ley fields
- high output per head and per hectare of surplus crops and animals.

Factory farming
- much capital input for buildings, light and heat
- few workers; high output per person and per hectare
- good road access essential.

Extensive cereal farming
- huge open fields, few workers, much machinery
- farms often owned by big business (for example, Kellog)
- high output per person, low output per hectare.

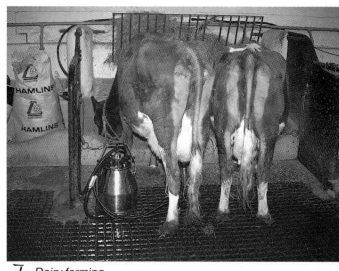

J Dairy farming

─ *I* *Farm system for extensive cereal farming*

EXTENSIVE CEREAL FARMING	For example: wheat for flour, barley for brewing

Large farms (and large fields) Few workers Much capital for fertilisers, seeds, machinery and storage of harvest and machinery High quality seed → Tractor ploughing, tilling, drilling, (planting), fertilising, spraying, harvesting Machine drying storing → Moderate output per hectare Very high output per worker → All grain for sale at high industrial prices

K Huge fields of cereals

Assessment FARM SYSTEMS AND DECISION MAKING

1 Name three characteristics of extensive animal ranching. (3) *RUSV*

....
....
.... `3 ` ` `

2 Study the details in Table A of a farm located in western Britain.
   (i) Summarise the features of this farm in the form of a systems diagram. (6) `3 `3 ` `

I_____S   W___K   O___S   M_____S

[ ] → [ ] → [ ] → [ ]

(ii) What is the major type of agriculture practised on this farm? (1) *RUSV*

.... `1 ` `

(iii) What factors have encouraged the development of this form of agriculture in western Britain? (4)

....
....
....
....
....
.... `2 `2 ` `

$\mathcal{A}$ *Facts about a farm in western Britain*

Size: 40 hectares

Farm buildings: farm house   3 hay sheds
                dairy   5 equipment sheds

Land use: 9% cereals (barley and oats for cattle)
           2% root crops (potatoes, swedes, kale for cattle)
          60% pasture
          29% hay

Stock: 52 Friesian dairy cows
       1 Hereford bull
     72 breeding ewes
      4 rams
    45 poultry

Fertiliser: 12 tonnes per year (nitrogen/phosphate/
               potash)

Foodstuff   cattle food   – 32 tonnes per year
brought in: wet sugar beet
           pulp   – 20 tonnes per year
           ewe/lamb/nuts – 2 tonnes per year

Equipment: 2 tractors   1 swede drill
          1 cultivator   1 fertiliser distributor
          1 disc plough 1 roller
          1 seed drill   1 spray for pesticides
          1 hay turner   1 mowing machine
          4 trailers   1 baler
          1 cattle trailer 1 manure spreader

Recent purchases: 12 milking cows
                      12 ewes

Recent sales: 100 lambs to abattoir
             12 tonnes potatoes to grocery chain
             80 tonnes hay to other farmers
             20 tonnes barley to brewery
             40 calves to abattoir

3   Study Diagrams B and C showing two   *RUSV*
different agricultural areas in East
Africa.

   (i) Both of these forms of agriculture
can be described as intensive. By
reference to both diagrams say why
the inputs and outputs of these
farms can be considered
intensive. (4)

....
....
....
....
.... | 1 | 1 | 2 | |

   (ii) Why is it significant that the market
garden is only eight miles from the
major Kenyan town of
Mombasa? (2)

....
....
.... | 1 | 1 | | |

   (iii) In what respects is the Tanzanian
sisal plantation typical of that form
of agriculture? (2)

....
....
.... | 1 | 1 | | |

   (iv) Explain which of the two forms of
agriculture listed in parts (ii) and
(iii) you consider to be most
beneficial to developing countries,
like those in East Africa. (3)

....
....
....
.... | | 1 | | 2 |
                                               | 8 | 10 | 5 | 2 |

$\mathcal{B}$ *Asian market garden, Digo, Mombasa*

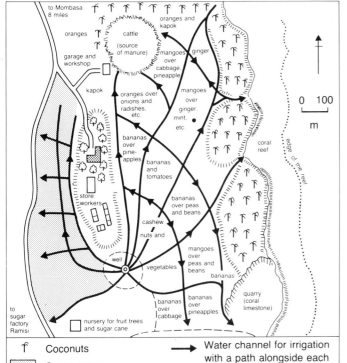

↑	Coconuts	→	Water channel for irrigation with a path alongside each
▒	Sugar cane		
▓	Manager's house	⌇	Ridges, cliffs (coral on coast)

$\mathcal{C}$ *Sisal plantation in Tanzania*

- - - - Light railway

workers' houses
railway line   workers' houses
main railway line
Dar es Salaam shredding sheds dispensary
drying yards store foremen's houses manager's house
fibre processing and baling sheds
railway line

Map A shows the pattern of **agricultural gross domestic product** (AGDP) per year throughout the world. This is the amount of wealth (measured in US dollars) made by farming in one year. It shows that the region which produces most from its farms is western Europe, followed by eastern Asia (mainly China), the USSR, North America, and southern Asia.

Table B shows the numbers of people who live in farming families in these and other major regions, their output per hectare and their output per person.

Map C shows a simplified pattern of world farming types.

Diagram D shows how to identify various types of farming.

Some interesting points to note are:

1 Western Europe produces a large amount per hectare and per person with a mixture of intensive and extensive farm methods plus modern technology and science. It is the main food producing region in the world but most of the food is needed to feed its own people.

2 Extensive farming in North America and Australia produces little per hectare but an enormous amount per person. These are the countries which have spare food to sell to the rest of the world.

3 Intensive farming in Japan, plus the use of modern technology and science, give it a huge output per hectare. It is all needed to feed the 100 million Japanese people who live on the small, rugged islands which make up that country.

4 Latin America, especially Brazil and Argentina, and the Middle East have a middle range output per hectare and per person. Their farming is a mix of poor subsistence farming in the more tropical regions and modern farming, both extensive and intensive, in the temperate regions.

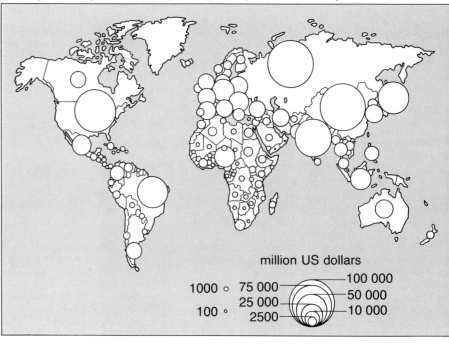

A Agricultural gross domestic product, 1981 (million US dollars)

million US dollars

1000 ○   75 000 ┐   ┌ 100 000
                 ├───┤
          25 000 ┤   ├ 50 000
100 ○   2500 ┘   └ 10 000

B Farming families and their output per year

Region	AGDP in thousand million US dollars	Millions of people in farming families	AGDP per hectare in US dollars	AGDP per person in US dollars
Western Europe	130	40	1350	3310
Eastern Asia	100	650	880	160
Latin America	100	125	600	800
USSR	100	45	430	2310
North America	100	6	400	15800
Southern Asia	80	600	380	130
Africa	70	280	380	220
Eastern Europe	50	30	1100	1610
Middle East	50	120	600	460
South East Asia	50	175	731	260
Japan	40	12	8150	3300
Australia	15	1	350	14000
World (approx)	900	2100	600	430

5 The poorer farming areas of the world, eastern Asia, southern Asia, south Asia and Africa, produce very little per person per year. This is because there are so many people in farming families 'on the land'. Over three-quarters of the world's farmers are in this group. They are mainly subsistence farmers, living from what they produce, with little left over to sell.

C Simplified pattern of world farming types

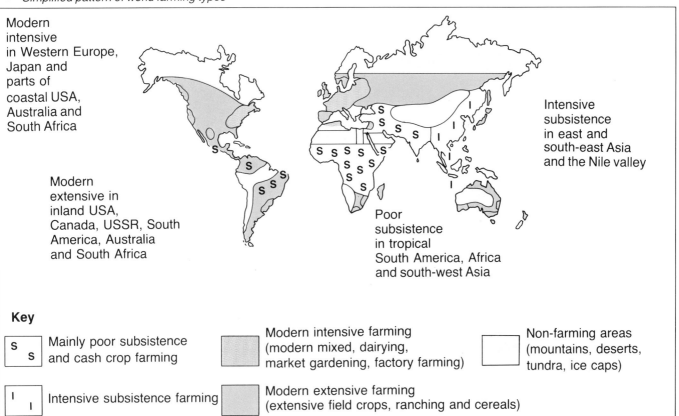

Modern intensive in Western Europe, Japan and parts of coastal USA, Australia and South Africa

Modern extensive in inland USA, Canada, USSR, South America, Australia and South Africa

Intensive subsistence in east and south-east Asia and the Nile valley

Poor subsistence in tropical South America, Africa and south-west Asia

Key

S / S	Mainly poor subsistence and cash crop farming	
I / I	Intensive subsistence farming	
(shaded)	Modern intensive farming (modern mixed, dairying, market gardening, factory farming)	
(shaded)	Modern extensive farming (extensive field crops, ranching and cereals)	
(white)	Non-farming areas (mountains, deserts, tundra, ice caps)	

D Farming key: How to identify the type of farming

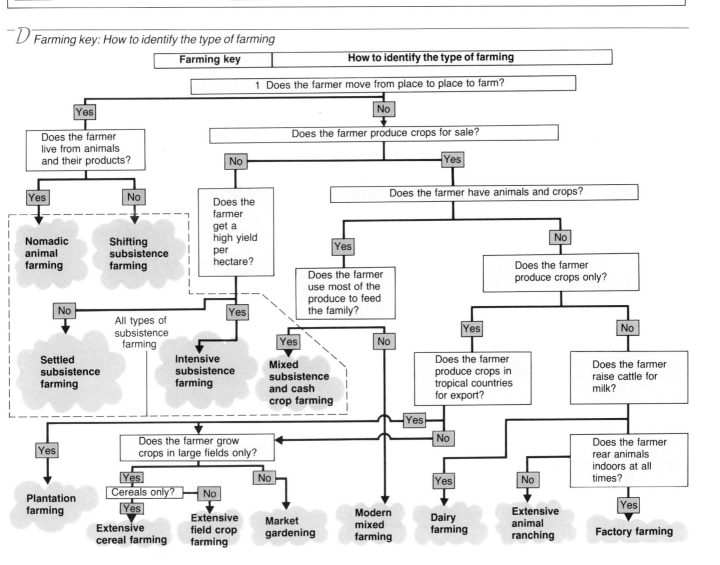

1   What do the letters AGDP stand for? (2)

RUSV

⬜ 2 ⬜⬜⬜

....

2   Study the table below.

Country	Percentage of labour force employed in agriculture	Value of exports per head of population (US dollars)
Brazil	30	200
France	8	1860
India	69	12
Italy	11	1400
Netherlands	6	4800
Nigeria	54	220
Norway	7	4550
United Kingdom	2	2000
West Germany	4	2840

(i)   Which country has the greatest percentage employed in agriculture? (1)

.... ⬜⬜ 1 ⬜

(ii) Which country has the highest value of exports per head of population? (1)

.... ⬜⬜ 1 ⬜

(iii) What is the relationship between the percentage employed in agriculture and the value of exports per head? (2)

....

....

....

.... ⬜ 1 1 ⬜

3   Study the maps of Japan (B and C) and the accompanying photographs (A and D).

A Japanese farming methods

B Distribution of population in Japan

People per square mile
- ⬛ Over 1000
- ▦ 500–1000
- ▨ 250–500
- ▥ 100–250
- ▤ 50–100
- ⬜ Under 50

Towns
- ■ Over 1 million
- ● 500 000 to 1 million

N ↑

0   300 km

C Relief of Japan

Highland ⬜ Over 600 ft
Lowland ⬛ 0–600 ft

Ishikari
Hokkaido
Sea of Japan
Honshu
Fujiyama 12 388 ft
Wakasa Bay
Biwa Lake
Kingu Plain
Kwanto Plain
Tokyo Bay
Ise Bay
Nobi Plain
Shikoku
Kyushu
Inland Sea

N ↑

0   300 km

(i)   What is the major system of farming in Japan? (1)

RUSV

⬜ 1 ⬜⬜⬜

....

(ii) State two major problems Japanese farmers face. (2)

....

....

....

.... ⬜⬜ 2 ⬜

D Cultivation in Japan using rotivators

(iii) Why is it important for a country like Japan to have as efficient an agricultural system as possible? (3) *RUSV*

....
....
....
....
....
....

| | 2 | | 1 |

(iv) Suggest how the Japanese manage to have such high agricultural production. (4)

....
....
....
....
....
....
....

| 4 | | | |

4 Study Table E which gives statistics on farming in Denmark. *RUSV*

Describe the main trends in Danish farming illustrated by these figures. (5)

....
....
....
....
....
....
....
....
....
....

| | 4 | 1 | |

5 Why is subsistence farming becoming less important throughout the world? (4)

....
....
....
....
....
....
....

| | 3 | | 1 |
| 7 | 12 | 4 | 2 |

E

Number and size of Danish farms

	0 – 5	5 – 10	10 – 30	30 –60	Over 60 hectares
1966	21 779	40 102	79 001	20 870	4554
1975	14 061	24 401	59 362	22 852	6478

Numbers of livestock on Danish farms (in thousand head)

	Milk cattle	Pigs	Sows	Hens	Broilers
1966	1350	8120	904	6197	9004
1975	1184	7682	892	5466	7174

Cropped area in Denmark (in thousand hectares)

	Wheat	Barley	Fodder beet	Grass leys	Permanent grass
1966	94	1112	293	559	316
1975	102	1443	181	464	277

IMPROVING AGRICULTURE IN DEVELOPING AND DEVELOPED AREAS

East Anglia is one of Western Europe's most productive farming areas. The pattern of farming and the physical and human advantages of the region are shown in Map A.

Map B shows some of the problems and the improvements being made to farming in north east Brazil.

Whether in tropical or temperate regions, rich or poor countries, there are many ways in which farmland can be improved. Nearly all of them give rise to argument, either with local people, with walkers, with conservationists worried about the long-term effects on wildlife or with people worried about cruelty to animals.

The following are some points to consider about farm improvements.

Division of land

There are different ways of owning, dividing up and using the land. In the plains of the USA and Canada, huge farms of 10 000 hectares each are owned by big firms such as Kellog. In southern Italy, one family might own and live from the produce of ten hectares of farmland, which is in ten small plots scattered around the local countryside.

Markets

There are different markets for farm produce and different ways of selling it. In Denmark, farmers sell their milk and bacon to government marketing boards, which give them a guaranteed price for their produce. In most parts of the world, however, farmers have to take their produce to a local market and see what price it will fetch on the day. If there is a lot of similar produce the price is likely to be low and the farmer will not make much money. If the farmer's produce is in short supply, the price is likely to be high. Either way it is a risky business.

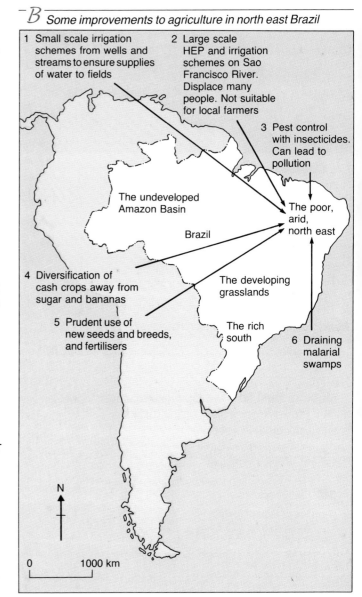

B *Some improvements to agriculture in north east Brazil*

1 Small scale irrigation schemes from wells and streams to ensure supplies of water to fields

2 Large scale HEP and irrigation schemes on Sao Francisco River. Displace many people. Not suitable for local farmers

3 Pest control with insecticides. Can lead to pollution

The undeveloped Amazon Basin

Brazil

The poor, arid, north east

4 Diversification of cash crops away from sugar and bananas

The developing grasslands

5 Prudent use of new seeds and breeds, and fertilisers

The rich south

6 Draining malarial swamps

N

0   1000 km

Output

There are great differences in farm output per hectare and per worker. Intensive farming can produce a great deal from small areas of land, century after century, but the output per worker is low. On extensive farms, output per hectare is low but output per worker is enormous because everything is done by machine and on such a big scale.

Capital input, technology and science

There are differences in the levels of **capital input**, **technology** and **scientific services** available to farmers.

A *East Anglian farming*

Physical advantages	Human advantages
1 Warm, sunny summers to ripen the crops	1 Accessible to markets of London, West Midlands and south-east England
2 Adequate rainfall (650 mm) with maximum April to August when needed for growing and ripening	2 Large efficient farms. Average area for arable farms is over 200 hectares
3 Wide variety of fertile soils	3 Guaranteed market with food companies such as Bird's Eye, who buy food for processing
4 Low, undulating land suitable for large fields, extensive mechanised farming	4 Farms owned by pension funds with capital for investment in new crops (oilseed rape), mechanisation, silo storage, irrigation, drainage, fertilisers and seeds
5 Cold, dry, frosty winters kill off diseases and break up the soil for ploughing	

Lincoln
0   20 km
fruit, bulbs, market gardening on fens
fruit, vegetables, cereals on greensand
forestry on breckland sands
sugar beet, potatoes, broads
cereals and sheep on East Anglian heights
dairying on boulder clay
vegetables and pigs on sand
dairying and market gardening near London
Kent
N

East Anglian farming

Capital is the money used to fund a business. Most farmers in the world have little capital. The larger farms in rich countries are often owned by pension funds and banks which have a lot of capital to invest. If capital is available, a farm manager can more easily adapt the farm to produce whatever is likely to bring in most profit. Scientific services, such as veterinary help with animals, and technological improvements, such as new farm machinery and storage bins, can be brought in or hired. They are expensive but give higher profits in the long run. A small, poor farmer just cannot afford to change like this and tends to carry on in the old ways.

Here are some common types of improvement to agriculture with some common disadvantages which come with them.

Water control

Dry land can be irrigated by ditch or sprinkler. Wetland (marshes) can be drained and used for agriculture, as in the fens.
Disadvantages
The irrigation water can evaporate off and leave harmful salts in the soil.
Valuable wetland wildlife has nowhere to live and dies out. The land can shrink, fall below river level and become a flood hazard.

Making the land more productive

Chemicals like nitrate and phosphate fertilisers or DDT pesticides can be added.
Disadvantages
The chemicals wash out into rivers, lakes and reservoirs, killing fish and causing weeds to grow and clog up the river or lake.
New, chemical resistant strains of pest may develop and these are even more troublesome.

Matching crops or animals to environmental conditions

To do this the farmer must know which seeds and breeds suit a particular climate.
Disadvantages
New seeds and breeds may give short-term gains but may lead to long-term problems. For example, new rice and maize seeds give huge crops for the first years but the soil is then exhausted and lots of chemical fertiliser is needed to maintain production.

Making farming methods more efficient

This means producing more crops or animals with fewer workers in less time with less manual work and an increased use of machinery.
Disadvantages
It causes rural unemployment. Younger people go off to the cities which destroys the fabric of rural village life. Machinery flattens the soil and makes it easier for wind and rain to remove the topsoil.

Factory farming

In this type of farming, animals (usually chickens, calves and pigs) are reared in warm, sheltered conditions and with the correct diet for rapid growth and fattening.
Disadvantages
Some people think factory farming is cruel, even when it is well run. When badly run, it is obviously cruel. If the resources used in factory farming of animals for meat were given over to grain or vegetable farming, far more people could be fed.

Matching product to demand

The product can be matched with what people want to buy. This ensures a more regular market price. The Milk Marketing Board does this for British dairy farmers.
Disadvantages
The farmer is tied to a bureaucratic organisation and has to spend a lot of time filling in forms.

Putting in an infrastructure

For example, roads can be built to transport resources into and products out of farms.
Disadvantages
Takes up valuable farmland, especially in densely populated areas like eastern China, where every square metre is vital.

Reorganising the pattern of land holdings

A farmer with larger fields can use machinery more effectively. Also it is better if a farmer has his or her land in one block rather than as many small scattered fields.
Disadvantages
To make fields and farms larger, hedgerows and trees are destroyed. These form windbreaks as well as providing a habitat for wildlife, so the new farms have problems with wind erosion and have no room for wildlife.

Agricultural education

Through education farmers can learn what alternatives are possible. For example, how to reduce soil erosion by tree planting.
Disadvantages
Farmers may be tempted to adopt new methods which do not work in their surroundings and find themselves worse off than before. Also, they often resent outsiders telling them how to farm.

Crop rotation

Planting a different crop each year in a field will keep the soil in good condition, especially if there are some years when the field is left fallow.
Disadvantages
It may go against tradition and is difficult to organise at first.

1   What is meant by
    (i) factory farming   *RUSV*

....

....

    (ii) marketing boards? (2)

....

....

....   2

2   Study Maps A and B which show an area
    of France before and after land reform.
    (i) State three characteristics of the
        agricultural landscape before land
        reform. (3)

....

....

....

....

....

....   3

(ii) What factors would have
     encouraged the development of
     such a pattern. (2)   *RUSV*

....

....

....

....   2

(iii) What are the advantages of the
      consolidated holdings in Map B? (2)

....

....

....

....   1   1

(iv) What disadvantages might result
     from this agricultural
     improvement? (3)

....

....

....

....

....

....   2   1

A Before land reform

B After land reform

Before

Lavergne
Sach
Borie Thomas
Taix
Riols
Lespinasse

After

Lavergne
Sach
Borie Thomas
Taix
Riols
Lespinasse

N

■ Holding of farmer X
▨ Holding of farmer Y

0   ½   1 km

C Before land reform

Before land reform

D After land reform

After land reform

3   Study Diagrams C and D which show
    how a government land reform scheme
    has helped with the development of a
    rural area in a developing country.

    (i) Name three changes made to the
         landscape as a result of the reform
         scheme. (3)

    ....

    ....

    ....

    ....

    ....

    ....

    RUSV

    | | 3 | |

    (ii) Suggest how a government would
         carry out a land reform scheme like
         the one shown. (4)

    ....

    ....

    ....

    ....

    ....

    ....

    | 4 | . | | |

    (iii) Explain why such a land reform
          scheme is not always easy to carry
          out. (6)

    RUSV

    ....

    ....

    ....

    ....

    ....

    ....

    ....

    ....

    ....

    ....

    ....

    ....

    | | 6 | |

    | 6 | 11 | 6 | 2 |

9. Industry

RESOURCES, RAW MATERIALS AND FUELS

Map A shows some of the **resources** of an area. A resource is anything which is useful. Sometimes resources are divided into two basic types, **raw materials** and **fuels**.

A raw material is something from the Earth which can be used to make things. It may be grown as a crop, like sugar beet, which is a raw material for sugar and fodder. Or it may be a mineral, such as clay, for brick making and ceramics.

A fuel is a resource which provides energy. Wood is used in many poorer parts of the world as fuel for heating homes. Wood is a fuel formed by plants growing today, and is therefore known as a **renewable fuel**. Coal, oil and natural gas are called **fossil fuels**. They are formed from swamp plants which grew millions of years ago. As the plants were buried under sand and mud, some of them slowly turned into fossils of solid coal. Others decomposed into liquid oil or gas. The coal, oil and gas became trapped between rock layers to form reserves of fossil fuels which can now be exploited. These fossil fuels can also be thought of as raw materials, as Table B shows.

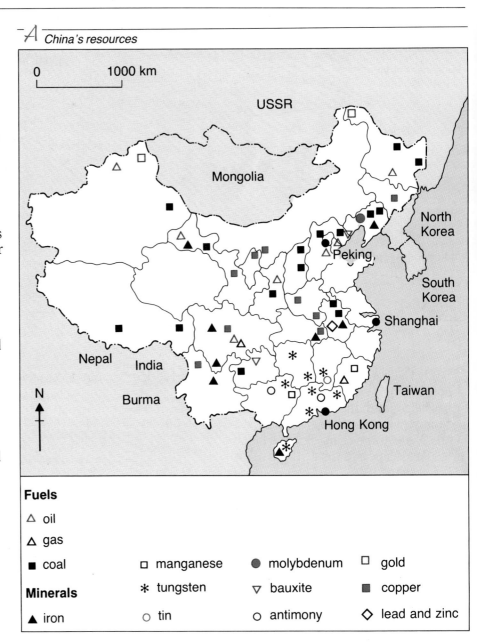

A China's resources

0   1000 km

Fuels

△ oil

△ gas

■ coal

Minerals

▲ iron

□ manganese   ● molybdenum   ▢ gold

✳ tungsten   ▽ bauxite   ▪ copper

○ tin   ⊙ antimony   ◇ lead and zinc

B Resources which can be fuels and raw materials

Resource	As a fuel	As a raw material
Wood	Firewood	Timber for building Wood pulp for paper making
Oil	Heating oil	Petrochemicals to make things like oil-based paints
Coal	House coal	To make tars and drugs
Natural gas	Cooking gas	To make acetylene for welding

The energy in fossil fuels is used in power stations to generate electricity, which is fed into a system of power lines (called the National Grid in Britain). The grid feeds electrical energy to houses, offices and factories in all parts of Britain, so people have a convenient source of power 'at the flick of a switch'.

Uranium is another type of fuel which is used to produce electricity. It is the fuel for the twenty nuclear power stations which produce electricity by nuclear fission in Britain today. The uranium is imported from Namibia (South West Africa) and Australia.

Map C shows some of Britain's major energy resources and the location of power stations.

Table D shows the main raw materials used in the world's industries.

Table D contains some non-renewable resources. These are resources such as oil which, once used up, cannot be replaced in the near future. Table D also contains some renewable resources, such as wheat, and resources which can be recycled, such as iron ore. Diagram E shows what is meant by **renewable** and **non-renewable** resources and also what is meant by **recycling**.

D Main raw materials used in the world's industries

Resource	Amount produced in 1980 (millions of tonnes)	Chief producer
Coal and lignite	3500	USSR
Crude oil	3000	USSR
Iron ore	600	USSR
Limestone	500	USSR
Wheat	420	USSR
Rice	400	China
Maize	350	USA
Potatoes	300	USSR
Barley	180	USSR
Salt	150	USSR

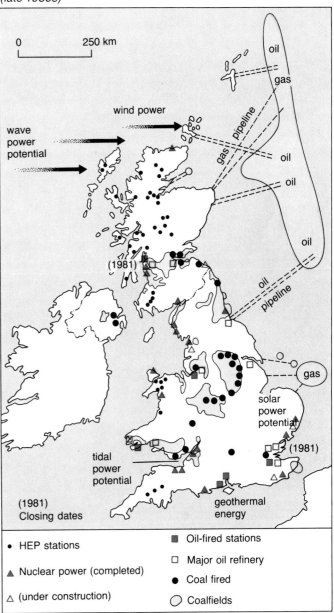

C Britain's energy resources and power generation stations (late 1980s)

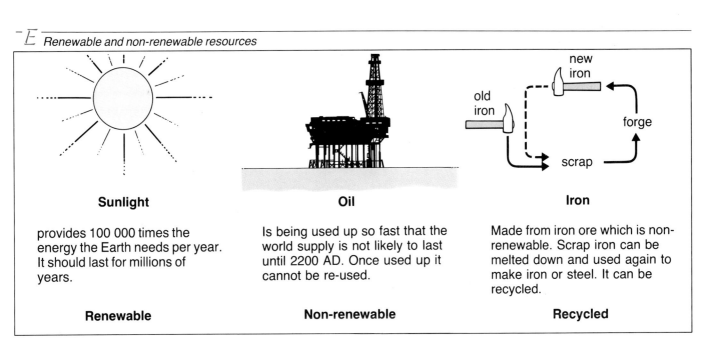

E Renewable and non-renewable resources

Sunlight — provides 100 000 times the energy the Earth needs per year. It should last for millions of years. **Renewable**

Oil — Is being used up so fast that the world supply is not likely to last until 2200 AD. Once used up it cannot be re-used. **Non-renewable**

Iron — Made from iron ore which is non-renewable. Scrap iron can be melted down and used again to make iron or steel. It can be recycled. **Recycled**

1 Study Map A showing southern Ghana, Photograph B of the Akosombo Dam and Photograph C of the Valco aluminium smelter at Tema, both also in Ghana.

RUSV

(i) Name:

(a) one raw material produced in Ghana

....

(b) one renewable resource found in Ghana

....

(c) one non-renewable resource found in Ghana

....

(d) the main fuel supply in Ghana. (4)

.... ☐ ☐ 4 ☐

(ii) Suggest why the building of the Akosombo Dam was necessary for the exploitation of Ghana's resources. (3)

....
....
....
....
....
.... 1 2 ☐ ☐

(iii) In which ways can Lake Volta itself be considered a resource? (2)

....
....
....
.... 1 1 ☐ ☐

A Southern Ghana

Ivory Coast

Lake Volta

Togo

Berekum
Dormaa-Ahenkro
Hohoe
Amedzofe

Kumasi   Timber
Bibiani   Al   Al
Timber   Au   Konongo   R. Birim
Awaso   Au   Obuasi   Keta
Al
R. Ancobra   Kade
Dunkwa   Timber   Koforidua
R. Pra
Oda   Tema
Prestea   Timber   Accra
Au   Tarkwa
Mn   Elmina
Nsuta   Cape Coast
Mn
Axim   Takoradi

Al   Bauxite
Mn   Manganese
Au   Gold
◆   Diamonds
▨   Main cocoa and timber areas today
—   Railways
═   Dam

N

0   500 km

Scale

B Akosombo Dam in Ghana

C   Valco aluminium smelter in Ghana

2   The building of the Akosombo Dam and
    the Volta aluminium smelter was only
    possible with American aid.   *RUSV*
    (i) Why was the USA willing to help a
         developing country like Ghana? (2)

....

....

....

.... | 2 | |

    (ii) Do you think the exploitation of the
         resources of a developing country
         (like Ghana) using foreign aid is a
         good thing for the country
         itself? (4)

....

....

....

....

....

....

....

.... | 2 | | 2 |

3   Many developed countries are
    searching for alternatives to fossil fuels
    as a source of energy.   *RUSV*
    (i) Name one fossil fuel. (1)

.... | 1 | | |

    (ii) Name one alternative energy
         source. (1)

.... | 1 | | |

    (iii) Explain why developed countries
          are searching for alternative
          sources of energy. (5)

....

....

....

....

....

....

....

....

....

.... | 4 | 1 | |

    (iv) Explain why a complete change
         from fossil fuels to alternative
         sources of energy is likely to take a
         long time. (3)

....

....

....

....

.... | | 3 | |

                                              | 8 | 11 | 4 | 2 |

INDUSTRY: A SYSTEM AT A VARIETY OF SCALES

Unit 6.2 shows how farming can be thought of as a system. In a similar way, an industrial business can be seen as a system. Diagram A shows this in simple terms and Diagram B shows what the system would be for a small local business (making garden ornaments).

Where to locate a small firm like this is one decision the owner has to make. There must be a balance between the various costs and conveniences. Diagram C shows some of the thoughts which might occur.

Industries are often put into the following five categories because of their function (the job they do).

A Simple systems diagram

	Feedback	
Decisions	← New ideas	Profit (or loss!)

Input	→	Process	→	Output	→	Market

B A system for making garden ornaments

A system for making garden ornaments

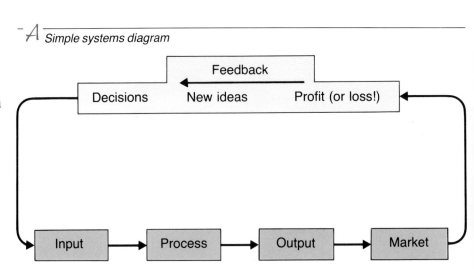

Inputs	**Processes**	**Output**	**Market(s)**
Resources			
(a) Raw materials (bought from Builders' Merchants) Cement Sand Colouring	Negotiating and buying from builders' merchant	Gnomes Sundials Birdtables Fountains	Garden centres Department stores Householders Public parks
(b) Energy supply Electricity (bought from Electricity Board)			

Feedback

1 Need to make greater range of items
2 Must build bigger store
3 Profit down on last year

Capital investment
Site ¼ hectare
Storage/work building
Office shed } Building and maintenance

Mixer } Mixing
Moulds } Moulding
Drier } Drying

Transport
Lorry }
Van } Transporting

Office equipment
Calculator } Estimating prices
Word processor } Letter writing
Account files } Book keeping

Labour
Owner/Managing Director
1 worker

Grants
Nothing, except a loan from a bank

Primary (or extractive) industries

An example is iron ore mining, where a resource is taken from the ground.

Secondary (or manufacturing) industries

An example is clock making, where raw materials are put together to make goods which people want to buy.

Secondary (or power-producing) industries

An example is a coal-fired power station, where fuel from coal is used to generate electricity, which is a more convenient source of power in houses, offices and factories.

Tertiary (or service) industries

An example is teaching, where a service and not goods is provided.

Quaternary (or information technology) industries

An example is the production of software for computers.
Table D shows how these industries can be seen as systems.

C Locating an industry

Costs
How much will it cost to:

buy or rent the site?
buy the plant (equipment)?
buy the resources?
transport them to the site?
employ a worker?
sell the products?
transport them to the markets?
get rid of waste on tips?

Convenience
Where do I want to work:

within 5 km of home?
not too close to other homes? near a main road ?
looking out on to green fields?

D The five types of industry as systems

Industry	Input	→ Process	→ Output	→ Market	→ Feedback
Iron ore mining	Explosives Diggers Energy	Quarrying or mining	Iron ore	Steelworks	Profit Quality of the ore
Clock and watch making	Components made from plastic and metal Microelectronics skills	'Factoring', i.e. fitting the bits together so they work Designing new clocks	Clocks	Department stores Homes Special users (e.g. schools)	Profit Which designs sell best Reliability
Coal-fired power stations	Coal Water (for the turbines) Huge buildings	Coal heats water Water → steam Steam turns turbines in magnetic field	Electricity	Domestic (home) and industrial buildings	Profit Reliability of electrical supply
Teaching	School buildings Chalk, paper, books and equipment Skill	Supervising Communication Learning	Educated people Exam passes and other achievements	Parents and their children	Quality of the teaching Relevance to the real world
Software writing	Computer system Skill	Creative writing	Programs Documentation	Industry Home users	Profit Usefulness

A   *Potters in northern Nigeria*

1   Study Photograph A of potters in northern Nigeria.   *RUSV*
    (i)   Briefly explain why pottery is a cottage (or craft) industry. (2)

....

....

....

....   2 ☐ ☐ ☐

    (ii)   Complete the following diagram to show how pottery making acts as a system. (4)   ☐ 4 ☐ ☐

☐ → ☐ → ☐ → ☐

(iii)   How may cottage (or craft) industries in the developed world differ from those in the developing world? (5)   *RUSV*

....

....

....

....

....

....

....

....

....

....

....   2 3 ☐ ☐

B

2 Study Photograph B.
   (i) Which category of industry is
       illustrated here? (1)

RUSV

`1 | | |`

....

   (ii) Draw a labelled diagram to show
        the following features of the
        photograph: the coastline, spoil
        tips, the works. (4)

`| | 4 |`

   (iii) Why would planning regulations be
         important inputs in the
         development of an industry such as
         that shown on the photograph? (3)

....

....

....

....

....

....

`| 1 | 2 |`

3 Ford Motors is an example of a large
   scale multinational (or transnational).
   (i) What is a 'multinational'? (1)

RUSV

....

....

`1 | | |`

   (ii) What are the advantages to a
        company like Ford Motors of
        operating on such a large scale? (5)

....

....

....

....

....

....

....

....

....

....

....

`3 | 2 | |`

`9 | 10 | 4 | 2`

FACTORS WHICH INFLUENCE THE LOCATION OF INDUSTRY

Map A shows Western Europe's most important manufacturing regions. There are many reasons why each of these locations has become important, but the same few factors are involved in each case. These factors are capital, resources, communications, markets, skills, environment and government policy.

Capital is the money available to set up and run new industries.

Resources are things like coal or iron ore which are used to make goods and to provide services.

Communications are movements of people, goods and ideas along natural and artificial routeways.

Markets are where goods and services are sold.

Skills are the organisational and technical talents needed to get jobs done. This factor can also be called 'labour'.

Environment is the site (the land the industry is built on) and its surroundings. Modern industries are prevented by law from polluting the environment with their waste products in certain ways. People, especially those with advanced skills, are not prepared nowadays to live in places which are polluted or otherwise unpleasant. So the new industries which are growing up tend to have decent environments.

Government policy often encourages new industries to go to less developed areas, which tend to be the poorer parts of a country, or to areas where unemployment is higher than average. Where governments have no such policy, they are letting 'market forces' decide where new industries should be located.

A Western Europe's most important manufacturing regions

0   500 km   N

Key

1	Stockholm
2	Glasgow
3	Tyne-Tees
4	Lancs-Yorks
5	West Midlands
6	South Wales
7	London
8	Hamburg
9	Raandstad
10	Ruhr
11	Northern France, southern Belgium
12	Paris
13	Lyon
14	Turin
15	Milan
16	Marseilles
17	Bilbao
18	Barcelona
19	Rome
20	Naples

B Factors influencing the growth of the Ruhr

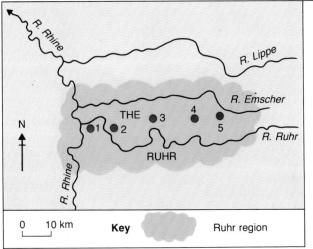

R. Rhine
R. Lippe
R. Emscher
THE ●1 ●2 ●3 4 5 R. Ruhr
N
R. Rhine
RUHR

0   10 km   **Key**   Ruhr region

Environment

The River Ruhr has exposed coal seams in its valley. They are now exhausted. Newer mines are deep ones sunk into the Emscher and Lippe valleys. The area is low, undulating land, easy to build on and to landscape, and is surrounded by pleasant farming country.

Accessibility

Via River Rhone to coast for imports of raw materials and for exports of manufactured goods. Via rail and autobahn (motorway) to the rest of Western Europe.

Capital

North Germany became a rich farming area using scientific methods in the 19th century. There was money available for 'risk capital' to set up new, risky industries. Lots of capital was needed for coal mines, steelworks and infrastructure (roads, railways, canals).

Resources

1 Thick seam of coal for
(a) fuel in power stations
(b) raw material for steelworks
(c) raw material for chemicals.
2 Water from rivers for use in steel and chemical industries (20 tonnes of water needed to make 1 tonne of steel)
3 Local iron ore in the 19th century is now replaced by imports
4 Local limestone for 'flux' in steelmaking

Government policy

Coal mining, steel making, engineering and chemicals have been privately developed in the Ruhr but governments have supported firms by putting in infrastructure where necessary and supporting prices in lean years.

Markets

The industrial areas of Western Europe, North America and Japan. Also capital cities and developing parts of the third world.

Two European examples

The Ruhr Planning Region is an area covering North Rhine and Westphalia. Here the River Ruhr flows into the River Rhine from the east at the port city of Duisburg, which is 100 km upstream from the Rhine's mouth near Rotterdam, in Holland. For 80 km along the Ruhr east of Duisburg, and for 30 km to the north of the river is Western Europe's greatest traditional concentration of heavy industry. It was based on coal mining and steel making. The region has a population of six million people. Map B shows the factors involved in its growth.

Environmental problems

The growth of the Ruhr Planning Region brought problems. Huge areas were covered by spoil heaps from the mines and steelworks. Factories poured out smoke and soot over people's houses and liquid waste into the River Ruhr.

Improving the environment

The people living in the area have been transforming it from a dirty industrial scene into a pleasant place to live. Now there are large green belts between the main cities, five area parks with multi-purpose leisure facilities, and twenty other major sports and leisure parks in the Ruhr Planning Region.

Change

Over the last twenty years, the traditional coal and steel industries have been closing down and tens of thousands of jobs have been lost. New, advanced 'high-tech' industries are rapidly taking their place, using the engineering and scientific skills already present.

Success

Unlike other areas of declining heavy industry (for example, South Wales and North East England) the Ruhr is changing successfully into an area of modern industry. The main reason is that it is centrally placed in Western Europe, so it is close to the whole European market and firms want to set up there.

Industry in North and South Italy

Italy is another major European industrial nation. The north of Italy is prosperous, with flourishing industry. In contrast, the south is poor, and has received a great deal of government help to encourage new industries to set up. Maps C, D and E show these two regions and give details of some of the main factors at play in each one.

D Growth of industry in the Mezzogiorno (mezzogiorno means 'midday')

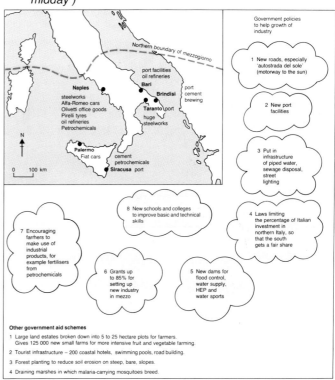

Government policies to help growth of industry

1 New roads, especially 'autostrada del sole' (motorway to the sun)

2 New port facilities

3 Put in infrastructure of piped water, sewage disposal, street lighting

4 Laws limiting the percentage of Italian investment in northern Italy, so that the south gets a fair share

5 New dams for flood control, water supply, HEP and water sports

6 Grants up to 85% for setting up new industry in mezzo

7 Encouraging farmers to make use of industrial products, for example fertilisers from petrochemicals

8 New schools and colleges to improve basic and technical skills

Naples — steelworks, Alfa-Romeo cars, Olivetti office goods, Pirelli tyres, oil refineries, Petrochemicals

Bari — port facilities, oil refineries

Brindisi — port, cement, brewing

Taranto — port, huge steelworks

Palermo — Fiat cars

Siracusa — cement, petrochemicals, port

Other government aid schemes

1 Large land estates broken down into 5 to 25 hectare plots for farmers. Gives 125 000 new small farms for more intensive fruit and vegetable farming.
2 Tourist infrastructure – 200 coastal hotels, swimming pools, road building.
3 Forest planting to reduce soil erosion on steep, bare, slopes.
4 Draining marshes in which malaria-carrying mosquitoes breed.

E Factors involved in development of Fiat at Turin

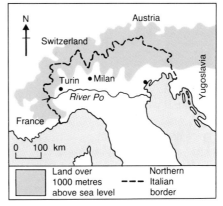

Only **resource** is HEP from the Alps, other resources have to be imported

Government policy is to leave north Italian industry to private firms

Land over 1000 metres above sea level · Northern Italian border

Traditional metal working (e.g. swords, guns) and design **skills** (artists) in northern Italy

Strong local **market** for cars and trucks in rich and densely populated north west and Lombardy provinces

Accessibility: the nearest part of Italy to the markets of France, West Germany and Britain, with excellent rail and road links

The **environment** is low, fertile, undulating farmland in the Po valley near attractive mountain scenery

Rich farming in the 19th and 20th century provided risk **capital** for the setting up of new industries

C Provinces of Italy in order of income per person

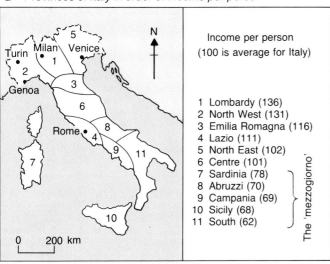

Income per person (100 is average for Italy)

1 Lombardy (136)
2 North West (131)
3 Emilia Romagna (116)
4 Lazio (111)
5 North East (102)
6 Centre (101)
7 Sardinia (78)
8 Abruzzi (70)
9 Campania (69)
10 Sicily (68)
11 South (62)

The 'mezzogiorno'

1 (i) Copy the list below of factors which   *RUSV*
are important when locating an
industry:
power supply;
source of raw materials;
large market;
ready supply of labour.
Against each factor, write one of
the following industries which might
be attracted to a location with this
factor.
Aluminium smelting, electronics
manufacture, baking bread, sugar
beet refining. (4)

....

....

....

.... | 4 | | |

(ii) For each industry, give a reason
why it is attracted to that particular
location. (4)

....

....

....

....

....

....

....

.... | 4 | | |

2 Study Map A which is based on a
newspaper advertisement. It is
designed to attract industry to West
Yorkshire.
(i) Name two types of industry that
are likely to have developed in an
area like West Yorkshire. (2)

....

.... | 2 | | |

(ii) Suggest why the towns and cities of
West Yorkshire need to advertise
for new industry. (3)

....

....

....

....   *RUSV*

....

.... | 1 | 2 | | |

(iii) Using map evidence only, describe
the advantages of West Yorkshire
for new industry. (4)

....

....

....

....

....

....

.... | | | 4 | |

(iv) What additional information would a
company require before moving to
West Yorkshire? (4)

....

....

....

....

....

....

.... | 1 | 2 | | 1 |

(v) Map B and Photograph C show
that West Yorkshire is a
government assisted area. Explain
how the government encourages
industry to move to such an
area. (4)

....

....

....

....

....

....

.... | 2 | 2 | | |

| 8 | 12 | 4 | 1 |

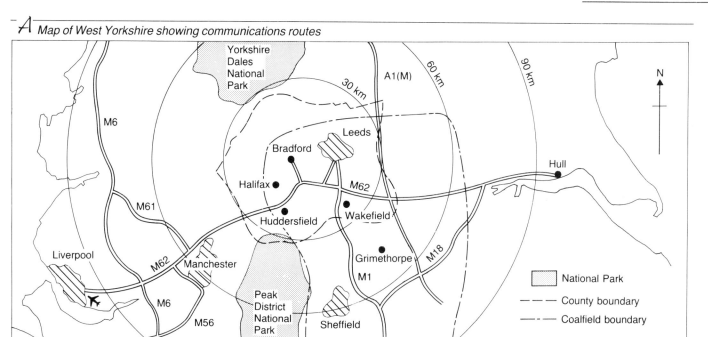

A *Map of West Yorkshire showing communications routes*

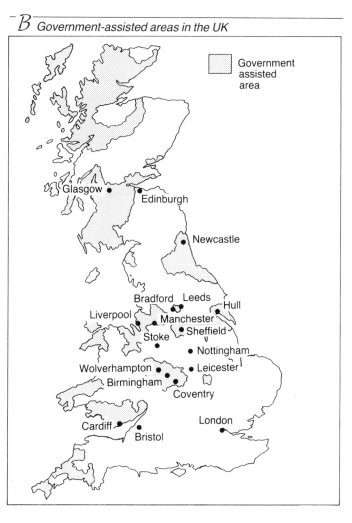

B *Government-assisted areas in the UK*

C *Mantra House, Keighley – a former mill redeveloped with the aid of a Government grant*

FROM MANUFACTURING TO SERVICE INDUSTRIES

Table A shows how the percentages employed in Britain in the four industrial sectors, and those unemployed, have changed from 1945–1985. Note that primary (extractive) industry includes agriculture.

A Employment in Britain, 1945–1985

	Primary (1) (extractive)	**Secondary (2)** (manufacturing)	**Tertiary (3)** (services)	**Quaternary (4)** (information technology)	**Unemployed**
1945	8	52	34	1	5
1965	6	42	46	2	4
1985	3	27	48	7	15

(The figures show the percentage of each group in the UK economy 1945–1985)

B Wistow Colliery, Yorkshire – a primary extractive industry

C Lea Hall Colliery, Staffs, supplies coal to the nearby Rugeley Power Station – a secondary power industry

Location of these types of industry

Primary extractive industry

Extractive industries are always located as near to the site of the resources that they use as possible. For instance, the new colliery in Photograph B is sited over the coal seams of the Selby coalfield.

Secondary manufacturing industry

Sometimes a manufacturing industry will locate near a raw material or fuel that is expensive to transport. In the 19th century, it was expensive to move coal from the collieries. Manufacturing industry, which used coal as its main fuel, moved to the coalfields. Coal-fired power stations (Photograph C) have **raw material locations**. Apart from coal, Britain's mineral resources are either exhausted or more expensive to produce than foreign imports. So inland firms closed down and new ones have been built on the coast, where the imports can be unloaded straight into the works. An important example is found in the steel industry. Map D shows how inland steelworks have closed down, leaving almost all British steelworks on the coast. This is called a **coastal location** and is shown in Photograph E.

D Iron and steel in Britain

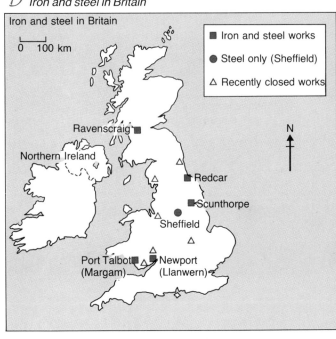

Iron and steel in Britain

0   100 km

■ Iron and steel works
● Steel only (Sheffield)
△ Recently closed works

N

Ravenscraig ■
Northern Ireland
Redcar ■
Scunthorpe ■
Sheffield ●
Port Talbot ■ (Margam) △ ■ Newport (Llanwern)

The only steelworks left inland is at Sheffield, in South Yorkshire. It is still inland because of **geographical inertia**. Inertia means resistance to movement. Even though the location is poor for modern times, the skills of the local workforce are able to keep the industry there by making special steels which keep the firms in profit.

Nowadays, most factories are powered by electricity from the National Grid. Small manufacturing industries, such as light engineering, can be located almost anywhere in the country. Factories like these are said to be 'footloose'. They usually set up in **industrial estates** (Photograph F) either in the old industrial parts near city centres or in trading estates on the edges of cities near main roads. These sorts of location are called **market locations**, as they are near their customers in the city.

Tertiary service industry

Tertiary industries are located in cities, where people want to buy their goods and services. They have a market location. Restaurants, for example, need their customers to be able to reach them easily, so they locate in busy city centres or in suburban high streets. Large office blocks housing insurance firms and building societies are often built in the city centres (central business districts) (Photograph G).

Quaternary information technology industry

The newer information industries, such as software writing, are not strongly tied to a market location. As their products are cheap to move, by post, telephone or computer link-up, they are able to locate almost anywhere. Often, small, pleasant towns near motorway junctions are chosen, so their workers can move around the country to share or pick up new ideas.

E   The Port Talbot steelworks: coastal location. Secondary manufacturing industry

G   Centre of Sydney, Australia – CBD. Tertiary service industry, offices and shops in CBD.

F   An industrial estate outside Basingstoke, Hampshire. Secondary manufacturing and market location.

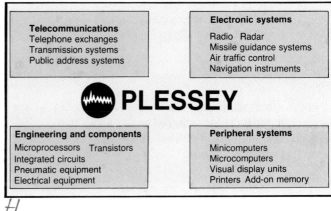

Telecommunications	Electronic systems
Telephone exchanges	Radio Radar
Transmission systems	Missile guidance systems
Public address systems	Air traffic control
	Navigation instruments

PLESSEY

Engineering and components	Peripheral systems
Microprocessors Transistors	Minicomputers
Integrated circuits	Microcomputers
Pneumatic equipment	Visual display units
Electrical equipment	Printers Add-on memory

H

A *Employment structure in various countries*

1 Study Column Graph A which shows the structure of employment in certain countries.
RUSV

  (i) Explain the meaning of:
    (a) primary industries
    (b) secondary industries
    (c) tertiary industries
    (d) quarternary industries. (4)

....
....
....
....
....
....
....
....
                      `4`

  (ii) What percentage of the working population is employed in primary occupations in India? (1)

....
....
                      `1`

  (iii) What percentage of the working population is employed in secondary occupations in the United Kingdom? (1)

....
....
                      `1`

  (iv) How does the employment structure of developing countries differ from that in the developing world? (3)
RUSV

....
....
....
....
....
                      `2` `1`

  (v) What problems does the developing world have in encouraging the growth of secondary industries? (4)

....
....
....
....
....
                      `4`

  (vi) Do you consider that quarternary occupations are likely to occur in the developing world in the near future? Explain your answer. (2)

....
....
....
....
                      `1` `2`

2 Study Photograph B, Maps C and D and Table E which refer to the Ruhr industrial area of West Germany.

RUSV

(i) Suggest how the maps and table explain the development and eventual decline of the industrial landscape shown in Photograph B. (5)

....
....
....
....
....
....
....
....
....
....

| 2 | 2 | 1 | |

(ii) What factors have encouraged the development of the present day pattern of industry in this region? (4)

....
....
....
....
....
....
....
....

| 1 | 3 | | |

| 8 | 11 | 4 | 2 |

B Ruhr industrial area

C Cross section of the Ruhr region to show its coalfields

Changes in mining

North

Late twentieth century mines
Few actual mines in a semi-rural environment
Advanced mechanisation gives high output per miner
High investment
Conservation of environment important

Late nineteenth and twentieth century mines
Greater mechanisation giving higher output per miner
Rationalisation of smaller mines
Many closures 1960–80

Nineteenth century and early twentieth century mines
Most coal seams exhausted
Those remaining tend to be thin, faulted and liable to flooding
Extraction has become very costly
Out-of-date equipment
Mining towns decaying

South

Newer rocks
Flammkohlen
Gaskohlen
Fetikohlen
Ebkohlen

Type of coalfield

| concealed | concealed | exposed |

Type of mining

| Deep shafts reaching down to 1000 metres | Shafts cut vertically down to coal seams, under 500 metres deep | Some open-cast, mainly adit mines – horizontal galleries where coal was exposed on valley sides |

◀——— 50 km ———▶

N-S cross-section of map D

E Employment in the Ruhr region since 1939

	1939	1950	1984
Essen			
Total number employed	281 751	250 485	261 144[1]
Percentage employed in mining	17.9	20.3	3.1[2]
Percentage employed in iron & steel	7.5	5.5	
Bochum			
Total number employed	151 206	146 027	152 708
Percentage employed in mining	23.6	28.0	0.2[2]
Percentage employed in iron & steel	15.8	12.0	6.0[2]

[1] Estimated
[2] Business with more than 20 employees

D Coalfields and mines in the Ruhr region

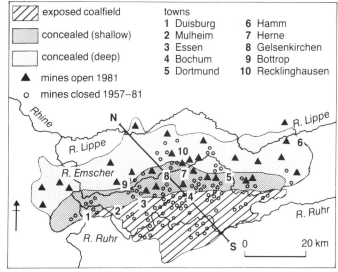

exposed coalfield
concealed (shallow)
concealed (deep)
▲ mines open 1981
o mines closed 1957–81

towns
1 Duisburg
2 Mulheim
3 Essen
4 Bochum
5 Dortmund
6 Hamm
7 Herne
8 Gelsenkirchen
9 Bottrop
10 Recklinghausen

10. Communications

TRANSPORT AND TRANSPORT ROUTES

Transport is the movement of goods and people.
  Diagram A shows the ten main types of transport in use in the world.

A

Factors influencing transport routeways

Routeways are influenced by four main factors:
the shortest route;
physical obstructions;
political obstructions;
other economic considerations.

Shortest route

The shortest route should be the cheapest and therefore should be the one chosen, all other things being equal. Oddly, this is not always the case, as will be shown.

  If there are just two places to be joined, a straight line is the shortest and cheapest route. For instance, the rail route across the Eucla Basin Plain in Southern Australia is dead straight for over 800 km!

If more than two places are to be joined, the shortest route pattern may be an unusual shape. This diagram shows the shortest routes for three places, and for four places forming the corners of a rectangle.

Routes may be built by different companies who are competing with each other. Also routes tend to be built from one place to the next, rather than to fit mathematical patterns. So the overall shortest route pattern is not always found. Map B shows the rail link between Dallas, Houston and San Antonio in Texas.

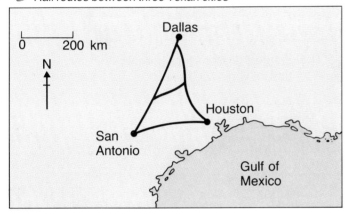

B *Rail routes between three Texan cities*

Physical obstructions

Mountains

It is often cheaper for routes to go round uplands rather than over or through them. If a route has to rise up a very steep slope, a zig-zag route may be needed to keep the gradient low enough for traffic to make it up the slope. Tunnels can be dug through mountains to shorten routes, but these are expensive to build and are only used on routes with heavy traffic. Map C shows the tunnel route through the Alps from Bern in Switzerland to Milan in Italy.

Marsh

Marshland causes routes to sink unless they are provided with expensive foundations reaching down to solid rock. Modern routes have to have expensive foundations anyway, so marshes are not such an obstruction, but in most parts of the world routes still bend around marshy areas.

Water

Land routes avoid water wherever possible, as bridges and tunnels are expensive to build and maintain. A bridge or tunnel crossing of the English Channel has been suggested many times, but the costs have put firms off for many years. Now, finally, after many years of discussion a tunnel is going to be built to connect Great Britain and France. Roll-on roll-off ferries are often a cheaper way of crossing long stretches of water. Bridges are better for rivers or narrow estuaries which obstruct routes bearing heavy traffic, such as the ones across the River Severn from London to South Wales.

Land

Sea routes obviously have to detour around headlands which lie in their way. Canals can shorten these detours where the amount of saving is high. Map D shows the importance of the Suez and Panama canals. However, canals are expensive to build and maintain and also to widen, so large modern ships do not use them.

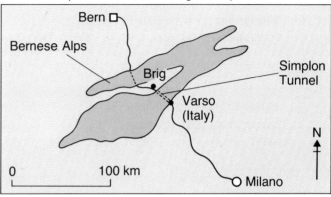

C *The Simplon Tunnel route through the Alps*

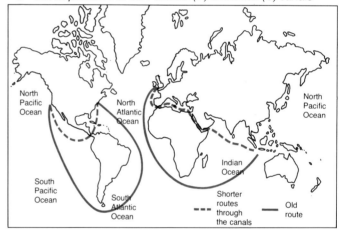

D *The importance of the Panama (P) and Suez (S) canals*

Political obstructions

Routeways often have to bend around 'unfriendly' territory. In 1985 a civilian airliner was shot down when it strayed over a forbidden area of Eastern USSR and nearly 400 people were killed. In 1956 the ruler of Egypt closed the Suez canal to shipping. Since then, shipping lines have been wary of such actions and have invested in huge supertankers to take long sea routes rather than offer the money to widen and deepen a Suez canal which could be closed to them by a sudden political decision.

Environmental obstructions

If local people feel that a transport route would spoil the landscape too much it may be diverted or hidden. Pipelines or cables can be laid underground, for instance.

Other economic considerations

Low local taxes may encourage transport firms to choose less obvious routeways. Irish tax concessions have attracted some trans-Atlantic airlines to Shannon airport rather than other West European airports, for example.

1 (i) Which two oceans are linked by the Panama Canal? (1) *RUSV*

....

....

(ii) Which river is crossed by the South Wales motorway? (1)

....

....

(iii) Through which tunnel does the railway from Bern to Milan pass? (1)

....

.... |3| | | |

2 Study Map A showing the railways of West Africa.
(i) Describe the pattern of railways shown on the map. (4)

....

....

....

....

....

.... |2|2| | |

(ii) Which two countries does the railway route from Ouagadougou to Abidjan link? (2) *RUSV*

....

....

....

.... | |2| | |

(iii) In what respect is this route not as economic as it could be? (1)

....

.... | |1| | |

(iv) Suggest reasons for the route of this railway. (2)

....

....

....

.... |1|1| | |

A Railways of West Africa

Key:
- – – – Rivers navigable all the year
- ——— Rivers navigable part of the year
- +++++ Railways
- ——— International road

0 — 800 km

3   Study Map B and Photograph C of the
    Tanzam railway in South East Africa
    (between Tanzania and Zambia).
    (i) Suggest why Zambia needed the
        railway. (2)

....

....

....

....   ☐☐1 1

    (ii) What advantages could Tanzania
         get from the railway? (2)

....

....

....

....   ☐2☐

    (iii) Suggest why this route was
          chosen. (4)

....

....

....

....

....

....

....

....   3 1☐

4   With reference to specific examples,
    show how motorway engineers have
    overcome physical obstacles. (6)

....

....

....

....

....

....

....

....

....

....

....   3 3☐☐

                                             7 12 6 1

RUSV

B The Tanzam railway in south east Africa

Legend:
- ▨ Land over 1400 metres
- ▬ Tazara railway
- –·– Country boundaries
- 0 ___ 300 km
- ░Cu░ Copper mining area
- N ↑

C   Chinese workers on the Tanzam railway

LAND TRANSPORT: PATH, TRACK, ROAD AND RAIL

A *Carrying water from a well*

Photograph A shows a typical scene in the developing world. People are walking along a path, carrying water from a well to their homes. This is quite a normal event in the lives of many of the world's people. Compared to other types of transport it is slow and hard on the people involved, requiring a lot of effort per tonne or kilometre. It is cheap, however, and people can alter the path to suit wherever they want to go, so it is the most flexible method of transport.

Photograph B shows animals being used to carry goods along a path. This is less wearing on the people involved. It is slow but flexible.

Photograph C shows one of the most useful inventions in history, the wheeled cart. Pulled by a horse, mule or ox, it is an efficient way of shifting goods over short distances. The wheels make moving heavy weights easy but they need a specially hardened surface, so cart tracks are not as flexible as paths.

Photograph D shows a very common scene in the developed world, people travelling in motorised road vehicles.

B *Animals carrying goods*

C Wheeled cart

D Motorised road vehicles

Building roads is expensive. In the UK, motorways cost two million pounds per kilometre. A roads cost one million pounds per kilometre and small secondary roads cost half a million pounds per kilometre. The cost is met from the rates by county authorities, plus government funds raised from everyone's taxes. All motorists have to pay a licence fee each year, some of which goes on the upkeep of roads. On some motorways in France and Italy, motorists have to pay a toll which is used to pay for roads.

Road transport relies on cheap petrol and diesel refined from crude oil. Before 1973, crude oil was very cheap, which encouraged huge investment in roads all over the world. In rich countries, where a dense road network had been built, road transport was very flexible. Once the road pattern was laid it was easy to travel from any place in the country to any other, door to door. This is road transport's biggest asset. The UK, for instance, has 340 000 kilometres of roads, compared to 17 230 kilometres of railway track. No wonder that 80 per cent of all goods tonnage and 95 per cent of passengers go by road in the UK.

However, there are problems associated with so much transport by road. Many British roads are now congested. They are damaged by the wheels of heavy lorries and need frequent, expensive maintenance, which slows up the traffic. Large stretches of good farmland and useful city space have been taken for road use in recent years.

Table E shows how road vehicle production has changed in recent decades.

The fastest train in the world is the Paris to Lyon TGV (Train á Grande Vitesse). It is an all-passenger express with twenty services per day, travelling at up to 275 kilometres per hour. Like most rail services in the world, however, it loses money.

Railways can only pay where there is a high, regular flow of people or goods between any two places. In reality, this means that railway traffic is limited to three types of movement. Firstly, commuters travelling daily from densely populated suburbs into city centres to work and returning home in the evenings. Secondly, large numbers of passengers travelling from one large city centre to another. Thirdly, goods moving from ports or centres of production to places where they are regularly used. The best example in the UK is the movement of coal from collieries to coal-fired power stations, which makes up 70 per cent of all rail freight.

There is a view that more heavy traffic should be put on the railways, but this would mean huge investment in new railway tracks. Also, there is no guarantee that, when the new tracks are laid, the patterns of movement would not have changed. With the present road networks in rich countries, it is easier to adapt to new patterns of movement.

E Number of vehicles produced in the world (millions)

	1965	1975	1985
Cars	25	29	33
Commercial vehicles	6	9	12

1 Study Map A which shows the autobahns in West Germany.
(i) What is an autobahn? (1)

....
.... [1 | | |]

(ii) Which city would you pass when travelling from Frankfurt to Nuremburg along the autobahn? (1)

....
.... [| | 1 |]

(iii) How does the map suggest that there are many important resources in both the Cologne – Duisburg – Dortmund area and the area south west of Frankfurt? (2)

....
....
....
.... [| | 2 |]

(iv) What are the advantages of autobahns over other types of road? (3)

....
....
....
....
....
.... [3 | | |]

(v) What kinds of traffic or cargoes would you encourage and what kinds would you discourage from using autobahns? Give reasons for your answers. (5)

....
....
....
....
....
....
....
....
.... [2 | 3 | |]

R U S V

A Autobahns in West Germany (1985)

B British Rail: passenger and freight receipts and traffic

	Unit	1979	1981	1983	1985
Passenger receipts	£000s	799.7	1022.7	1137.5	1295.5
Freight receipts	£000s	562.9	623.6	633.3	596.2
Passenger journeys	Millions	748.2	718.5	693.7	697.4
Freight traffic	Million tonnes	170.5	155.1	146.0	122.9
Coal and coke	Million tonnes	93.5	95.2	87.9	65.9
Iron and steel	Million tonnes	25.1	18.2	15.9	14.1

Source: *Annual Abstract of Statistics* (HMSO, 1986), p. 200

2 Study the figures above showing passenger and freight receipts and traffic on British Rail (Table B).

   (i) Complete a line graph to show the tonnage carried in the years between 1979 and 1985. (3)

....
....
....
....
....
.... ☐ ☐ 3 ☐

   (ii) Describe the pattern of passenger and freight receipts and traffic in the period 1979 to 1985. (3)

....
....
....
....
....
.... ☐ 3 ☐ ☐

   (iii) Give reasons for the pattern you have described. (3)

....
....
....
....
....
.... ☐ 3 ☐ ☐

RUSV

C

RUSV

3 Study Photograph C which shows a boy from Nepal who earns his living by carrying loads on foot up into the foothills of the Himalayas. He is looking at a new road being built with British aid.

Describe the effects this new road will have on the boy and on a developing country like Nepal. (4)

....
....
....
....
....
....
....
.... ☐ 2 ☐ 2

☐ 6 ☐ 11 ☐ 6 ☐ 2

TRANSPORT BY AIR AND WATER

Major world air-traffic routes

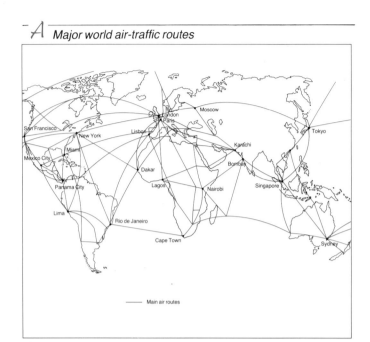

— Main air routes

Ideal situation and conditions for an airport

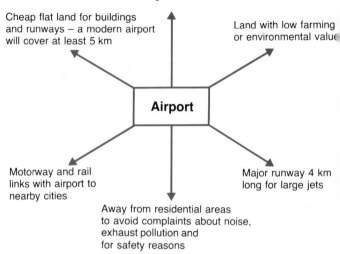

Low incidence of frost, fog, low cloud, snow and high winds

Cheap flat land for buildings and runways – a modern airport will cover at least 5 km

Land with low farming or environmental value

Airport

Motorway and rail links with airport to nearby cities

Away from residential areas to avoid complaints about noise, exhaust pollution and for safety reasons

Major runway 4 km long for large jets

Air

Aeroplanes are fast, and that is their main advantage. They are more expensive than other forms of transport per tonne per mile (the cost of moving a tonne through one mile) but speed is also valuable. On a package holiday, for instance, you cut down holiday travel time if you go by air.

Concorde is very expensive, noisy and uses huge amounts of fuel. Yet nine Concordes are still in use because people want to experience the novelty of travelling at over 2000 kilometres per hour. Highly-paid business people can fly from Europe to the USA, do a day's business, and fly back on the same day, and to them time is money.

There are two mass markets for air travel. One is in large, rich countries such as the USA, where lots of people wish to travel across the large distances between American cities. The other is in trans-oceanic flight between countries in the developed world. Map A shows the major world air-traffic routes.

Another use for aeroplanes is to transport high value, low bulk goods securely and quickly over long distances. Jewellery, documents and flowers are some of the goods carried by air.

The disadvantages of air travel are cost and airport location. To build a modern international airport costs up to 1000 million pounds and few countries can afford this outlay. Also, not many people want an airport on their doorstep! Diagram B shows some of the factors needed for an ideal airport and some of the main objections which local people raise.

Map C shows the location of the top ten UK airfields. All ten are near large or capital cities except Aberdeen, where there is a great deal of air transport to the North Sea oil and gas fields.

The major UK airports

■ Major international airport

○ Major regional UK airport

▲ Mainly package holiday airports

Airport	Passengers (millions)			
1 Heathrow	29.5	6 Aberdeen		1.7
2 Gatwick	14.1	7 Birmingham		1.7
3 Manchester	6.0	8 Belfast		1.6
4 Glasgow	2.8	9 Edinburgh		1.5
5 Luton	1.8	10 Bristol		1.4

Water

Ships

Ships are the cheapest way of transporting heavy loads for long distances. Diagram D shows the principle behind this. One problem though, is that it is costly to load and unload ships and barges. This 'goods handling' is cheapest when the goods are liquid, like oil. Map E shows the top fifteen freight seaports in the UK. All of Sullom Voe's tonnage and much of that of London, Teesside, Milford Haven, Orkney and Forth is made up of imports of crude oil. Another large part of the tonnage is made up of imports of iron ore for coastal steelworks.

Some solids, like grain, can be pumped on and off the ship as if they were liquid and are also cheap. Oddly-shaped, delicate goods are the most expensive to load and store securely.

Nowadays this problem is less important than it was because goods are often pre-packed into aluminium containers by transport firms. Each container measures 6 m × 2.5 m × 2.5 m. Lorries take the containers to the docks. At dockside container terminals they are swung quickly into the holds of ships by large cranes and are easily stored. Roll-on roll-off (ro-ro) terminals are even simpler. Lorries with their containers drive onto the ship and park. At the end of the sea route, they drive off and continue their land journey.

Container terminals are used mainly for long distance water transport, whereas roll-on roll-off terminals are better for short ferry routes across the English Channel or North Sea, for example. Felixstowe and Harwich in East Anglia are the UK's most important container and roll-on roll-off ports. They export and import expensive manufactured goods as part of the trade with the rest of Europe.

Barges

At ports like Europort, in Rotterdam, ships and barges exchange goods for import and export. Barges, often in 'trains', ply the River Rhine and the other main rivers and canals of Europe, creating a cheap bulk delivery system. They are useful for taking raw materials to riverside industrial firms.

Hovercraft

Across short stretches of water, hovercraft compete with ferries for passengers. They are small (carrying only 50–100 passengers) but are faster than ferries, averaging up to 60 kilometres per hour. Dover and Ramsgate in Kent are two major 'hoverports' for quick cross-channel travel to France.

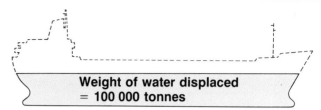

D The cheapest way of transporting heavy loads for long distances is by ship

Weight of water displaced = 100 000 tonnes

Explanation: So much of the ship is filled with air that it is less dense than water (it does not weigh as much as the same volume of water would). Therefore the ship floats. All the engine has to do is to move the floating ship forward.

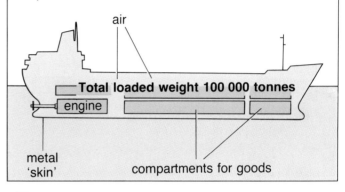

air

Total loaded weight 100 000 tonnes

engine

metal 'skin'

compartments for goods

E The major UK seaports

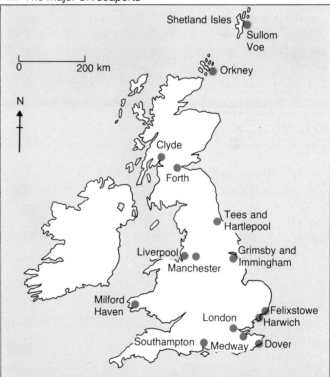

Port	Freight (mid 1980s) (millions of tonnes)
1 Sullom Voe	59.5
2 London	48.0
3 Tees and Hartlepool	32.5
4 Milford Haven	32.0
5 Forth	30.0
6 Southampton	27.5
7 Grimsby and Immingham	27.0
8 Orkney	16.0
9 Medway	11.5
10 Liverpool	11.0
11 Manchester	11.0
12 Clyde	10.5
13 Dover	10.0
14 Felixstowe	9.5
15 Harwich	8.0

1 (i) Explain the meaning of: *RUSV*
        (a) ro-ro (2)

....
....
....
.... ☐2☐☐☐

        (b) container traffic (2)

....
....
.... ☐2☐☐☐

    (ii) Why are these important
          developments in water
          transport? (2)

....
....
....
.... ☐☐2☐

2   Study Map A and Photograph B of
    Europort, Rotterdam.
    (i) Name the waterway in the
         foreground of the photograph. (1)

....
.... ☐☐1☐

    (ii) What appears to be a major import
          into Europort? (1)

....
.... ☐1☐☐

(iii) Give three pieces of evidence to   *RUSV*
       support your answer. (3)

....
....
....
....
....
.... ☐☐3☐

B The port complex of Europort, Rotterdam

A Europort, Rotterdam

THE
NORTH SEA

Industrial areas
Built-up areas
21.6 Depths in metres
Old Rotterdam
┼┼┼┼ railways

21.6

Hook of Holland   container terminal

Maasvlakte

Rotterdam   Rijnhaven
Parkhaven
Lekhaven
Schiedam

Vlaardingen

Maashaven

Beer Kanaal   Benelux   5th petroleum   7th petroleum
                Haven   haven   haven

4th petroleum
haven

Rozenburg   New Waterway 16.2   Old Maas

Botlek   Derdehaven   Tweedhaven

Eemhaven   Waalhaven   Wilhelminakade

0   8 km

(iv) Why is water the most economic form of transport for this type of commodity? (3)

RUSV

....
....
....
....
....
....

| 1 | 2 | | |

(v) Why has Rotterdam become so important for the import of this commodity? (2)

....
....
....
....

| 2 | | | |

3 Photograph C shows Gatwick Airport. Stansted has been chosen as London's third airport.

RUSV

(i) Why is there a need to build a third airport for London? (3)

....
....
....
....
....
....

| | 3 | | |

(ii) Discuss the advantages and disadvantages of siting a major international airport near Stansted in rural Essex. (6)

....
....
....
....
....
....
....
....
....
....
....

| 1 | 3 | | 2 |
| 9 | 11 | 4 | 2 |

C Gatwick airport

Route patterns

The lines which routes make on a map can be called a **route pattern**. A network is a pattern of routes which cross each other like the strands of a net. Route patterns show how well an area has been opened up to modern transport. Networks show how well an area is served by its routeways.

The simple Maps A1 to A6 form a model of how routes may develop from the coast inwards in a country. It is called the Taffe model, after the person who helped invent it when studying a number of African countries. The six stages of development are described below.

1   Small ports develop. Each port has a small **hinterland** with paths and trackways along which people bring in the local produce and take back goods imported from foreign countries in exchange. There is little trade between neighbouring ports as they produce the same things.

2   Some ports link up with inland centres of production by railway or road. This makes their hinterlands much larger. Places along these routes grow in size as a result of the increased traffic. The other ports stay small.

3   The inland places which expand fastest link up with each other. Smaller routes explore the neighbourhoods of expanding places.

4   Routes spread to join up villages and towns between the expanding places.

5   As times change, people need different routeways. Some of the linked centres will become more important than others and new types of routeway grow between them, missing out the smaller towns and villages in between.

6   **High-priority links** join up the fastest growing cities, missing out the smaller cities in between.

A real example is given in Diagram B which shows how the major routeways of Sri Lanka are developing. An atlas will help you to find the place names and smaller routeways.

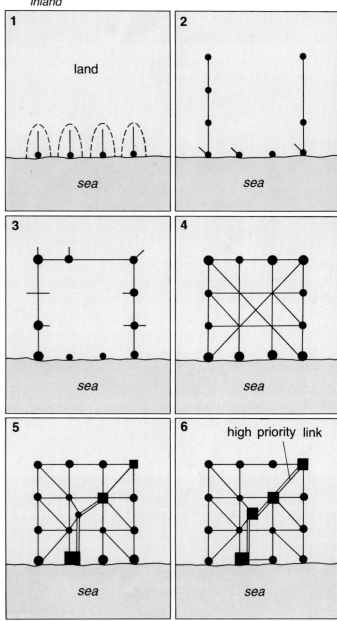

A Model of development of national routeways from the coast inland

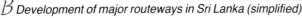

B Development of major routeways in Sri Lanka (simplified)

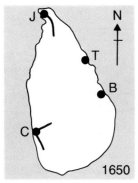
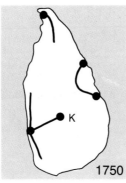
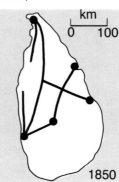
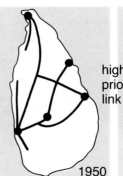
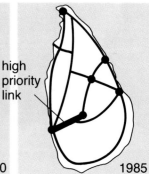

Diagram C shows the high priority links in the UK, France and Japan. An atlas will show the rest of the major routeways in these three countries and will allow you to name the important cities shown.

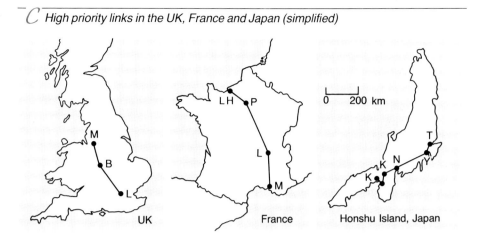

C *High priority links in the UK, France and Japan (simplified)*

UK France Honshu Island, Japan

Transport networks

Maps D and E show simplified versions of the networks of motorways in West Germany and the UK. Here are some methods for finding out which network seems to be best. In such studies of networks, measurements are taken of **nodes** (places joined up by the routes studied), **routes** (lines linking nodes) and the **area** of the region studied.

Route length density

This shows the length of routeways per 1000 square kilometres. It is calculated by:

$$\text{Route length density} = \frac{\text{Length of routeways}}{\text{Area of country}}$$

The higher the number, the denser the network, and the better the transport possibilities, other things being equal.

Beta index

This is a mesure of the number of choices of route within a network. It is calculated as follows:

$$\text{Beta index} = \frac{\text{Number of routes}}{\text{Number of nodes}}$$

The higher the beta index, the more choices of route there are. This is a measure of how well connected the network is.

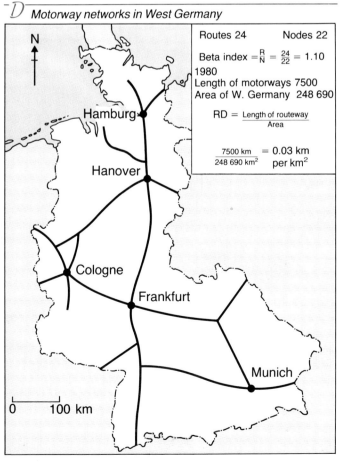

D *Motorway networks in West Germany*

Hamburg
Hanover
Cologne
Frankfurt
Munich

Routes 24   Nodes 22

Beta index $= \frac{R}{N} = \frac{24}{22} = 1.10$

1980
Length of motorways 7500
Area of W. Germany 248 690

$RD = \frac{\text{Length of routeway}}{\text{Area}}$

$\frac{7500 \text{ km}}{248\ 690 \text{ km}^2} = 0.03$ km per km^2

0   100 km

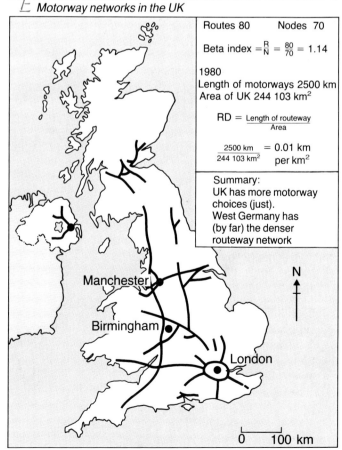

E *Motorway networks in the UK*

Manchester
Birmingham
London

Routes 80   Nodes 70

Beta index $= \frac{R}{N} = \frac{80}{70} = 1.14$

1980
Length of motorways 2500 km
Area of UK 244 103 km^2

$RD = \frac{\text{Length of routeway}}{\text{Area}}$

$\frac{2500 \text{ km}}{244\ 103 \text{ km}^2} = 0.01$ km per km^2

Summary:
UK has more motorway choices (just).
West Germany has (by far) the denser routeway network

N

0   100 km

1   Study Map A of the transport network
of Ghana.
   (i)   Name three types of transport
illustrated on the map. (3)

....

.... | | | 3 | |

....

....

....

....

   (ii)   State the formula for the beta
index. (2)

....

....

....

.... | 2 | | | |

   (iii)   Work out the beta index for the
railway network of Ghana. (3)

....

....

....

....

....

.... | | 3 | | |

   (iv)   What does this tell you about the
railway network of Ghana? (2)

....

....

....

.... | | 2 | | |

   (v)   Suggest what stage of the Taafe
model Ghana's railway network
appears to be in. (1)

....

.... | 1 | | | |

   (vi)   Suggest two disadvantages of the
railway network illustrated. (2)

....

....

....

.... | | | | 2 |

RUSV

A Transport network of Ghana

National parks

▨ Existing

▨ Projected

+++ Railways

—— Main roads

▲ Lake port

– – Country boundary

0   100 km

   (vii)   What developments to the railway
network might occur in the future
if Ghana follows the Taafe
model? (3)   *RUSV*

....

....

....

....

....

.... | 1 | 2 | | |

B British Rail services (May 1982): topological map of rail network

Principal services May 1982
Times shown are fastest
journey from or to London

═══ Railair Link coaches
O O Outer London pick-up set-down points
□ National Exhibition Centre

Inverness 10hr 40
Aviemore
Perth
Stirling
Glasgow 5hr 16
Carlisle 3hr 48
Motherwell
Blackpool 3hr 49
Lancaster
Preston 2hr 35
Wigan
Liverpool 2hr 37
Warrington
Runcorn
Holyhead Chester
Crewe 1hr 55
Stockport
Stoke-on-Trent 1hr 48
Stafford
Chesterfield
Shrewsbury
Wolverhampton 1hr 53
Birmingham International 1hr 17
Nuneaton
Worcester 2hr 18
□ **Birmingham** New Street 1hr 34
Cheltenham Spa
Gloucester 1hr 41
Coventry 1hr 06
Rugby
Hereford
Bristol Parkway
Watford
Oxford 43min
2hr 39
Swansea
Cardiff 1hr 41 **Newport** 1hr 24
Bath 1hr 09
Swindon
Bristol 1hr 25
Reading
Slough
Paddington
Weston-super-Mare
Taunton
Newton Abbot
Exeter 2hr 10
Plymouth 3hr 07
Torquay 2hr 52 Salisbury
Bournemouth 1hr 36
Paignton
Penzance 4hr 57
Weymouth
Southampton 1hr 07
Portsmouth 1hr 26
Brighton 58min

Manchester 2hr 36
Bradford 2hr 31
New Pudsey
Leeds 2hr 10
Wakefield
Sheffield 2hr 30
Alfreton & Mansfield
Derby 1hr 57
Parkway
Milton Keynes
Kettering
Luton
Stevenage
Euston **King's X**
St Pancras
Victoria **Charing X**
Waterloo
Heathrow Airport
Bromley
Woking East Croydon
Gatwick Airport 42min

Aberdeen 7hr 17
Dundee
Edinburgh 4hr 35
Newcastle 2hr 54
Berwick Middlesbrough
Harrogate
Durham
Darlington 2hr 30
York 1hr 58
Hull 2hr 34
Doncaster 1hr 35
Grimsby 3hr 36
Retford
Newark Cleethorpes
Lincoln
Grantham
Nottingham 1hr 55
Leicester 1hr 22
Peterborough 50min
King's Lynn
Norwich 1hr 52
Cambridge 1hr 03
Ipswich 1hr 05
Colchester Harwich
Chatham
Canterbury
Folkestone
Dover 1hr 28

C Conventional map of rail network

Inverness
Aberdeen
Perth Dundee
Glasgow Edinburgh
Berwick
Londonderry Larne
Belfast Carlisle Newcastle
Darlington Middlesbrough
to Dublin Scarborough
York
Preston M
Liverpool D G
Holyhead Sh
Crewe Norwich
P KL
Birmingham C Harwich
Hereford
Swansea O London
Cardiff
Bristol Southampton Dover
Exeter Po Brighton
Plymouth
Penzance
0   200 km

M   Manchester
D   Doncaster
G   Grimsby
Sh Sheffield
KL Kings Lynn
P   Peterborough
C   Cambridge
Po Portsmouth
O   Oxford

2 Study Maps B and C of the British Rail network. *RUSV*

(i) State two ways in which these maps differ. (2)

....
....
....
....

[1 | 1]

(ii) From which London station would you travel to Sheffield? (1)

....
....

[| | 1]

(iii) How long would the journey last? (1)

....
....

[| | 1]

(iv) Describe the networks of Scotland, Wales and Northern Ireland, and suggest why they differ from the network in England. (5) *RUSV*

....
....
....
....
....
....
....
....
....
....

[2 | 2 | 1]
[6 | 10 | 7 | 2]

11. Quality of life – welfare and leisure

WHAT IS 'QUALITY OF LIFE' ?

We all know people who are 'better off' and 'worse off' than ourselves. When we compare like this we are thinking about the 'quality of life' that people have. We notice where they live, how big their house is, what car they own, what clothes they have, how much time they have for leisure and so on. Photographs A and B might represent people near the 'top' and 'bottom' of a 'Quality of Life League Table', of which several types exist.

A warning is needed, though. Rich does not necessarily mean happy, or poor, miserable. Howard Hughes, one of the world's richest men, died as a recluse, afraid to meet people. But generally it is more difficult to be happy if you are poor.

A Top of the 'quality of life league table'?

B Bottom of the 'quality of life league table'?

When we study people's quality of life from place to place, we often look at welfare and leisure. Welfare is how well people are provided with the things they need to exist in the modern world. Leisure is how people enjoy life when they take time off from providing for themselves. Some of the more important factors associated with welfare and leisure are shown in Table C.

C Factors influencing welfare and leisure

Welfare factors	
Basic needs	Food, water, clothing, shelter, security
Secondary needs	Health, education
Public needs	Roads, sewers, power supply
Major wants	Income, transport (car), work
Leisure factors	
Social needs	Friends, family, play, entertainment, leisure time, recognition for achievements
Minor wants	Labour saving devices
Luxuries	Holidays, sport, home entertainment, hobbies

If there is an unfair distribution of these things between people, there may be unrest in the community. Those who feel they are being deprived may strive to improve conditions. They may try by argument, but if they feel that this has achieved nothing, they may use violence. Usually, it is in everyone's interest for all members of the community to feel that they have adequate welfare and leisure for themselves and their families.

One problem is that people sometimes feel they are not being treated fairly, even when they are. Governments and other organisations collect statistics to see what is really the case. Every ten years, and most recently in 1981, there is a compulsory **census of population** in the UK, in which all householders are asked to fill in a form giving information about their families. This information is processed in many ways and then published for anyone to see. Similar surveys are carried out by various government departments and private firms each year. They are summarised in *Social trends*, a useful publication by the Central Statistical Office, a government service. Government workers, political parties, and pressure groups such as the Child Poverty Action Group, can study these figures to see if there is evidence to support their case. Table D shows an extract from the 1985 version of *Social trends*.

D Consumers' expenditure on various products

	Percentage of people's spending per year					
						1983
Category of product	1976	1978	1980	1982	%	£ (millions)
Food	18.4	18.0	16.7	15.4	14.9	27 148
Alcoholic drink	7.5	7.3	7.3	7.2	7.3	13 372
Tobacco	4.1	3.9	3.5	3.5	3.4	6 208
Clothing and footwear	7.7	7.9	7.2	6.6	6.6	12 114
Housing	13.4	13.2	13.8	15.5	15.0	27 326
Fuel and power	4.7	4.6	4.6	5.2	5.2	9 395
Household goods and services	7.6	7.6	7.3	6.7	6.7	12 274
Transport and communication	14.8	15.3	16.4	16.5	17.3	31 475
Recreation, entertainment and education	9.1	9.4	9.2	9.3	9.1	16 541
Other goods, services and adjustments	12.7	12.8	13.9	14.1	14.6	26 574
Total	100.0	100.0	100.0	100.0	100.0	182 427

Source *Social trends, 1985* (p. 96)

A Countries of the world by Physical Quality of Life Index

91–100   51–70

81–90   26–50

71–80   0–25

Data not available for Greenland, Mongolia, North Korea and Vietnam

1 Study Map A which classifies the countries of the world on the basis of a Physical Quality of Life Index (PQLI). The PQLI is based on life expectancy, literacy and infant mortality. It is scaled from 0 to 100. 100 is the best score 0 is the worst.

RUSV

(i) Explain the meanings of the terms 'life expectancy', 'literacy' and 'infant mortality'. (3)

....
....
....
....

| 3 | | |

(ii) Name two continents with a high PQLI. (2)

....
....

| | 2 | |

(iii) Name the country with the lowest PQLI in Western Europe. (1)

....

| | 1 | |

(iv) Which continent has the lowest PQLI? (1)

....

| | 1 | |

RUSV

(v) Explain why most people of this continent have such a low quality of life. (4)

....
....
....
....
....
....
....
....

| 4 | | |

(vi) Why may the figures for countries like South Africa or India, which suggest a poor quality of life, mask great variations in the quality of life in those countries? (3)

....
....
....
....
....
....

| 3 | | |

2   (i) Apart from those factors mentioned in question 1 (i), name three others that would influence a person's quality of life. Photograph B might help you. (3)

RUSV

....

....

....

....

....

....

| 3 | | | |

   (ii) Choose *one* of these factors and explain how it influences a person's quality of life. (3)

....

....

....

....

....

....

| | 3 | | |

(iii) How may a government best improve a person's quality of life? (5)

RUSV

....

....

....

....

....

....

....

....

....

....

| 1 | 2 | | 2 |

| 7 | 12 | 4 | 2 |

B *Another quality of life factor*

HUMAN WELFARE

There are many ways of describing how well people provide for themselves and their families. 'Welfare', 'social welfare', 'living standards' and 'social well-being' are some of the terms used. There are also many methods of trying to measure human welfare.

One way is to study the Gross National Product (GNP) per person. This is worked out as if the wealth created in a country in one year was shared equally among all the people in the country. In 1985, the GNP per person in the USA was 15 000 US dollars. So every person in the USA would have received 15 000 dollars if all the wealth created in the country had been shared out equally. In the UK the GNP per person was 10 000 US dollars.

Thus there seems to be good evidence that people in the USA are better off than those in the UK. However, using a measurement like this is on its own may be misleading. With GNP per person, for instance, it all depends on whether the wealth is shared out equally or not. It may be kept in the hands of a few super-rich people, while all the others are poor.

Table A shows some of the many things which can be used to measure human welfare, here called 'social well-being'. This table is used to find out if social well-being varies in Europe from country to country.

A *Social well-being in Europe: List of variables*

Variables	Loadings
Percentage of population aged 0–15 years	0.93
Percentage of populatons aged 15–64 years	−0.65
Percentage of population aged 65 years and over	−0.90
Number of births/1000 inhabitants	0.94
Infant mortality/1000 live births	0.93
Total fertility rate	0.92
Number of persons/room	0.91
Percentage of households with 5 or more persons	0.91
Percentage of total population classed as urban	−0.71
Number of doctors/10 000 inhabitants	−0.62
Number of people/hospital bed	0.79
Gross national product/person	−0.86
Number of of people/physician	0.71
Percentage of population economically active	−0.51
Percentage of working population in agriculture	0.96
Percentage of working population in services	−0.80
Consumption of steel/inhabitant	−0.57
Consumption of energy/inhabitant	−0.67
Number of cars/1000 inhabitants	−0.82
Number of telephone owners/1000 inhabitants	−0.80
Number of television receivers/1000 inhabitants	−0.91
Consumption of newsprint/inhabitants	−0.74

Source B W Ibery, *Geography*, 1984, p. 294

B *Socio-economic well-being in Europe*

> −1.00   Best
−0.5 to −0.99
0 to −0.49
0 to +0.49
+0.5 to +0.99
> +2.00   Worst

Component scores

0 500

N

GNP per person is in the table with twenty-one other variables. Variables with high positive loadings can be thought of as showing worse conditions. Those with high negative loadings show better conditions. For example, a 0.93 loading for the percentage of the population aged 0–15 years shows that having a large number of young children tends to be a sign of a 'worse-off' country. On the other hand, the −0.91 loading for televisions per 1000 inhabitants shows that having a lot of televisions *is* a sign of a 'better-off' country.

Map B is the map of human welfare in Europe produced when these variables were combined for the early 1980s.

Similar studies have been done for the world and for much smaller regions. Map C shows a map of the UK showing 'well-being' in the eleven regional planning regions in the early 1980s.

Table D shows five variables associated with human welfare in Avon. The variables have been simplified. In each case, the higher the percentage in the district, the worse-off it seems to be.

You must, of course, say which welfare variables you used to get the figures. Each single variable will give you a different picture from any other single variable. The more variables you can rank like this to get the total, the more chance you have of getting a real picture of the social welfare of an area.

In all the tables and maps above you have been looking at **relative welfare**. You have been comparing one group of people with another. However, there is also **absolute poverty**. This is when people have no home,

C How well-being may vary throughout the UK

| Over 4 |
| 2 to 4 |
| 0 to 2 |
| 0 to −2 |
| −2 to −4 |
| Below −4 |

'Better off'

'Worse off'

O = National average for 'well being'

1 Scotland
2 Northern
3 Yorks and Humber
4 North West
5 Wales
6 West Midlands
7 East Midlands
8 East Anglia
9 South West
10 South East
11 Northern Ireland

no food and no medical help. In the UK and Europe there is little absolute poverty as occurs elsewhere. However, the maps and tables above do show that human welfare is not equal, even in rich countries.

F Welfare rankings in Avon County districts

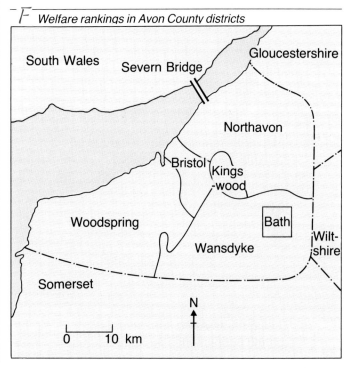

Another way of showing these differences is by putting the districts into rank order. By adding these rankings together, the welfare totals can be found. Table E shows how this can be done.

Map F shows what the values in Tables E and F mean for Avon on a map.

D Percentage of indicators of human welfare in districts in Avon

Variable	Bath	Bristol	Kingswood	North Avon	Wansdyke	Woodspring
Households with no car	32	30	20	15	21	22
Houses with more people than rooms	2.1	3.0	1.7	2.0	1.6	1.5
People seeking work	9.5	12.5	8.0	7.0	7.5	9.0
One parent families	17	18	9	8	10	11
Free school meals	19	20	8	9	10	11

E Table of rankings for welfare in Avon County districts

Variable	Bath	Bristol	Kingswood	North Avon	Wansdyke	Woodspring
Households with no car	6	5	2	1	3	4
Houses with more people than rooms	5	6	1	4	3	2
People seeking work	5	6	3	1	2	4
One parent families	6	5	4	1	2	3
Free school meals	5	6	1	2	3	4
Total	27	27	11	9	13	17

1 Explain the difference between absolute and relative poverty. (2)

$RUSV$

....

....

....

.... [2]

2 Study Map A of Italy and the accompanying Tables B and C which refer to the situation in the early 1950s.

   (i) What is meant by Gross National Product per person? (2)

....

....

....

.... [2]

   (ii) How does this differ from average income per person? (2)

....

....

....

.... [1][1]

   (iii) What is the income per head in Basilicata? (1)

....

.... [1]

   (iv) Name one region with an income of more than 250 000 lire. (1)

.... [1]

   (v) Describe the pattern of income in Italy. (3)

....

....

....

....

....

.... [2][1]

   (vi) Give one reason suggested by Table B for this pattern of income. (1)

....

.... [1]

A *Italy: average income per person*

Lire (thousands)

Over 250
200–250
150–200
100–150
Less than 100

0   200 km

B *The south and the rest of Italy compared, circa 1950*

	South	Centre and North
Total land area (per cent)	40	60
Total population (per cent)	38	62
Occupational structure – percentage employed in:		
agriculture	53	37
industry and transport	27	39
commerce, administration, etc.	20	24
Consumption of electricity (kWh per head):		
for lighting	27	64
for other purposes, especially industry	114	548
Radio subscribers per 1000 inhabitants	68	130
Cars, motor cycles and motorised bicycles per 1000 inhabitants	53	156
Average food consumption:		
meat (kg per head)	9	20
milk (litres per head)	18	68
sugar (kg per head)	7	17
Percentage of population below the 'poverty line' (an official survey)	27	3

(vii) What disadvantages do the people of central and southern Italy appear to suffer compared with those living in the north of the country? (3)   *RUSV*

....

....

....

....

....

.... | 2 | | 1 |

(viii) Use the figures in Table C to construct a map to show the contrasts in relative welfare in different parts of the south of Italy. (5) | 3 | 1 | 1 | |

3 To what extent does Table D suggest that there is a north/south divide in the pattern of welfare in Britain? (5)   *RUSV*

....

....

....

....

....

....

....

....

.... | 1 | 3 | 1 | |

.... | 8 | 10 | 6 | 1 |

C Regional contrasts within the south circa 1950

| | Occupational structure | | | | Land use: area in various uses | | | | | Consumption of electricity for lighting (kWh per capita) | Cars, motor cycles and motorised bicycles per 1000 inhabitants | Income per head (000s lire) |
	Agriculture %	Industry and transport %	Trade and services %	Total %	Arable %	Grazing %	Tree crops %	'Forest' and unproductive %	Total %			
Abruzzi-Molise	71	14	15	100	57	15	5	23	100	20	46	101
Campania	42	30	28	100	52	12	11	25	100	38	55	106
Apulia	49	29	22	100	46	13	35	6	100	24	59	110
Basilicata	72	15	13	100	47	27	4	22	100	15	23	97
Calabria	64	19	17	100	38	12	16	34	100	16	33	80
Sicily	48	25	27	100	62	11	20	7	100	27	59	110
Sardinia	48	22	30	100	27	45	3	25	100	30	48	129
Italy	43	32	25	100	47	18	9	26	100	51	117	188

D Some contrasts between north west and south east England, early 1980s

	Lancs	Surrey		Lancs	Surrey
Persons per sq km (1982)	451.9	603.9	full time) 1983		
Population (1982)	1384.1	1013.9	man over 21 (£)	151.0	176.1
Over retiring age (%)	19.9	18.2	woman 18 and over (£)	102.8	112.4
Live births (per 1000 population)	12.7	10.7	Education: pupils aged 16 staying		
Deaths (per 1000 population)	13.9	10.8	beyond leaving age (% 1982)	20	46
Perinatal (near birth) mortality rate (per 100 live births)	12.9	10.8	Housing:		
Population projections: (% change in 1981–1991)	3.6	0.3	owned by local authority 1981 (%)	19.0	18.0
			average domestic rates (1982/83)	148.0	281.0
Employment (%):			owning or buying house (%)	71.7	68.7
agriculture, forestry, fishing	1.5	1.4	renting from local authority (%)	19.8	19.0
metal manufacture, engineering, etc.	20.2	16.5	below bedroom standard (%)	5.2	2.8
other manufacturing	16.2	5.2	Car and van licences 1979 (per 1000 population)	282	358
construction, distribution, transport	27.3	33.4			
mining, quarrying, electricity, water	1.4	2.1	Commercial/industrial floorspace (%)		
other services	32.3	41.4	industrial	62	37
Unemployment rate (July 1981)	13.0	6.0	warehouses	20	29
Earnings (average gross weekly,			commercial offices	4	13

A — Leisure pursuits available near most towns and cities

Leisure is how people enjoy themselves when they are not earning a living. It could be said that the more leisure we have, the greater is our quality of life. The trouble is that in order to use the time to best effect, we need money. The time that unemployed people have is not really leisure time because of this.

The richer people get, the more time and money they are usually able to spend on enjoying themselves. As a result, more jobs are created to provide these leisure activities. If more people want to play golf, there will be an increase in golf course groundstaff and golf club makers, for instance.

Diagram A shows the range of leisure activities found in most of our cities and towns.

The list below shows some of the jobs created to provide for these activities.

Jobs created to provide for urban leisure
1 Recreational
Sports instructors
Keep-fit instructors
Martial arts/self defence instructors
Disc jockeys
Musicians
Actors/stage managers
Theatrical producers/directors
Fairground staff
Cinema staff: managers, usherettes, projectionists

2 Caterers
Chefs/kitchen staff
Waiters
Receptionists

3 Retailers
Garden centre suppliers
Sales staff
Sport shopkeepers
Sports equipment makers

These leisure activities are fairly local and do not cost much for each visit. Some, such as walking, are free. This probably explains why walking is the UK's most popular active leisure-time activity.

Other leisure pursuits are less local. They are only found in certain parts of the country. We have to make special visits to take part in them. Table B shows some of the more popular places to visit in the UK and the number of people who visit them each year.

Graph C shows the numbers of visitors from overseas who came to the UK to see the attractions displayed in Table B. Map D and Graph E show where British holiday-makers go for their holidays at home and abroad.

Table F shows how leisure jobs increased from 1971 to 1981 in the UK. It is likely that there will be a continued increase in jobs in leisure until the turn of the century. However, this increase cannot replace the jobs lost in manufacturing industry in the early 1980s.
Table G displays how much money a British family might spend on leisure per week on average through the year. In 1983 this expenditure on leisure was 15.6 percent of total household expenditure in the UK, for all household types.

Most rich countries share this pattern of increasing leisure. Most rich holiday-makers go to other rich countries for their holidays. Some seek the warm resorts of the Caribbean or the Indian Ocean and others go 'on safari' to the game parks of East and South Africa. There are dangers in countries relying on the income from tourism, however. It is easy for holiday-makers to be put off by terrorism, pollution or just because money is tight at home.

B *The most visited attractions in Britain*

Site	Type of attraction	Millions of people/year
Blackpool pleasure beach	Seaside resort	6.7
Windsor Castle	Historic building	3.5
Science Museum, London	Museum	3.3
National Gallery, London	Art gallery	2.9
British Museum, London	Museum	2.8
Natural History Museum, London	Museum	2.5
Madam Tussauds, London	Waxworks	2.0
Tower of London	Historic building	1.6
Alton Towers	Theme park	1.6
Tate gallery, London	Art gallery	1.3

C *Number of visitors to the UK from overseas*

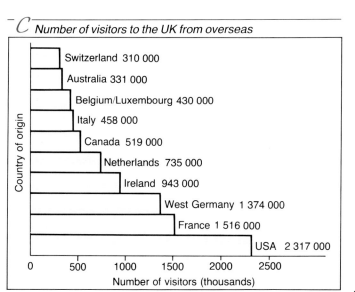

D *Where holiday-makers go in Britain and Ireland*

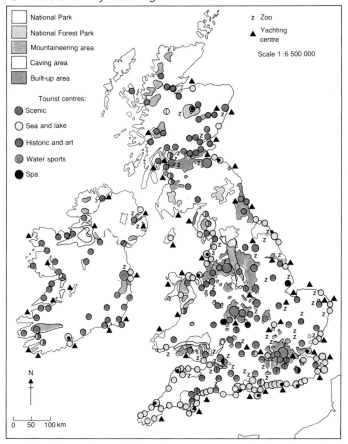

E *UK holiday choices abroad*

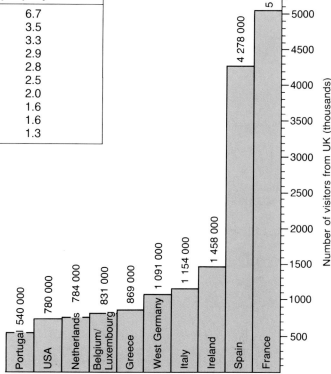

F *Increase in leisure jobs, 1971 – 1981*

Leisure industries	People employed in 1971	People employed in 1981	Percentage change 1971-81
Recreation	258 000	301 000	28
Catering	625 000	798 000	30

G *Money spent by British families on leisure*

Leisure activity	Average weekly expenditure (£)
Alcoholic drink (away from home)	5.04
Meals (away from home)	2.92
Books, magazines, papers	2.29
TV, radio, musical instruments	3.91
DIY	2.35
Holidays	4.07
Hobbies	0.10
Cinema admission	0.09
Theatre, concerts	0.22
Dance admission	0.12
Subs for participating in sport	0.42
Soccer admissions	0.08
Other spectating at sports matches	0.02
Sports goods (not clothes)	0.31
Other entertainment	0.26
Total	**22.21**

Source *Social trends*, p. 157

1 (i) State two reasons why leisure
activities are of increasing
importance. (2)

....

....

....

....

2 ☐☐☐

(ii) Explain how the 1983 figure of 15.6
per cent of total household
expenditure being spent on leisure
activity is likely to change in the
next few years. (2)

....

....

....

....

2 ☐☐☐

2 Study Graph A of the changes in
employment in leisure industries.

RUSV

A Employment change in leisure industries

thousands

275	
250	
225	
200	
175	
150	
125	
100	
75	
50	
25	
0	

1971 1973 1975 1977 1979 1981

hotels and
other residential
establishments

public houses

Restaurants,
cafes, snack bars

sport and
recreation

clubs

Cinema, theatre,
radio

betting and
gambling

B Protected areas of England and Wales

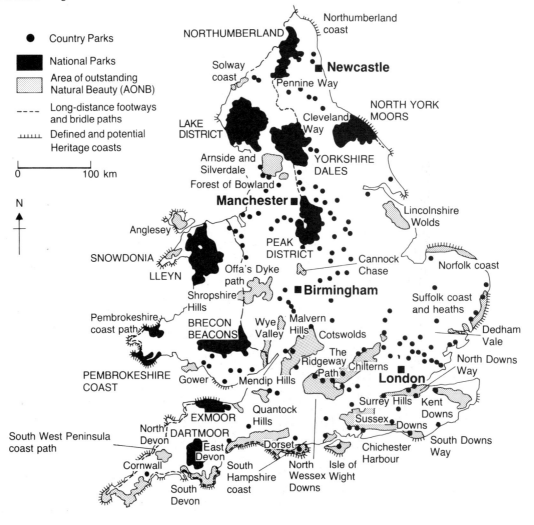

● Country Parks

■ National Parks

▨ Area of outstanding
Natural Beauty (AONB)

---- Long-distance footways
and bridle paths

⊥⊥⊥⊥ Defined and potential
Heritage coasts

0   100 km

N

(i) Which group of leisure industries employed the greatest number of people? (1)

RUSV

....

....

| | | 1 | |

(ii) Which leisure industry showed the greatest growth in employment? (1)

....

....

| | | 1 | |

(iii) Why is the general growth in employment in leisure industries important for the economy of the country? (3)

....

....

....

....

....

....

| 1 | 2 | | |

3 Study Map B of protected areas in England and Wales.
   (i) Why have these areas been protected? (2)

....

....

....

....

| | 2 | | |

(ii) State two types of leisure activity that may take place in protected areas. (2)

....

....

....

....

| 2 | | | |

(iii) Suggest how leisure activities in these areas may conflict with other uses of the land. (4)

RUSV

....

....

....

....

....

....

....

| | 4 | | |

4 Study Graphs C, D and E which concern Jamaica.
   (i) State one feature of Jamaica's temperature. (1)

....

....

| | | 1 | |

(ii) What is the rainfall total in July? (1)

....

....

| | | 1 | |

(iii) State two reasons why tourists are attracted to Jamaica. (2)

....

....

....

....

| | 2 | | |

(iv) Do you consider tourism to be a good basis for the economy of a developing country like Jamaica? Give reasons for your answer. (4)

....

....

....

....

....

| 2 | 1 | | 1 |

| 7 | 13 | 4 | 1 |

C Rainfall in Jamaica

D Temperature in Jamaica

E Sunshine hours in Jamaica

In all countries there are people whose quality of life is much higher than the average. In the USA, a western capitalist country, there are one million millionaires. These people form a 'better-off' group with large cars, boats and ranches. In the Eastern European countries, the better-off group is made up of senior Communist Party members. They have government limousines, passes for shopping in luxury stores and 'dachas' (holiday houses) in the countryside.

Even in Third World countries, some politicians and business people are able to have very comfortable lifestyles, as Photograph A shows. Yet the majority of people here are very poor.

This inequality is a fact of life. It has always been so and probably always will be. However, if people feel that they have no chance of climbing up the 'quality of life ladder' there is potential source of conflict. People will put up with unfairness so long as things seem to be improving. If not, there may be conflict.

Here are some of the most important potential sources of conflict between people.

A   An acceptable third world life style

Political ideas

There are major political differences between the two most powerful nations in the world, the USSR and the USA. The government of the USSR believe that capitalism allows businessmen to become rich and to hold on to their money (capital). Most people stay poor so that a few can be rich and live well. The government in the USSR think people should not aim to make profits for themselves from business, and they encourage people to work for the good of the State.

In the USA, more or less anything goes. People can earn a living at anything legal in almost total freedom. Those who do well make lots of money. Those who do not have a very poor quality of life in city or rural slums. There are no slums in the USSR, but little freedom either. Which country has a better quality of life is a question open to discussion.

These two great countries, the USA and the USSR, have 80 per cent of the world's armaments between them (Photographs B and C). Theirs is the greatest source of conflict on Earth: how wealth should be created and who should control it.

B   American armaments: a cruise missile launcher

Inequality of opportunity

In most cities of the world there are neighbourhoods which house the poorest citizens. Some may be work-shy, but most want to better themselves. If people have no jobs they do not have the opportunity to improve their way of life. They are forced to live in inadequate housing, often with many people to a room, without privacy, toilet facilities or a clean water supply.

Living like this breaks up families, causes hopelessness and leads to crime and a dreadfully low

C   Russian armaments: tanks on show at the May Day parade

quality of life. It is estimated that 20 million people in rich countries live like this. In the UK in 1986, it was estimated that 100 000 people had nowhere to live at all, so were officially 'homeless'. In the rest of the world some 500 million people live in poor urban conditions, mainly in shanty towns on the edge of Third World cities.

Some refugees have to live like this and also have to put up with the fact that they cannot live in their own country. Their bitterness can be a serious source of strife in the world. Some Palestinian people have been living in refugee camps for over 35 years. One million Afghan people fled to Pakistan since Russian troops invaded their country in 1980.

Pollution

Waste products from industry or consumers like us can pollute the environment and reduce our quality of life. The effect can range from crisp bags in the street to nuclear fall-out, as happened after the explosion at the nuclear power station at Chernobyl in Russia in 1986 (Map D).

Land use conflicts

Whenever someone changes the use of a piece of land, by design or by accident, someone else sees the change as a threat to their quality of life. The change of land use becomes a source of conflict. Diagram E shows a small scale example.

In all these cases of conflict, it is difficult to say what should happen. Usually, the groups with most money tend to get their way, unless the rule of law is strong enough to ensure that people are dealt with fairly.

D Pollution from Chernobyl nuclear power station, May 1986

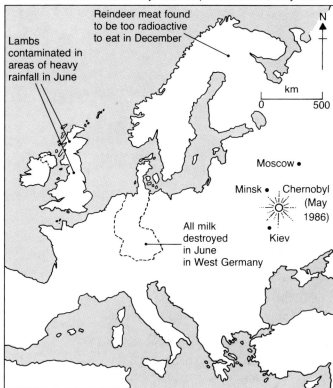

After an experiment went wrong, radioactive gas and particles were emitted from Chernobyl nuclear power station in the USSR. The 'cloud' was carried to the north and west. Radioactive material was washed down to the Earth in rainfall as far away as Lappland and the UK. There was widespread concern around the world about nuclear pollution.

E Land use conflict

Problem Dangerous traffic congestion on a major road between two cities where it passes through a town

Plan A by-pass. Two routes available.

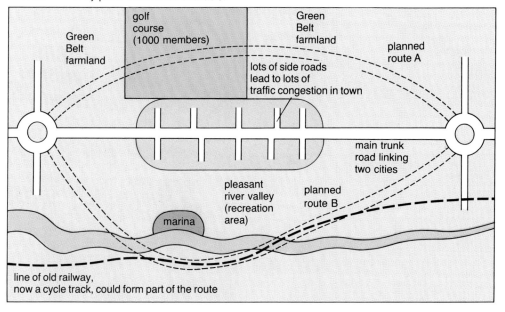

Conflicts

Both routes would pass through Green Belt farmland where development is discouraged.

Route A would pass through an existing popular golf course with 1000 members. A great deal of well-organised opposition comes from the club committee.

Route B would pass through a pleasant river valley designed as a recreation and tourist area. Local residents association organises opposition from local inhabitants.

Whose quality of life should suffer: motorists and people on the main road, golfers on route A, locals and tourists on route B?

1 Riots broke out in the inner city areas of
   Brixton (London), Mosside
   (Manchester) and Toxteth (Liverpool)
   during spring and summer of 1981.
   Study Photographs A and B, Diagram C
   and Table D.

RUSV

   (i) What was the male unemployment
   rate in Mosside? (1)

.... ☐ ☐ ☐1☐

   (ii) What percentage of the population
   of Merseyside was aged less than
   24? (1)

.... ☐ ☐ ☐1☐

   (iii) In what respects does the
   population of the inner city areas
   differ from that of the cities as a
   whole? (3)

....
....
....
....
.... ☐ ☐2☐1☐

   (iv) With the aid of Diagram C, suggest
   how the quality of life could be
   improved in these inner city areas
   in order to reduce the danger of
   further riots. (5)

....
....
....
....
....
....
.... ☐1☐2☐1☐1☐

A Moments of confrontation: the Brixton riots, 1981

B The Liverpool riots, 1981

C Reasons for the riots

D

Social statistic	Brixton	Inner London	Mos-side	Greater Manchester	Toxteth	Mersey-side
% population aged under 24	43.9	35.5	53.3	37.5	42.6	38.2
% men unemployed	17.4	12.8	27.1	12.6	33.8	17.8
% people in households with NCWP☆ head	43.3	18.8	40.0	3.9	11.2	1.0

☆ Born in New Commonweath or Pakistan.

E Nomads in Saudi Arabia

F Oil sheikh's jet

2 Photographs E and F show two aspects *RUSV*
of life in Saudi Arabia.
  (i) What do the photographs suggest
about the quality of life in Saudi
Arabia? (2)

....
....
....

☐ 2 ☐ ☐

  (ii) How may the apparent contrast in
the quality of life have come
about? (3)

....
....
....
....

☐ 3 ☐ ☐

G Sources of acid rain falling on Sweden during one year
recently

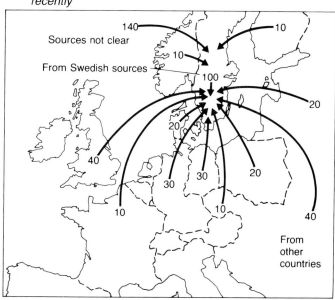

3 Pollution is a source of conflict. Study *RUSV*
Map G which shows the source of the
acid rain which fell on Sweden during
one year recently.
  (i) Name three factors which may have
caused acid rain. (3)

....
....
....
....
....
....

3 ☐ ☐ ☐

  (ii) Describe the damaging effect of
acid rain. (3)

....
....
....
....
....
....

2 1 ☐ ☐

  (iii) How could the problems of acid rain
be lessened? (4)

....
....
....
....
....

2 2 ☐ ☐

8 12 4 1

12. Development

DEVELOPMENT CAN BE DEFINED AND MEASURED IN DIFFERENT WAYS

Development means changing things to improve the way people live. Improvements can be made in farming, mining, manufacturing, transport, housing, and all the service industries, like teaching and tourism. Countries are often said to be **developed** or **developing**.

Maps A and B show some differences between a developing country (Nigeria) and a developed country (France). Notice how Nigeria's cities have developed along its main railway line, with most of the rest of the country undeveloped. France has more railways than are shown on the map. All the country is developed. Some regions (like the Paris Basin and the south east coast) are more developed than the rest.

Many countries, Brazil for example, have some 'developed' parts and some 'developing' parts. The developed regions are those where **natural resources** have been used to build up the community. Natural resources are things like minerals, forests and rivers, which can provide raw materials and energy for roads, railways, ports, other cities and manufacturing industries.

Roads and railways open up a country, making access to new resources easier. They are expensive to build but reduce transport costs once they are built. They also allow large quantities of materials like coal or iron ore to be transported quickly. A network of roads and railways links the capital city (often the biggest port) with inland resources.

Ports usually become the richest towns in poor countries and a port is often the capital.

The country's raw materials are exported to rich countries through the ports. Lagos used to be Nigeria's capital. It was the main outlet for forest products from the south and groundnuts (peanuts) from the north. It took in imports of manufactured goods from rich countries. Docks, warehouses, factories and government offices created job opportunities. The city workers became well off compared with the poor farmers inland.

As a country develops, however, its government often decides to make an inland place the new capital. The idea is to help the poorer parts of the country develop as well as the rich resource centres and ports. The small inland town of Abuja is now Nigeria's capital. Such moves of capital city are very expensive and take decades to complete.

There are many ways of measuring development and no one way is perfect. Measurements are usually of two types, those of 'economic development' and those of

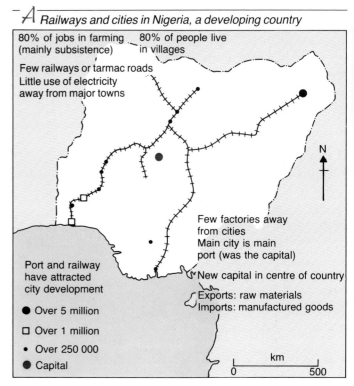

A Railways and cities in Nigeria, a developing country

80% of jobs in farming (mainly subsistence)
80% of people live in villages
Few railways or tarmac roads
Little use of electricity away from major towns

Few factories away from cities
Main city is main port (was the capital)
New capital in centre of country
Exports: raw materials
Imports: manufactured goods

Port and railway have attracted city development

● Over 5 million
□ Over 1 million
• Over 250 000
⬤ Capital

km
0   500

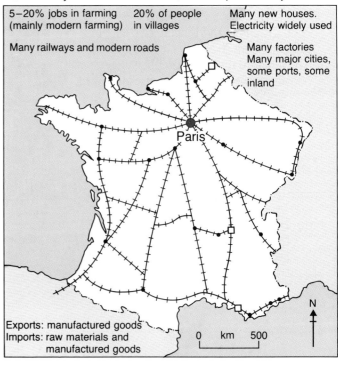

B Railways and cities in France, a developed country

5–20% jobs in farming (mainly modern farming)
20% of people in villages
Many new houses. Electricity widely used

Many railways and modern roads

Many factories
Many major cities, some ports, some inland

Paris

Exports: manufactured goods
Imports: raw materials and manufactured goods

0   km   500

'quality of life'. This is shown in Table C. Diagram D shows what some of these terms mean. Maps E and F show development in Brazil and how it is unequal from region to region.

One difficulty about measuring development is that averages make things look as if the people are equally well off. In many countries a few people control most of the wealth. They are rich, whereas most of the people are poorer than the average.

C Development measures for West Germany, Brazil and Chad

Economic development	West Germany	Brazil	Chad
GNP (million US dollars)			
GNP per person (US dollars)	10 000	2 000	200
Energy per person (kg)	7 000	1 000	50
People per car	3	50	1 000
Percentage in farming	8	50	90
Quality of life			
Life expectancy	73	60	45
Food intake (Kcals)	3 500	2 800	2 200
Patients per doctor	500	10 000	30 000
Percentage adult literacy	99	60	25
Percentage drinking safe water	99	50	10

D Terms used to describe economic development and quality of life

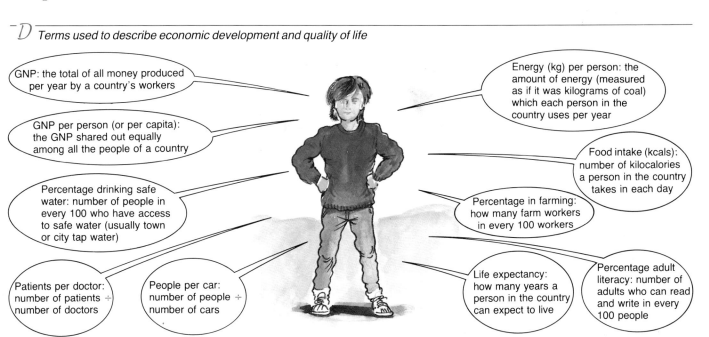

GNP: the total of all money produced per year by a country's workers

GNP per person (or per capita): the GNP shared out equally among all the people of a country

Percentage drinking safe water: number of people in every 100 who have access to safe water (usually town or city tap water)

Patients per doctor: number of patients ÷ number of doctors

People per car: number of people ÷ number of cars

Energy (kg) per person: the amount of energy (measured as if it was kilograms of coal) which each person in the country uses per year

Food intake (kcals): number of kilocalories a person in the country takes in each day

Percentage in farming: how many farm workers in every 100 workers

Life expectancy: how many years a person in the country can expect to live

Percentage adult literacy: number of adults who can read and write in every 100 people

E Brazil's regions and resources

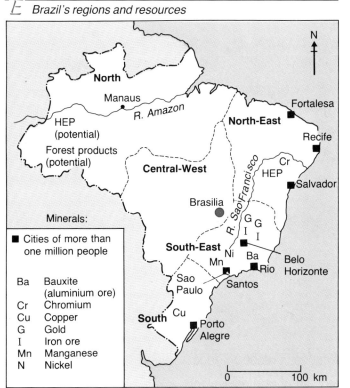

N

North
Manaus
R. Amazon
Fortalesa
North-East
HEP (potential)
Recife
Forest products (potential)
Cr
Central-West
HEP
Salvador
Brasilia
G G
I I
South-East
Ni
Ba
Belo Horizonte
Mn
Rio
Sao Paulo
Santos
South
Cu
Porto Alegre

Minerals:

■	Cities of more than one million people
Ba	Bauxite (aluminium ore)
Cr	Chromium
Cu	Copper
G	Gold
I	Iron ore
Mn	Manganese
N	Nickel

0 ___ 100 km

F Regional inequality in Brazil

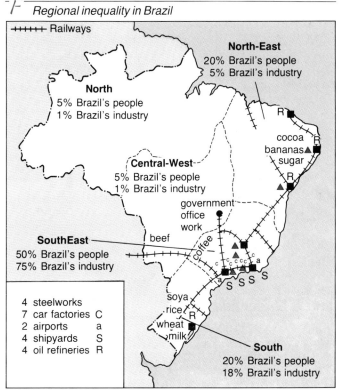

+++++ Railways

North-East
20% Brazil's people
5% Brazil's industry

North
5% Brazil's people
1% Brazil's industry

cocoa
bananas
sugar

Central-West
5% Brazil's people
1% Brazil's industry

government office work

SouthEast
50% Brazil's people
75% Brazil's industry

beef

coffee

soya
rice
wheat
milk

4	steelworks	
7	car factories	C
2	airports	a
4	shipyards	S
4	oil refineries	R

South
20% Brazil's people
18% Brazil's industry

1 A number of different criteria can be
used to measure development. They
include:
GNP per person (£ sterling)
Energy consumption per person (kg of
coal equivalent)
Daily food supply per person (calories)
Adult literacy (percentage)
　(i)　Name one of these criteria which
　　　measures each of:
　　　(a)　economic development
　　　(b)　quality of life. (2)

....
....

　(ii)　Choose one of the four criteria and
　　　explain how it shows the difference
　　　between developed and developing
　　　countries. (3)

....
....
....
....
....
....

RUSV

2 Study Graph A.
　(i)　What kind of graph is it – bar, line
　　　or scatter?

....

　(ii)　Draw a circle around a cross on the
　　　graph which represents a
　　　developing country. Label the circle
　　　'Developing country'. (1)

　(iii)　Draw a circle around a cross on the
　　　graph which represents a
　　　developed country. Label the circle
　　　'Developed country'. (1)

　(iv)　Explain the link shown between
　　　energy consumption by industry
　　　and average income. (2)

....
....
....
....

RUSV

-*A*

Graph A: scatter graph of Average income per person (£ sterling) against Energy used by industry (kg of coal equivalent)

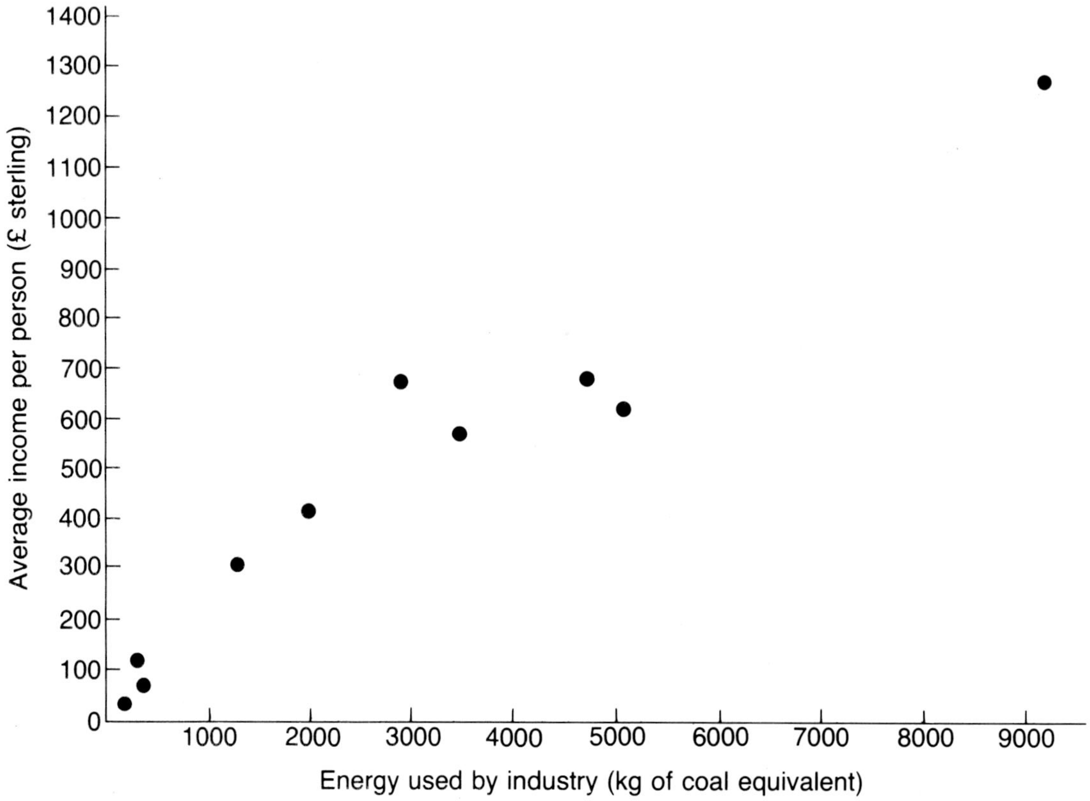

B Proportion of working population employed in agriculture

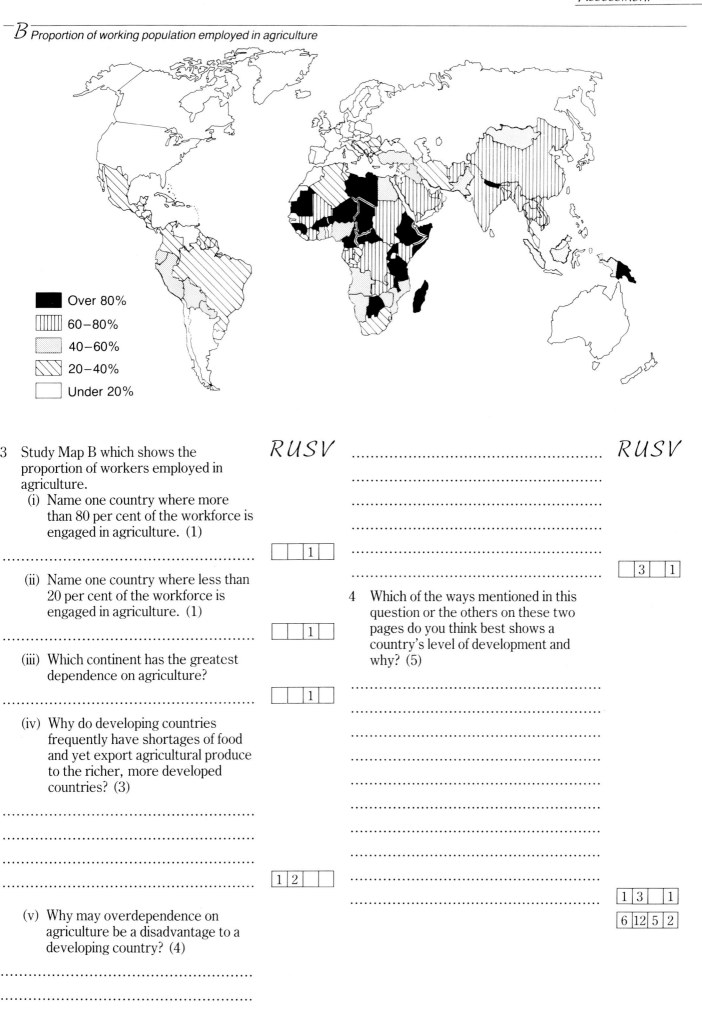

■ Over 80%

▥ 60–80%

▦ 40–60%

▨ 20–40%

☐ Under 20%

3   Study Map B which shows the proportion of workers employed in agriculture.

  (i) Name one country where more than 80 per cent of the workforce is engaged in agriculture. (1)

....

RUSV

☐☐1☐

  (ii) Name one country where less than 20 per cent of the workforce is engaged in agriculture. (1)

....

☐☐1☐

  (iii) Which continent has the greatest dependence on agriculture?

....

☐☐1☐

  (iv) Why do developing countries frequently have shortages of food and yet export agricultural produce to the richer, more developed countries? (3)

....
....
....
....

1 2 ☐ ☐

  (v) Why may overdependence on agriculture be a disadvantage to a developing country? (4)

....
....

RUSV

....
....
....
....
....
....

☐3☐1

4   Which of the ways mentioned in this question or the others on these two pages do you think best shows a country's level of development and why? (5)

....
....
....
....
....
....
....
....
....
....

1 3 ☐ 1
6 12 5 2

HOW DEVELOPMENT IS RELATED TO PHYSICAL, SOCIAL AND POLITICAL CONDITIONS

As Map A shows, most developed nations are to be found outside the tropics, whereas most developing countries are found within them. The reasons seem to be linked with three types of conditions. They are **physical** (environmental), **social** (how people get on with and learn from each other) and **political** (how people organise each other).

Physical conditions

Map A shows that hot areas tend to be under developed. In the tropics there are a number of physical problems which make progress difficult, which are not so severe in cooler areas. These all involve the water supply, as Diagram B shows.

Social conditions

Modern ways require new skills which were not important in the past. The best hunter does not always make the best builder. Literacy skills are vital for development. (Literacy is to do with reading and writing.) When people can read and write they can more easily gain other skills. If the people are aware of new skills, new technology and new ways of doing things, there is more opportunity for the country to develop. The social conditions which encourage development are ones which allow people to learn about and evaluate new ideas.

Sketch C shows a farmer trying to evaluate the pros (good points) and cons (bad points) of the 'green revolution'. Should he use the benefits of modern technology to improve farm output or not? It would mean planting new types of seed, irrigating his land and using chemical fertilisers to produce more food.

Political conditions

People disagree about what are the best political conditions for development. Here are three alternatives.

Capitalism
People work for the capitalists (who own most of a country's wealth). The idea is that the poor can help

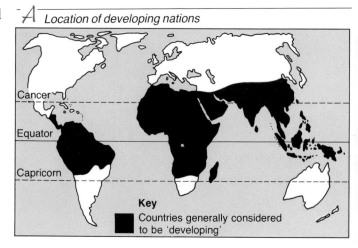

A Location of developing nations

Cancer

Equator

Capricorn

Key
Countries generally considered to be 'developing'

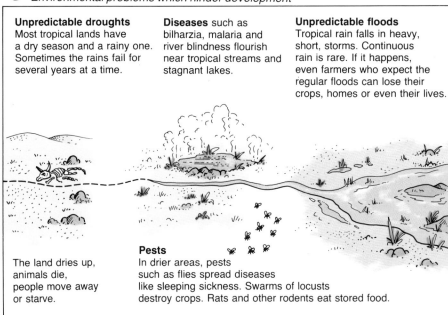

B Environmental problems which hinder development

Unpredictable droughts
Most tropical lands have a dry season and a rainy one. Sometimes the rains fail for several years at a time.

Diseases such as bilharzia, malaria and river blindness flourish near tropical streams and stagnant lakes.

Unpredictable floods
Tropical rain falls in heavy, short, storms. Continuous rain is rare. If it happens, even farmers who expect the regular floods can lose their crops, homes or even their lives.

The land dries up, animals die, people move away or starve.

Pests
In drier areas, pests such as flies spread diseases like sleeping sickness. Swarms of locusts destroy crops. Rats and other rodents eat stored food.

C The green revolution

Should I learn new farming skills? I might get it wrong. My soil might blow or wash away if I tire it out.

Should I risk my money buying expensive new seeds and fertiliser?

The money lender wants 20% of my profit.

Do I want to be left behind as all my friends get richer?

They say you get twice as much rice per hectare.

I might not get a loan or be unable to repay it.

themselves to get rich by making the rich richer. Anyone can go from poor to rich – or rich to poor! Rich countries often finance big projects (like dams) in developing countries. These poor countries then export their goods back to the rich countries, usually very cheaply.

Communism

Everyone is employed by the state. All development is planned by the government and civil servants.

Mixed economy

Some things (power supplies, for example) are controlled centrally. Other parts of the economy are open for control by business people.

All three systems encourage people to gain and use new skills, but people argue about which system is most effective. One important question is whether development takes place better with help on a small scale, to individual families, or by big projects, such as dams and irrigation schemes. Diagrams D and E show the arguments for and against these options.

D *Big project development*

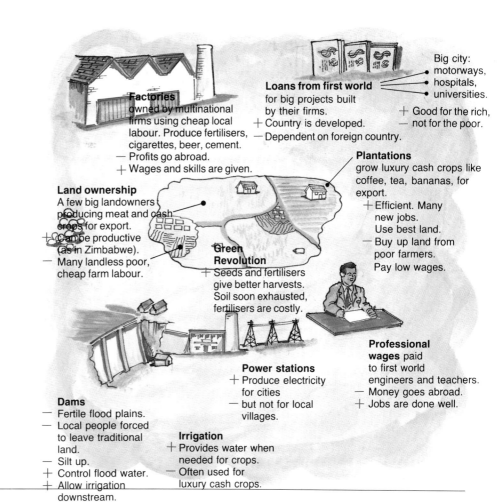

Factories
owned by multinational firms using cheap local labour. Produce fertilisers, cigarettes, beer, cement.
– Profits go abroad.
+ Wages and skills are given.

Loans from first world
for big projects built by their firms.
+ Country is developed.
– Dependent on foreign country.

Big city:
• motorways,
• hospitals,
• universities.
+ Good for the rich,
– not for the poor.

Land ownership
A few big landowners producing meat and cash crops for export.
+ Can be productive (as in Zimbabwe).
– Many landless poor, cheap farm labour.

Plantations
grow luxury cash crops like coffee, tea, bananas, for export.
+ Efficient. Many new jobs. Use best land.
– Buy up land from poor farmers. Pay low wages.

Green Revolution
+ Seeds and fertilisers give better harvests. Soil soon exhausted, fertilisers are costly.

Professional wages paid to first world engineers and teachers.
– Money goes abroad.
+ Jobs are done well.

Power stations
+ Produce electricity for cities
– but not for local villages.

Dams
– Fertile flood plains.
– Local people forced to leave traditional land.
– Silt up.
+ Control flood water.
+ Allow irrigation downstream.

Irrigation
+ Provides water when needed for crops.
– Often used for luxury cash crops.

E *Small scale development*

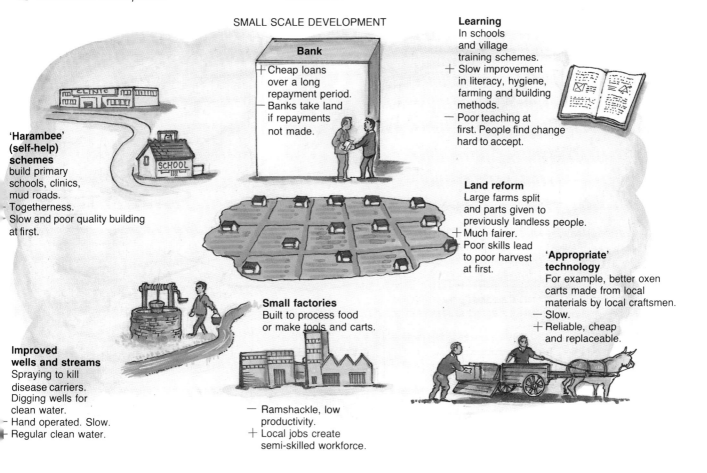

SMALL SCALE DEVELOPMENT

Bank
+ Cheap loans over a long repayment period.
– Banks take land if repayments not made.

Learning
In schools and village training schemes.
+ Slow improvement in literacy, hygiene, farming and building methods.
– Poor teaching at first. People find change hard to accept.

'Harambee' (self-help) schemes
build primary schools, clinics, mud roads.
– Togetherness.
– Slow and poor quality building at first.

Land reform
Large farms split and parts given to previously landless people.
+ Much fairer.
– Poor skills lead to poor harvest at first.

'Appropriate' technology
For example, better oxen carts made from local materials by local craftsmen.
– Slow.
+ Reliable, cheap and replaceable.

Small factories
Built to process food or make tools and carts.
– Ramshackle, low productivity.
+ Local jobs create semi-skilled workforce.

Improved wells and streams
Spraying to kill disease carriers. Digging wells for clean water.
– Hand operated. Slow.
+ Regular clean water.

1 Study Table A, Maps B and C and Graph D which show aspects of the geography of Indonesia in South East Asia.

  (i) State *four* facts about the relief and climate of Indonesia as shown by the maps and statistics. (4)

....

....

....

....

....

....

.... | 2 | 2 | |

  (ii) How may the facts you have listed in part (i) hinder the development of a country like Indonesia? (2)

....

....

....

.... | 2 | |

RUSV

  (iii) State *one* feature of population distribution in Indonesia. (1)

....

.... | 1 | |

  (iv) How may the population pattern described in part (iii) hinder development in certain parts of the country? (2)

....

....

....

.... | 2 | |

RUSV

A The population of Indonesia

Island	Population (000s)	Area (000 km^2)
Kalimantan	6700	550
Sulawesi	10400	230
Sumatra	28000	524
Java and Madura	91000	134
Small islands	11100	597
Total	147200	2035

B Indonesia

C Distribution of the population of Indonesia

N

People per km²
- **More than 500**
- 101–500
- 51–100
- 0–50

0 500 km

Sumatra
Kalimantan
Sulawesi
Moluccas
West Irian
Java

D The climate of Djakarta, Indonesia

Djakarta
Annual Rainfall total = 179.8 cm
Temperature
0 20 40 60 80 °F
J F M A M J J A S O N D
0 5 10 15 20 25 cm
−20 −10 0 10 20 30 °C

2 Environmental and social problems have often resulted in a vicious circle of poverty. *RUSV*
  (i) Complete Diagram E to show a vicious circle of poverty by putting the correct word or phrase in the appropriate box. Choose from the list below. One has been filled in for you. (4)
  Earns very little
  Produces very little
  No money
  Poor equipment/seeds
  No savings

  2 2

E The vicious circle of poverty

No money

3 (i) What is the 'green revolution'? (1) *RUSV*

....

.... 1

  (ii) State two advantages that the green revolution may bring to an area. (2)

....
....
....
.... 2

  (iii) Explain two disadvantages of using green revolution techniques. (4)

....
....
....
....
....
.... 4

4 Why are small rather than large-scale projects often more appropriate to the needs of the developing world? (5)

....
....
....
....
....
....
....
....
.... 2 3

3 15 4 3

COUNTRIES ARE INTERDEPENDENT IN TRADE

Interdependence

There are 150 or so nations of the world involved in world trade. Each country sells (exports) goods to other countries and buys (imports) goods from other countries. Trading nations must stay friends with each other to make sure that the trade contract is fulfilled. The more two countries trade, the more dependent they become on each other. Another way of saying this is that countries involved in trade are **interdependent**. The trade pattern is shown by Diagram A. Each arrow represents trade of more than 1500 US million dollars per year.

Trade

It is clear that Western Europe, North America and Japan dominate world trading. The poorest half of the countries of the world are involved in only 20 per cent (one-fifth) of the world's trade. They export raw materials which the rich countries cannot produce enough of for themselves. The prices they can charge are low. In return, the Third World countries buy manufactured goods, mainly from the First World. The prices they have to pay are high.

Multinationals

There is no doubt that in this pattern of trade the rich, First World countries have the advantage. It is their business people who set the prices for goods. Many Third World exports are produced by huge firms, like Kellog or Unilever. These firms run from First World countries such as the USA, UK and Japan. As they operate in many nations, they are called **multinational** or **transnational** firms. They develop the resources and help pay for improvements to roads, railways and ports such as Tema in Ghana, West Africa (Map B). One-third of all world trade is between transnational firms.

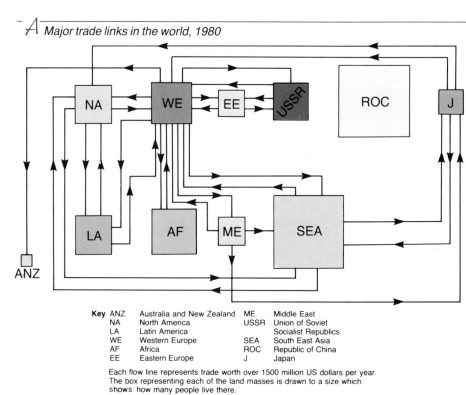

A Major trade links in the world, 1980

Key			
ANZ	Australia and New Zealand	ME	Middle East
NA	North America	USSR	Union of Soviet
LA	Latin America		Socialist Republics
WE	Western Europe	SEA	South East Asia
AF	Africa	ROC	Republic of China
EE	Eastern Europe	J	Japan

Each flow line represents trade worth over 1500 million US dollars per year. The box representing each of the land masses is drawn to a size which shows how many people live there.

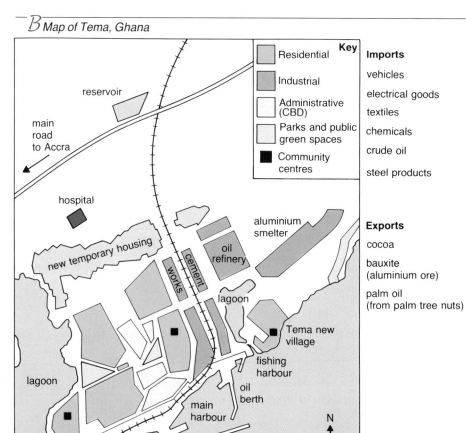

B Map of Tema, Ghana

Key
- Residential
- Industrial
- Administrative (CBD)
- Parks and public green spaces
- Community centres

Imports

vehicles

electrical goods

textiles

chemicals

crude oil

steel products

Exports

cocoa

bauxite (aluminium ore)

palm oil (from palm tree nuts)

Trading groups

It is also possible for other groups to have an effect on world trade. The twelve Oil Producing and Exporting Countries (OPEC) set the price of crude oil. In 1973 they raised its price by 400 per cent! Table C shows the OPEC countries. A price-fixing group like this is called a **cartel**.

Rich countries were able to pay this increased oil cost but they could not trade as much as before. The poor countries could not pay and also had less trade from the rich countries, so became much poorer. Since this time, firms have saved more energy and OPEC has had to cut its oil prices. Some OPEC countries, like Nigeria, have fallen into debt. They started development schemes which they cannot now afford. The debts are almost all to banks in rich countries like the USA, West Germany and France.

The Persian Gulf

The five South West Asian OPEC countries border the Persian Gulf between Iran and the Arabian Peninsula. The Gulf is one of the busiest waterways in the world. Crude oil is exported from the countries given in Table C to the rich countries of North America, Western Europe and North Eastern Asia. Throughout most of the 1980s, however, Iran and Iraq, both OPEC countries, were at war. Some Gulf states sought protection from United States and Western Europe warships to increase the safety of their tankers. This was an example of interdependence in wartime trade.

The EEC

The EEC (European Economic Community) is made up of twelve countries in Western Europe. It protects its own farmers by keeping out cheaper foreign farm produce, unless it cannot be produced in Europe. This makes it harder for Third World countries to export to the EEC. Map D shows the countries of the EEC.

Diagram E shows how rich and poor countries are interdependent. See if you can work out what it means.

C OPEC countries in 1980 and their production of oil

OPEC country	Percentage of world crude oil production	World region
Saudi Arabia	16.0	South West Asia
Venezuela	4.2	South America
Iraq	4.0	South West Asia
Libya	3.1	North Africa
Nigeria	3.0	West Africa
Indonesia	2.5	South East Asia
Iran	2.4	South West Asia
United Arab Emirates	2.0	South West Asia
Algeria	1.5	North Africa
Qatar	0.6	South West Asia
Gabon	0.5	West Africa

D EEC countries

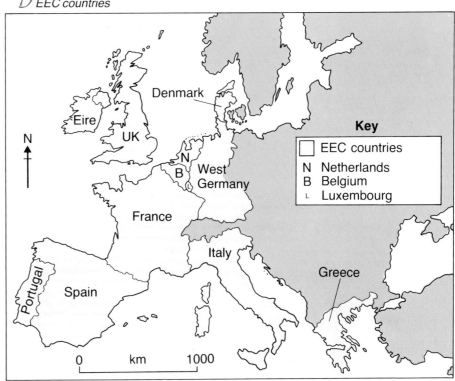

E 'Do you realise I have you under my control.'

1 Study Graphs A and B, showing the trade of Singapore and Sierra Leone, two former British colonies which both gained independence in 1959.

    (i) Where is Singapore situated? (1)

RUSV

....
....

| 1 | | | |

    (ii) Where is Sierra Leone situated? (1)

....
....

| 1 | | | |

    (iii) What is the percentage, by value, of Sierra Leone's coffee exports? (1)

....

| | | 1 | |

    (iv) What commodity makes up 11 per cent of the value of Singapore's imports? (1)

....

| | | 1 | |

    (v) What type of goods dominate Sierra Leone's exports? (1)

....

| | 1 | | |

    (vi) How does the pattern of imports into Sierra Leone show a lack of development in the manufacturing industry of that country? (2)

....
....
....
....

| | 2 | | |

    (vii) State one disadvantage of Sierra Leone's type of trade. (1)

....

| | 1 | | |

    (viii) In what ways does the pattern of Singapore's trade show that Singapore has reached a much higher level of development than Sierre Leone? (3)

....
....
....
....
....

| 1 | 2 | | |

    (ix) Choose either Sierra Leone or Singapore. For the one chosen state one part of the world this former colony is likely to trade with. (1)

RUSV

....

| 1 | | | |

    (x) What advantages do the trading partners chosen above get from each other as a result of this trade? (3)

....
....
....
....
....

| | 3 | | |

2 Study Table C which shows the total value of trade, the total production and the value of trade per person in the different parts of the world.

    (i) Draw a bar graph to show the value of trade per person in the different areas. (5)

| | | 5 | |

    (ii) What does the graph suggest about the developing world's share of world trade? (2)

....
....
....

| | 2 | | |

    (iii) Why do many developing countries claim that much of world trade seems to benefit the developed world more than them? (3)

....
....
....
....
....

| 2 | | | 1 |

| 6 | 11 | 7 | 1 |

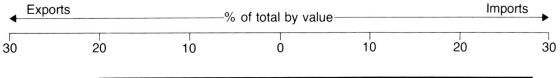

A The trade of Singapore

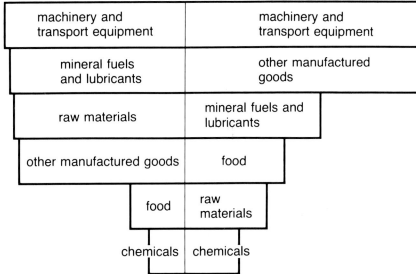

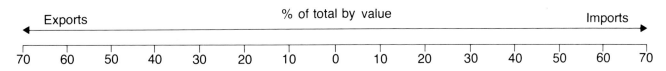

B The trade of Sierra Leone

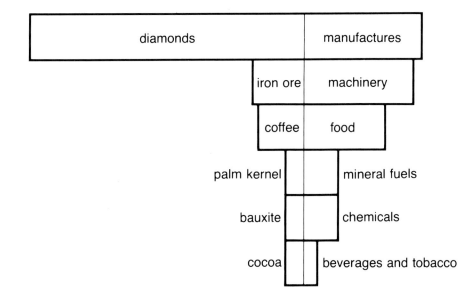

C Value of trade and population figures for the different parts of the world

Region	Total value of trade (millions of US dollars)	Total population (millions)	Value of trade per head (millions of US dollars)
Western Europe	1 679 150	350	4798
Northern America	595 200	251	2371
Eastern Europe and USSR	307 800	378	814
Africa	203 400	417	487
Asia	556 400	2475	224
Latin America	200 600	366	548
Australasia	55 100	22	2504

REDUCING INEQUALITY BETWEEN AND WITHIN COUNTRIES

Geographical inequality is to do with wealth. Some places are rich and some are poor. Children born in different places do not have the same opportunities to develop their talents and gain a rewarding way of life. Map A shows the inequalities in GNP per person in the world. Map B is another way of looking at these world inequalities. Within each region, Western Europe for example, there is inequality. Western Europe is not uniformly rich. The 'core' in northern France, Belgium, the Netherlands and West Germany is rich. The outlying parts of Western Europe (the 'periphery') is relatively poor, as Map C shows.

Should richer people help those in poorer regions? Most of us would answer 'Yes', but how to do it is a difficult problem. There are three main channels for such help (or aid).

Bilateral aid

Bilateral aid is aid between two countries. Aid is given by a rich 'donor' country to a poor 'receiver' country. A common problem is that such aid is given on the condition that firms from the donor country get building contracts in the receiver country. Or aid may depend on the use of ports or airfields as military bases for the donor country. Or the new schemes and equipment may need new imports, oil, for example, from the donor country to keep them going. Nearly three-quarters of all aid is given from one country to another bilaterally.

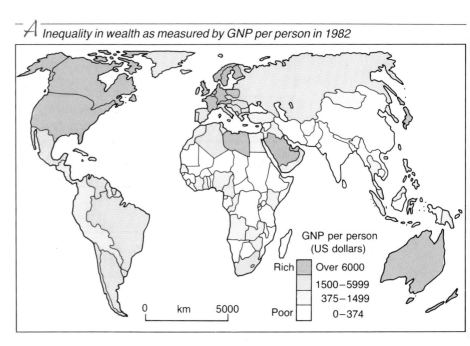

A Inequality in wealth as measured by GNP per person in 1982

GNP per person (US dollars)

Rich	Over 6000
	1500–5999
	375–1499
Poor	0–374

0   km   5000

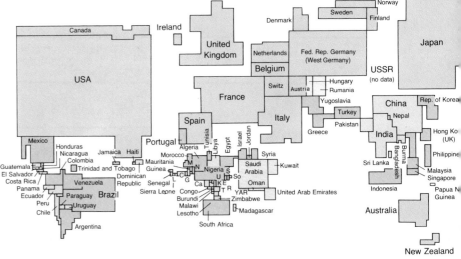

B Inequality in wealth – size of countries shown as proportion of world GNP

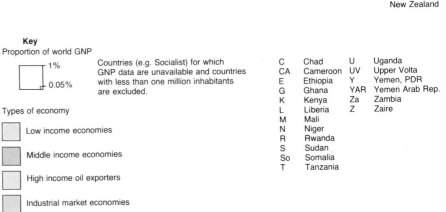

Key

Proportion of world GNP

1%
0.05%

Countries (e.g. Socialist) for which GNP data are unavailable and countries with less than one million inhabitants are excluded.

C	Chad	U	Uganda
CA	Cameroon	UV	Upper Volta
E	Ethiopia	Y	Yemen, PDR
G	Ghana	YAR	Yemen Arab Rep.
K	Kenya	Za	Zambia
L	Liberia	Z	Zaire
M	Mali		
N	Niger		
R	Rwanda		
S	Sudan		
So	Somalia		
T	Tanzania		

Types of economy

Low income economies

Middle income economies

High income oil exporters

Industrial market economies

East European non-market economies

C   The core and peripheral regions of the EEC

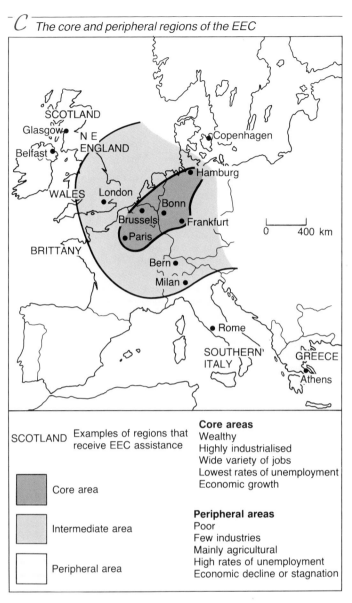

SCOTLAND   Examples of regions that receive EEC assistance

▨ Core area

▧ Intermediate area

☐ Peripheral area

Core areas
Wealthy
Highly industrialised
Wide variety of jobs
Lowest rates of unemployment
Economic growth

Peripheral areas
Poor
Few industries
Mainly agricultural
High rates of unemployment
Economic decline or stagnation

Multilateral aid

Multilateral aid is aid from many countries. Money is collected as taxes by various governments and is pooled to help the poorer regions. 20 per cent of all aid is of this type. For instance, the European Economic Community Regional Development Fund gives money to help poorer European regions. One major world aid organisation is the FAO (Food and Agriculture Organisation), a branch of the United Nations. One problem with aid given like this is that it tends to get lost in the bureaucracy of the system.

Charities

The Save the Children Fund, Oxfam and World Vision, among others, raise money from ordinary people in the rich world. This aid is usually given to small village projects and benefits ordinary people in the poor world, but it is only 5 per cent of all aid.

The aid given may be short term, to help in an emergency. This takes the form of food, transport, medicines, clothing and simple shelters such as tents. This sort of aid can cause big problems to those local people who are still working. Local farmers may not be able to sell their produce at a fair price when free food is being given out, for instance.

Longer term aid may take the form of building clinics, roads, irrigation schemes and factories. It may pay for skilled engineers, teachers and doctors, not only to work in the country, but also to train up local people in these skills. Aid may also be given to help pay off a poor country's debts, so that it can spend its own income on development. As poor countries develop, they can increase trade with rich countries, and so increase their real wealth. Diagram D shows how aid can turn into trade.

D   From aid to trade

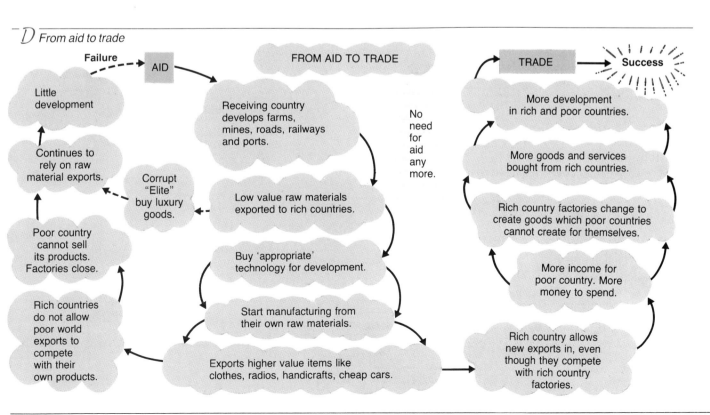

1   Explain the difference between bilateral and multilateral aid. (2)   *RUSV*

....

....

....

.... 2 | | |

2   The Brandt Report, '*North – South: A programme for survival*' separated the world into the two areas shown on Map A.
  (i) Name two characteristics of the so-called 'North'. (2)

....

....

....

.... 2 | |

  (ii) Name two characteristics of the so-called 'South'. (2)

....

....

....

.... 2 | |

  (iii) One of the recommendations of the Brandt Report was that developed countries should give 0.7 per cent of their GNP as aid. Briefly explain what this means. (2)

....

....

....

.... 2 | |

  Study Table B.
  (iv) How much countries have reached the target of 0.7 per cent? (1)

....

.... 1

  (v) Which country gave the highest percentage of its GNP in aid? (1)

....

.... 1

3   Study Advertisement C.   *RUSV*
  (i) How much does it cost to sponsor a child? (1)

....

.... 1

  (ii) Name two international aid agencies or charities apart from Action Aid who give money to developing countries. (2)

....

....

....

.... 2 | |

  (iii) State one advantage and one disadvantage of charities advertising in this way. (2)

....

....

....

.... 1 | 1

  (iv) Describe other forms of aid, apart from financial help, that the developing world may receive. (4)

....

....

....

....

.... 4 | |

  (v) Discuss the values and the dangers of external aid to the developing world. (6)

....

....

....

....

....

....

....

.... 5 | 1

  8 | 12 | 3 | 2

A The Brandt Report's division of the world into north/south

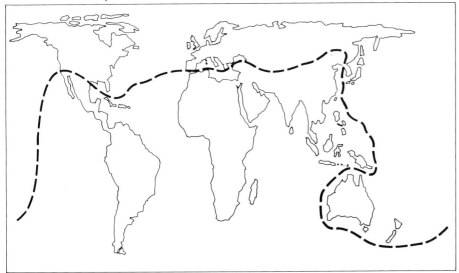

B Aid given by donor countries in 1980

Country	Value (£ million)	Aid as percentage of GNP
United States	3570	0.27
France	2025	0.62
West Germany	1760	0.43
United Kingdom	890	0.34
Netherlands	790	0.99
Sweden	460	0.76
Italy	335	0.17
Denmark	235	0.72
Norway	235	0.82
Austria	85	0.22

Mwende is 8. She now has the chance of a brighter future. You.

Mwende Kamana lives in a small rural village in Kenya. Her father is dead. And her mother tills the dry, meagre soil in a struggle to feed her 8 children. She desperately wants Mwende to go to school, and to have the chance of a better life. You can give her that chance. Through ActionAid's Child Sponsorship Programme.

As an ActionAid sponsor you give direct, continuing help to an individual child in a poor community. Sponsors give £7.92 a month – every penny of which is spent overseas to benefit the children in their communities. It's not much – the cost of a newspaper or a small loaf of bread a day. But it's all that's needed for action Aid to provide a child with an education and practical training for a more self-reliant future.

When you sponsor a child in need you'll know his or her name. You'll have a photograph to keep. And you'll receive regular news of his or her well-being and of the essential work being done to improve life for the whole community. Moreover, you'll know you are helping a child, a family and an entire village toward a more secure and productive future.

So please, cut out the coupon below and post it today. Your help will make a world of difference to a child like Mwende. Isn't that worth £7.92 per month?

ActionAid, 208 Upper Street,
London N1 1RZ.

Appendix A

EXAMINATION SKILLS

Use drawings

The word 'geography' means 'earth drawings'. So geography is a subject which gives you an opportunity to show your graphical skill, that is, your ability to draw maps, sketches and diagrams. Often what you know about a particular topic can be shown quickly and clearly by means of a simple drawing, although it would take a great deal of writing to record it.

So that drawings do not become cluttered up and difficult to read, they often have a key, or labels and notes giving additional information. 'Annotated maps' are simply maps with notes on. In an examination, detailed notes are not needed on a diagram, so long as the main features are clearly pointed out. Map A is an example of reasonable examination diagrams.

If a question actually asks for a map or diagram, marks will be reserved for it and these marks will be lost if no diagram is included in the answer. On the other hand, extra marks will usually be given for a diagram or map which makes a relevant (to do with the question) point, even if a drawing has not been asked for.

Use examples

In order to gain the highest grade you will need to recall facts in detail and back them up with plenty of examples at a suitable scale, from local to international. In addition you will need to apply ideas learnt in a variety of situations.

Use graphs

As well as being able to draw quick, clear maps, sketches, and diagrams, you need to show your ability to use various graphical and statistical techniques. You should be able to draw bar, line and scatter graphs from tables of figures to make sensible comments about information shown in tables and graphs.

Give balanced judgements

The examiners want to see that you can select and classify information so as to arrive at a well-reasoned conclusion. This will show that you appreciate all sides of an argument and can make an unbiased judgement.

On the other hand, if you can recall the basic outline of things you have been taught and find it difficult to explain the reasoning behind this information, the examiner will still award you a grade, although a lower one. At this grade you should show that you can collect geographical information and record it in simple sketch maps or diagrams such as a bar graph. You should show that you realise there are different points of view even if you find it difficult to make a judgement of your own.

Annual wheat production in the USA and USSR from 1978 to 1980

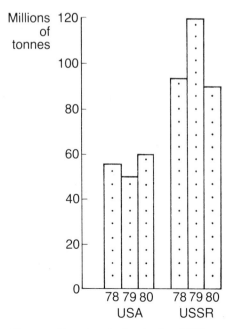

Comments

1 The USSR produced more wheat than the USA in each of these years.
2 In 1979 the USA wheat production fell, whereas the USSR production rose.
3 The USSR production varied between 90 and 120 million tons over the three years.
4 The USA production varied between 50 and 60 million tons over the three years.

Source: *Year book*, Australia, 1982.

Appendix B

EXAMINATION TECHNIQUES AND REVISION

The most important thing about GCSE examinations is that you need to show the examiner what you know and can do. Marks will *not* be lost for anything that you do wrongly.

Give a fact for each mark
The examination paper usually shows the number of marks available for a question or part of a question. In the majority of answers once complete fact is worth one mark. If the answer includes a list, for example of industries or crops, the items in the list are likely to be marked at half a mark each up to a maximum of two. Facts need to be specific. Marks will not be awarded for vague terms such as 'wet' and 'hot' when referring to climate, unless you give examples, for instance:

'Moscow has a cold winter climate (January average = $-10.8°C$). Even the top of Ben Nevis is warmer (January average = $-4.4°C$).'

This depth of detail should be used wherever possible. Similarly, when dealing with agriculture, words like 'fertile' and 'infertile' should be avoided and replaced by terms such as 'alluvial', 'loam', 'clay' and 'waterlogged'.

Give relevant answers
Answers must be relevant. In order not to waste time putting down information which will gain no credit, it is essential to recognise key words in the question. If the question begins with terms such as 'list', 'state' or 'name', all that is required is the basic information without any need to expand it further. If you are asked to 'describe' or 'explain', a longer answer is needed. However, there is a difference between 'describe' and 'explain'. Imagine being asked to describe a friend. You would say what he or she looks like. On the other hand, if you had to explain that same friend, you would have to give details of what makes them the kind of person they are. In the same way, being asked to describe a corrie is different from being asked to explain the formation of a corrie.

Make clear decisions
Other key words are 'discuss' and 'consider', which mean you must write down at least two points of view and say which one you favour. These harder questions in GCSE examinations are designed to give you a chance to show what values you hold and what ability you have for judgement. They rely on your being able to make quick decisions, even if you do not really know all the facts. (This is true of most of the decisions you will take in life anyway!)

Keep to time
In answering a question, you need to show the examiner what you know and how well you can use this information with different problems and situations. You must show that you can work under pressure and make maximum use of the available time. It is important not to waste time by writing irrelevant material ('waffling'). Work out how much time is available for each question and try to stick to it. A common fault is to go over time on the first question. It is very important to have sufficient time for the last question. If you run out of time and miss out this question you will have lost valuable marks. Table A shows timing plans for two examination papers.

Apply your knowledge
Your final grade will depend on what your answers show you know, what skills you can display, how well you can make a considered judgement, and how well you can apply knowledge. You will have learnt things about particular parts of the world. The examination questions may ask about parts of the world you have not studied. The examiner wants you to show that you can apply the ideas and concepts you have learnt to any location.

Full marks can be gained if you are able to set down the facts and explanations found in the mark scheme, even if your English grammar is not perfect.

A Timing plans for two examination papers

Paper 1 Time 1¾ hrs (105 mins)	Marks	Time (mins)
Reading		10
Question 1	40	35
Question 2	10	8
Question 3	10	8
Question 4	10	8
Question 5	10	8
Question 6	10	8
Question 7	10	8
Checking		12
		105 mins

Paper 2 Time 2 hrs (120 mins)	Marks	Time (mins)
Reading		10
Question 1	25	25
Question 2	25	25
Question 3	25	25
Question 4	25	25
Checking		10
		120 mins

2.1 Types of OS map

1 (i) 1:50 000(1)
        1:25 000(1)

   (ii) Landranger
         Examples: Hiking long distances,
         planning a local car journey.(1)
         Pathfinder
         Examples: Walking the dog on local footpaths,
         land use survey.(1)

2 (i) 1:50 000(1)

   (ii) 2.7 km(1)

   (iii) 6.2 km(1)

   (iv) Electricity pylon.(1)
         Church with tower.(1)
         Golf course.(1)

   (v) 6807(1)

   (vi) 712064(1)
         628081(1)

   (vii) Woodland.(1)

   (viii) ENE(1)

   (ix) Pylons, railway cutting, railway bridge, built up
         area, footpath, church without tower or spire,
         roundabout. (One mark each = 7.)

   (x) 407 metres(1)

   (xi) 178 metres(1)

   (xii) SW(1)

Total 25

2.2 Maps and landforms

1 Concave(1)
   Convex(1)
   Regular(1)

2 (3 marks)

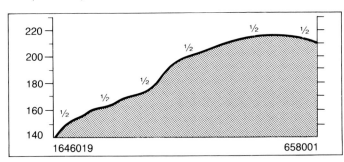

3 (8 marks)

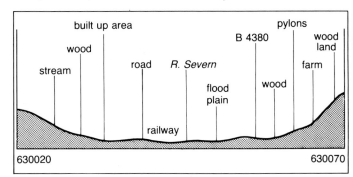

4 Ironbridge X section is:
   narrower(1)
   steeper sided (more of a gorge)(1)
   without a flood plain/flat valley bottom.(1)

5 No.(1)
   Flat land of Wrekin is in between.(1)

6 (6 marks)

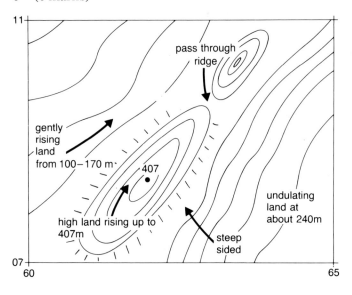

Total 25

2.3 Maps and land use

1   (i) (4 marks)

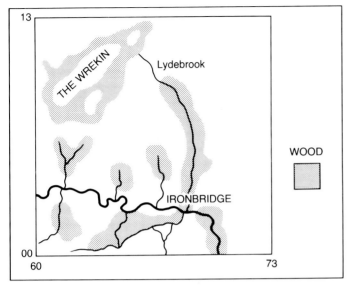

(ii) Found along steep slopes of the Wrekin.(1)
Also the valley sides of the River Severn and its tributaries.(1)

(iii) Steep sides unsuitable for agriculture or settlement.(1) Some woodland left to improve environment of built up area of Telford.(1) Some evidence of planting in plantations of Bannister's Coppice.(1)

2   (i) (4 marks)

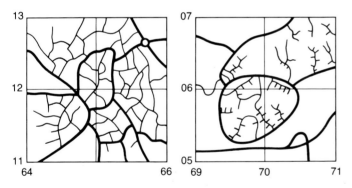

(ii) Wellington: Streets and houses are without a regular pattern.(1)
This shows they are unplanned/older.(1)
Brookside: Streets are curved/crescent shaped.(1)
This shows they are planned/modern.(1)

3   Large areas of quarrying(1)
in North Eastern part of map,(1)
expensive to build on.(1)

Map
Locating quarrying on map.(1)
Putting it in N.E. corner.(1)
Showing built up area of Telford.(1)
Neatness and accuracy of map.(2)

Total 25

2.4 Maps, photographs and images

1   (i) Sandbanks.(1)

(ii) Built up area, next to coastline, with farmland inland. (Any two, one mark each.) (2)

2   (i) Brownsea Island.(1)

(ii) A   Built up area.   B   Woodland.
C   Sandy beach.   D   Island lake.
E   Offshore deposition.   (5 × 1 = 5)

3   A   0389(1)   Pier/two piers/with lightbuoy.(1)
B   9990(1)   Works.(1)
C   0090 or 0190(1)   Poole/Poole quay/built up.(1)   (Total 6)

4   ½ mark for title. ½ for giving direction of view.
½ for artwork accuracy.
½ each for three correct labels, as shown on sketch.   (Total 3)

5   ½ mark for each point stated clearly. ½ for each accurate example. ½ for each accurate grid reference. At least two advantages and two disadvantages for full marks, for example:

Advantages:
Sandy beaches for holiday makers.
Large, sheltered, inland harbour for safe water sports.
Unspoilt, wooded, unbuilt up island for holiday exploring.
Boating lake (0290) for youngsters.
Plenty of mooring space for small boats.
Hotels.
Ferries.
(Or any suitable alternative.)

Disadvantages:
Possible pollution from ferries and motor boats.
Possible pollution from works on inland coastline.
Built up nature of most of the coastline.
(Up to a total of 6 marks.)

Total 25

3.1 **Tectonic activity and people**

1 Magma: molten material moving up from inside the Earth. (1)
   Richter scale: scale to measure the force of an earthquake. (1)
   Plate: one of the large masses of which the Earth's crust is made. (1)

2 All found in definite zones or belts. (½)
   Found around the Pacific Ocean. (½)
   Found throughout the Mediterranean. (½)
   Found down through S.E. Asia. (½)
   Represent the edge of the plates where the Earth's crust is weakest and the effect of the moving plates is felt. (1)
   Expect balance between explanation and description. (1)

3 (i)   Plate boundary. (1)

   (ii) Point on the Earth's surface vertically above the point of movement. (1)

   (iii) Shock waves have to travel through the Earth's crust. (1)
         Rome is further from the epicentre. (1)
         Therefore waves take longer to get there. (1)

   (iv) Collapse of housing. (1)
         Exposure to cold (November) weather. (1)

   (v)   Reinforced buildings. (1)
         Better medical facilities, temporary shelter. (1)

   (vi) Loss of population. (1)
         Destruction of housing. (1)
         Breakdown of local economy. (1)

   (vii) Volcanoes. (1)
         Lava flows. (1)

4 Tourism. (1)
   Spectacular scenery. (1)
   Rich fertile soils (lava and ash breaks down very easily). (1)
   Central heating (Iceland). (1)

Total 25

3.2 **Rock types and structures**

1 (i)   Metamorphic. (1)

   (ii) Sedimentary. (1)

   (iii) Igneous. (1)

2 (i)   Folding. (1)

   (ii) The raw materials are in the rocks. (1)
         They outcrop near the surface. (1)

   (iii) Coal-mining on coalmeasures. (1)
         Caves, disappearing streams and cement works on limestone. (1)
         Moorlands on sandstone. (1)

3 (i)   B: large amount of surface drainage, many streams and rivers, lake. (Any 2 points for 2 marks.)
         C: little surface drainage, intermittent drainage, disappearing streams, dry valleys. (Any 2 points for 2 marks.)

   (ii) Impermeable rock. (1)
         Porous/permeable rock. (1)

   (iii) Clay/shale. (1)
         Limestone/chalk. (1)

   (iv) Farming. (1)
         Quarrying. (1)

4 Advantages: employment, improved communications, spin-off to local economy.
   Disadvantages: spoiling the environment, loss of farmland, increased lorry traffic on local roads.
   (6 sensible separate ideas for 6 marks.)

Total 25

3.3 Rock structure and landscape

1 (i) Rift valley (1),   e.g. Rhine, Central Scotland. (1)
   (ii) Syncline (1),   e.g. South Wales coalfield,
       London Basin, Paris Basin. (1)
   (iii) Anticline (1),   e.g. Weald. (1)

2 Rocks at the top of an anticline are stretched (1) and
   so are less resistant to erosion. (1) Rocks at the
   bottom of a syncline are compressed (1) making them
   more resistant. (1)

3 (i) Rift valley. (1)

   (ii) Series of parallel faults (1) all of which allowed a
       portion of the Earth to drop, each by a different
       amount. (1)

   (iii) Different land uses on different steps: (1)
       meadow lands on the lowest step near the
       river (1)
       vineyards on higher slopes which face east, so
       have more sun (1)
       steepest slopes left forested. (1)

   (iv) Climate: area is sheltered by Vosges and Black
       Forest, so has higher temperatures and less
       rainfall. (1)
       Soil type: different soil types in different parts of
       the valley, for example, damp alluvium on the
       floodplain is ideal for meadows; rockier soils on
       the slopes of Vosges and Black Forest are used
       for vineyards or forests. (1)
       Communications: flatter land between mountains
       used for roads and railways. (1)

4 Rift valley; coalfields; basis of industry iron and steel;
   sheltered, therefore major farming area; densely
   populated, containing main settlements in Scotland.
   (5 sensible and separate points for 5 marks.)

Total 25

3.4 Rock types and resource opportunities

1 (i) Granite. (1)

   (ii) Chalk. (1)

   (iii) Limestone. (1)

2 (i) Caves, underground waterfalls, gorge.
       (2 of these for 2 marks.)

   (ii) Limestone karst scenery: chemical weathering,
       formation of swallow holes, rivers disappearing
       underground, continued solution underground
       leading to formation of caves.
       (4 developed points for 4 marks.)

   (iii) E.g. underground lighting, shops, restaurants,
       guided trails. (Any 3 for 3 marks.)

   (iv) Quarrying, sheep, grazing. (Any 2 for 2 marks.)

3 (i) Completed and labelled sketch. (5)

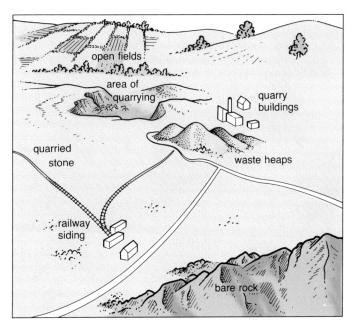

   (ii) Example: limestone. (1)

   (iii) Example: Peak District or any suitable
       example. (1)

   (iv) Employment, more money brought into the
       area. (2)
       Less land available for farmland, spoilt
       environment. (2)

Total 25

4.1 *Weathering and its effect on the landscape*

1 The breakdown (1) of solid rock into smaller pieces. (1)

2 (i) (a) Biological. (1)
   (b) Physical (mechanical). (1)
   (c) Chemical. (1)

   (ii) (a) E.g. vegetation on cliff face at coast or similar. (1)
   (b) E.g. mountain cliffs (Lake District or similar). (1)
   (c) E.g. Mendips, Peak District or similar. (1)

3 (i) Cold nights make rocks contract. (½)
   Hot days make the rocks expand. (½)
   Minerals in rock do not expand equally. (½)
   So the rocks sometimes split with a crack. (½)

   (ii) At snowline the temperature fluctuates above and below freezing point. (½) The water in cracks freezes and expands (½) forcing cracks to widen, breaking the rock. (½) Shattered rock (scree) falls to the base of the slope. (½)

4 (i) Simple sketch of photograph. (2)

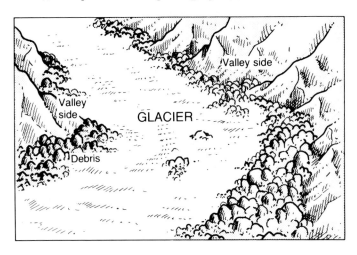

   (ii) Labels. (4 × 1)
   (iii) Weathering provides the load for agents of erosion. (1) Weathering weakens rock. (1) Weathering and mass movement constantly reveal fresh rock (1) which can then be weathered. (1)

5 Discolouration of building. (½)
   Example. (½)
   "Pitting" of surface. (½)
   Example (e.g. of statue). (½)
   Rusting of metal. (½)
   Example. (½)
   (Or similar sensible points.)

Total 25

4.2 *Landforms created by rivers*

1 Raised river bank. (1)

   Becoming young again. The river takes on characteristics of the upper course (e.g. waterfalls and gorges) in the lower part of its valley due to a fall in sea level. (1)

   Changes in river flow over the year. (1)

2 (i) 44 mm (1, or ½ if units omitted.)

   (ii) 6 hours (1, or ½ if units omitted.)

   (iii) 3.0 cubic metres per second. (1)

   (iv) Time was taken to get into the river via the surface (1) or by percolating through the rock. (1)

   (v) Greater volume of water, therefore able to carry greater loads so able to erode more. (1)
   Faster flowing. (1)
   Smaller proportion of cross sectional area is affected by friction with the bank and bed, so is available for erosion. (1)

3 (i) Limestone, (1) sandstone. (1)

   (ii) Plunge pool. (1)

   (iii) Undercutting of less resistant rock (1) leaving an overhang of resistant capping. (1) This drops due to lack of support, (1) so progressively the Falls are eroded backwards. (1)
   Gorge. (1)

   (iv) Knickpoint as a result of rejuvenation. (1 mark for either term.)

4 Railways use cuttings and embankments to maintain level gradient. (1) and must be away from the danger of flooding. (1) Settlement on river terrace or valley side above the flood plain. (1) Industry on low lying land near river. (1) Steep sides left wooded. (1) Flat area of valley where there is no danger of flooding provides farmland. (1)
   (Up to a maximum of five marks.)

Total 25

4.3 Ice creating landscape opportunities

1 Breaking up of rock by water freezing and expanding in cracks. (1)

Thin ridge between two corries. (1)

Line of glacial debris dumped at furthest extent of glacier. (1)

2 (i)

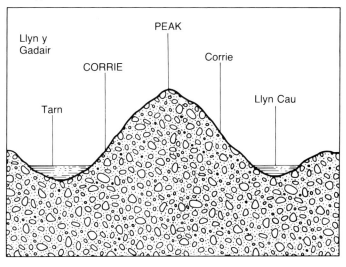

(3 × 1 mark for correctly labelled features. 1 mark for very generalised cross section.)

(ii) Either: Glacier created the valley. (1) Terminal moraine deposited at furthest point reached. (1) Meltwater dammed back (1) to form lake taking shape of valley. (1)
Or: Over-deepening (1) of valley floor (1) in area of less resistant rock (1) by a glacier. (1)
(Total 4 marks.)

(iii) Freeze-thaw process on valley sides (1) leading to break up of rock (1) which falls to base of slope to form scree. (1)

3 (i) From east, westwards. (1)

(ii) Ground moraine and boulder clay (till) would have been under the ice. (1) Sand deposits of the west are outwash from terminal moraine (1) deposited by meltwater from front of the glacier. (1)

(iii) Boulder clay in higher parts – good for farming. (1)
Boulder clay in low parts – bogs and marshland. (1)
Sandy soils – heathland. (1)
Sandy soils when fertilised can be arable. (1)
(Up to maximum of 3 marks.)

4 Suitable example (e.g. Alps). (1)
Tourism. (1)
Water supply. (1)
Hydro Electric Power (HEP). (1)
Boulder clay for farming. (1)
Water sports in lakes. (1)
(Up to a maximum of 5 marks.) Total 25

4.4 Coastal landforms and land uses

1 Zig-zag movement of coastal material parallel to the coast. (1)
Isolated pillar of rock left after erosion of headland by marine action. (1)
Submerged glaciated valley. (1)

2 (i) Sandspit. (1)

(ii) Longshire drift (1) bringing material down the coast (1) and depositing it parallel to the coast (1) causing the river to be diverted southward. (1)

(iii) Groynes (1): barriers built (1) out from the coast (1) to stop further movement of material (1) along the coast, (1) keeps beach for tourists. (1)
(Up to a maximum of 4 marks.)

(iv) Holiday resorts on the coast: sand (1), caravan sites on flattish land. (1)
Industrial development on the river. (1) allowing river transport because there is less problem of silting. (1)
(Up to a maximum of 3 marks.)

3 Sea walls. (½) Example. (½)
Break waters. (½) Example. (½)
Marram grass on sand dunes. (½) Example. (½)
(Up to maximum of 2 marks.)
Judgement on effectiveness. (1)

4 Example (e.g. Nile Delta). (1)
Seasonal flooding. (1)
Regular enrichment of soil due to flooding. (1)
Streams and marshes – difficult accessibility. (1)
Danger of river flooding for settlements. (1)
Low lying: danger of flooding from sea surges. (1)
Very rich soil – high crop yields. (1)
Very rich soil – more than 1 harvest per year. (1)
(Up to a maximum of 6 marks.)

Total 25

5.1 *Elements of the weather*

1   Sunshine (1), cloud type (1) and cover (1), precipitation (1), relative humidity (1), wind force (1) and direction (1), temperature. (1)
(5 of these.)

2   Relative humidity: the amount of moisture the air contains expressed as a percentage of its maximum capacity. (1)
Precipitation: moisture from the atmosphere falling to the Earth in one of several forms – rain, hail, snow, sleet. (1) (0 for rain.)
Pressure: force exerted by the air measured in millibars. (1)
Stratus: layered type of cloud. (1)

3   (i)   Heavy snow in December. (1)
Torrential rain in January. (1)

    (ii)   Between 20 and 30 mm. (1)

    (iii)   It is at the confluence of a number of rivers (1), each rising in the Pennines (1), where there is heavy rain and snow. (1) The single river is unable to cope with the increased volume of water. (1)

    (iv)   Homelessness (1), evacuation (1), damage to carpets (1), mud deposits (1), disruption of communications (1), higher insurance premiums (1). (Any 4.)

4   ½ for sensible point.
½ for specific example.
e.g.
Heavy rain – Flood barriers erected. (½)
                       Example. (½)
                   – Evacuation from low lying areas. (½)
                       Example. (½)
Ice   – Roads gritted. (½)
                       Example. (½)
Snowfall   – Snowploughs on roads. (½)
                       Example. (½)
Fog   – Fog warnings. (½)
                       Example. (½)
                       Speed restrictions on motorways. (½)
                       Example. (½)
Hurricanes – Evacuation. (½)
                       Example. (½)
(Up to a maximum of 5 marks.)

Total 25

5.2 *Measuring the weather*

1   (i)   Barometer: pressure. (1)
Anemometer: wind speed (wind force). (1)

    (ii)   (One mark for each of these up to a total of 4.)
8 octas cloud (accept 8/8ths cloud or overcast). (1)
South west wind direction. (1)
Force 7 wind. (1)
Thunderstorm. (1)
6°C (temperature). (1)

2   (i)   (4)

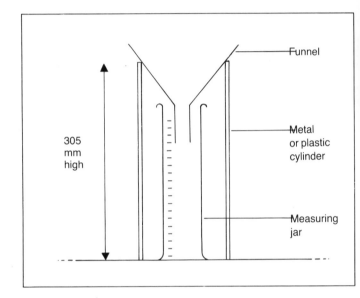

    (ii)   Sheltered by building and trees. (1) Trees may reduce amount or increase amount with drips. (1) Rain may splash off paved area into gauge. (1)

3   (i)   To allow water to evaporate (1), which brings the temperature down. (1)

    (ii)   Find the difference between wet and dry bulb temperatures (1) and use a set of tables to find the percentage figure for relative humidity. (1)

    (iii)   Day 2. (1)
Day 8. (1)

4   (i)   A clear sunny day (1) with good visibility. (1) Very calm (1) but very cold. (1) Severe frost. (1) Dry. (1) (Up to 4.)

    (ii)   Winter. (1)

    (iii)   Anticyclone. (1)

Total 25

5.3 Air masses and high and low pressure systems

1 A mass of air which takes on the characteristics of the region where it originated (its source region). (1)

2 (i) Tropical Maritime (mT). (1)
       Polar Continental (cP). (1)

   (ii) mT air originates over the warm waters of the Atlantic (1) and so brings warm moist conditions to the British Isles. (1)
       cP air originates over the cold dry areas of Siberia and Northern Russia (1) and so brings very cold, dry conditions to the British Isles. (1)

3 (i) A. (1)

   (ii) Isobars. (1)

   (iii) North west. (1)

   (iv) Light winds (1), clear skies (1), dry (1), warm. (1) (Up to 3.)

   (v) South and west Wales: warm and humid (½), winds from the South West. (½)
       North and east Wales: South East winds. (½)
       Cooler clearer. (½)

   (vi) Depression: September. (1)
       Anticyclone: May. (1)

4 (i) (6)

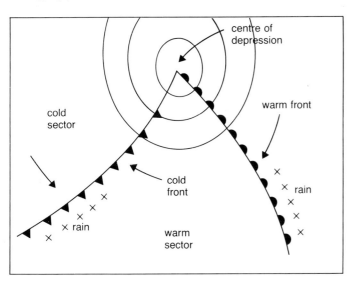

5 They give an overall picture (1) and allow greater accuracy in forecasting weather approaching this country. (1)

Total 25

5.4 Climate and location

1 Weather is the day to day changes in air conditions (1) whereas climate is the average of the different weather conditions over a period of time. (1)

2 Altitude (1), latitude (1), distance from the sea (continentality) (1), ocean currents (1), prevailing winds. (1) (One mark per point up to 4 marks.)

3 (i) 21°C (1)

   (ii) −14°C (1)

   (iii) 35°C (1)

   (iv) Away from the modifying influences of the sea, as it is situated in the centre of a large land mass. (1) In the winter the land cools down more rapidly than the sea (1), whereas in summer the land heats up more rapidly. (1)

4 (i)

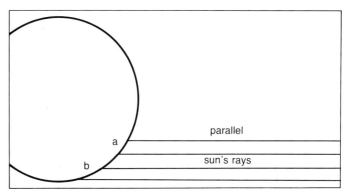

At lower latitudes the Sun's rays are concentrated in a smaller area (a) (1) whereas at higher latitudes the heat is dispersed over a larger area (b) and so is less effective. (1) (Reserve 2 marks for diagram.) (2) (No marks for saying southern Chile is further from the Sun.)

   (ii) Offshore winds blowing for most of the year. (1) Cold waters of the Humbolt current offshore will reduce evaporation so the water content of the air is low. (1)

   (iii) Winter. (1)

   (iv) Dry summers would suggest low cloud cover and so high sunshine totals ideal for ripening. (1) Dry summers mean water shortage and need for irrigation. (1)

   (v) Effect of altitude. (1)

   (vi) Effect of aspect. (1) The north-facing slopes in the Southern Hemisphere will face the Sun, increasing temperature and therefore reducing the period of snow cover. (1) The south-facing slopes will remain in the shade for much longer and so temperatures will be correspondingly lower. (1)

Total 25

6.1 *Population density, distribution and environmental opportunities*

1 Number of people in an area. (1)

2 (4)

	Area	Population	Population density	
Norway			13	(1)
Bangladesh	150			(1)
Australia		15000		(1)
Singapore	0.5			(1)

3 (i) P: hot desert. (1)
Q: mountain. (1)
R: arctic. (1)

(ii) (a) Very dry. (1)
Rain unpredictable. (1)
High evaporation. (1)
Stony surface – no soil for farming. (1)
Sand dunes form obstacles to communication. (1)
(One mark per point up to a maximum of 3 marks.)

(b) Digging wells ⎱ to improve
Piping/tanking water in ⎰ water supply.
Planting drought resistant grasses and shrubs.
(One mark for idea, two marks for explained idea.)

(iii) Mineral wealth. (1), oases. (1), irrigation in desert. (1)
Plantation agriculture in hot wet lands. (1)
One mark for answer. One mark for explanation or example. (Up to 2 marks.)

4 (i) Cash crop farming in the south provides jobs so greater population density. (1)
Mines for minerals in the south provide jobs. (1)
Railways provide jobs. (1)
Ports provide jobs. (1)

(ii) Unequal development leads to lack of opportunity for people of northern Ghana. (1)
Southern cities suffer traffic congestion. (1)
Shanty towns around southern cities have inadequate services. (1)
The most talented youngsters leave the poorer north, making the decline worse. (1)
Political/tribal dissatisfaction about the rich south benefitting most. (1)
Most taxes spent on southerners. (1)
No development in the north. (1)
New industry sets up in the richer southern cities. The rest of the country remains poor. (1)
(One mark per point up to a maximum of 5 marks.)

Total ☐25

6.2 *Natural increase: causes and effects*

1 (i) Number of births per 1000 people. (1)

(ii) Number of deaths per 1000 people. (1)

(iii) (3)

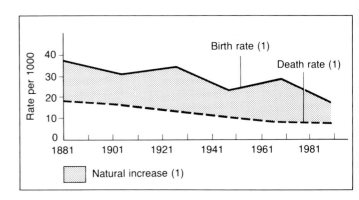
Natural increase (1)

(iv) 1921 or 1961. (1)

(v) Gain or loss from migration. (1)

(vi) Declining birth rate, (1) low rate of natural increase. (1)

(vii) Ageing population (1), greater demand on medical and welfare services. (1) Fewer skilled young/middle-aged workers. (1)

(viii) Rapidly increasing rate of growth due to high birth rate. (1) Medical advances reducing death rate. (1) Social and economic advantages (1) of a large family. (1)

2 (i) Population pyramid/age and sex ratio pyramid. (1)

(ii) 8%. (1)

(iii) Developing country. (1) Large number of young people because of high birth rate (1), small number of old people because high death rate in fairly recent past. (1)

(iv) 2 (1)

(v) (3)

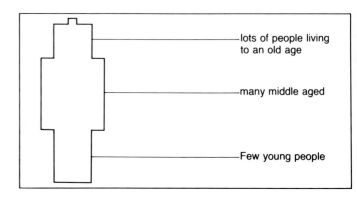

Total ☐25

6.3 *The population explosion and available resources*

1 Excess of births (1) over deaths. (1)

2 (i) South America (1), Africa. (1)

   (ii) Europe. (1)

   (iii) The birth (1) and death rates (1), medical improvement (1), social and welfare facilities. (1)

3 (i) Advertising (1), tax incentive gifts (1), medical advisory teams. (1)

   (ii) India (1), China (1) or any other suitable example.

   (iii) Tradition of having large families (1), insurance for parents' old age (1), potential wage earners (1), social prestige (1), high infant mortality (1) so large number of births in order that some may survive. (1)
   (Up to 3 marks.)

   (iv) Planning for increasing population. Greater output of food through irrigation (1), use of fertilisers (1), super seeds. (1) Increased output from industries (1) to provide employment (1) and foreign exchange to provide food. (1)
   (Up to 3 marks.)

4 Mao: no problem with large and increasing population (1) because production increases at the same rate and so provides for everybody. (1)
Also, the more Chinese, the more important China is. (1)
Shao Li-tsu: need to introduce birth control (1) in order to keep population growth low. (1)
This would give people a chance to overcome the problems of drought, floods and poor communications. (1) It would also allow them to increase production of goods and services to give everyone a better standard of living. (1)
(One mark for each sensible point up to a total of 5.)

Total 25

6.4 *Migration*

1 Push factors: problems at home that encourage migrants to move to another area. (1)
Pull factors: features of another area which seem to offer advantages to the migrant. (1)

2
Push factors	Pull factors
E (1)	A (1)
F (1)	B (1)
	C (1)
	D (1)

3 (i) India. (1)

   (ii) 14% (1)

   (iii) 11% (1)

   (iv) Majority of migrants are men. (1) Most migrants are aged 25 (1) to 29. (1)

4 (i) Students (1), better employment opportunities, (1) prejudice (1), discrimination (1), loneliness (1), difficulties with climate (1), language. (1) (Up to 3 marks.)

   (ii) Short term contracts (1), education (1), engineers (1), VSO help to underdeveloped countries. (1) (1 of these.)

   (iii) Seasonal movement for harvest (1), greater employment prospects (actual or imagined), (1) cities provide a greater range of facilities (1). Lack of prospects in country. (1)

   (iv) Inbalance between different parts of the country. (1)
   Resources in one area not being fully exploited. (1)
   Decline of birth rate if males migrate. (1)
   More money being put into one part of the country. (1)
   (Any 3 of these.)

Total 25

7.1 *Factors affecting site, situation and layout of settlements*

1   Defence (1), building supplies (1), water supply (1), agricultural land (1), shelter. (1) (Up to 4 marks.)

2   (i)   Reasonable labelled sketch (1½), position of river (½), position of castle (½), position of bridge. (½)

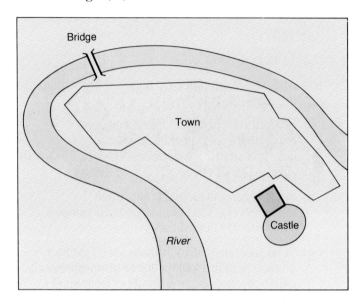

    (ii) Defensive site (1), protected by river (1) on three sides (1), river entrenched to provide additional protection. (1)

    (iii) Traffic problems (1), limited room for expansion. (1)

3   Site: the actual land (1) on which the settlement is built. (1)
Situation: where the settlement is (1) in relation to the surrounding area. (1)

4   (i)   Little Baddow: linear village (1) built along the road. (1)
Galleywood: compact village (1), new development on the outskirts of Chelmsford. (1)

    (ii) Heart of city around cathedral between rivers Can and Chelmer. (1) Growth around the town hall (1), growth along the railway south westwards towards the college and museum (1), and north eastwards towards the prison (1), shown by straight, regular street pattern. (1) New developments on modern estates (1) with geometric layout (1), e.g. Great Baddow. (Up to 4 marks.)

Total ⟨25⟩

7.2 *Settlement patterns and processes*

1   (i)   250 (1)

    (ii) 15 000 (1)

    (iii) The higher the population (1) the greater the number of shops. (1)

    (iv) Putting settlements in order (1) according to certain criteria. (1) For example, number of shops (½), type of shops (½), population. (½) (Up to 3 marks.)

    (v)   No indication of the type of shops. (1) Shops may only be low order, convenience shops. (1) Dormitory settlements may have a large population but few shops. (1)

2   (i)   Post office (1), grocer (1), general store. (1) (Any two.)

    (ii) The shops require a larger market area. (1) The shops will have large ranges and thresholds and so need a larger population to remain profitable. (1)
People are prepared to travel greater distances to obtain goods or services from higher order shops. (1)

    (iii) Greater range of shops in B (1), certain low order shops found in both but higher order shops restricted to B. (1)
Comparison foods more common in B. (1)
Credit any examples. (1)

3   (i)   City – 4th order in urban hierarchy. (1)

    (ii) Investigation of bus/train services (1), delivery areas of local shops (1), catchment area of local schools (1) or hospitals (1), circulation area of local newspapers (1), questionnaire techniques in towns and surrounding villages. (1) (Up to 5 marks.)

Total ⟨25⟩

7.3 Urban settlements: processes and patterns

1 (i) Densely populated (1), little open space (1), mixture of industry and housing (1), main roads through built-up area. (1)

   (ii) Inner city. (1)

   (iii) Nineteenth century. (1)

   (iv) Unemployment (1), poor standard of housing (1), lack of play space (1), traffic congestion (1), lack of car parking. (1)
   (Up to 3 marks.)

   (v) Improving the standard of housing, or improving the environment. (1)

   (vi) Maintains sense of community (1), does not create a dead heart in the centre of the city where nobody lives and which becomes empty at night. (1)

2 (i) Essonne. (1)

   (ii) Built-up area on the outskirts of an urban area. (1)

   (iii) Capital of France (1), largest economic centre (1), attraction of job opportunities, actual or imagined (1), cultural and educational facilities. (1)

   (iv) Declining population (1), people moving out. (1)

   (v) Greater mobility of the population (1), more pleasant surroundings (1), cheaper land. (1)
   (Up to 2 marks.)

3 Award marks as follows up to a total of 5:
   Mainly like the sector model. (1)
   e.g. sector to south (1)
   e.g. sector to south east (1)
   e.g. sector to east (1)
   Some parts like concentric model. (1)
   e.g. in north (1)
   e.g. in west (1)
   Some evidence of nuclei model. (1)
   e.g. near shopping centres in south west (1)
   (If an annotated map answer, mark generously.)
   Total 25

7.4 Problems caused by too many people living in cities

1 (i) 21 million. (1)

   (ii) 26 million. (1)

   (iii) 2 (1)

   (iv) Expectation of employment (1), decline in opportunities on the land (1), better welfare and social facilities (1), increasing tradition of movement to towns (1), expectation of better life. (1)

2 (i) Makeshift settlement made of a variety of building materials, housing immigrants into the city. (1)
   (Or similar description.)

   (ii) Outskirts. (1)

   (iii) Reserve 2 marks for specific detail: disease due to lack of sewers (1) and piped water (1), unemployment (1), crime (1), breakdown of family life (1), high infant mortality (1), low life expectancy. (1)
   (Up to 6 marks.)

   (iv) Advantages: better facilities (1), more work. (1) Disadvantages: growth of shanty towns (1), use of agricultural land because of urban sprawl (1), strain on resources of country (1), increasing inbalance between city and rural areas. (1)
   (Up to 4 marks.)

3 Separation of industrial and urban areas. (1) Traffic-free areas. Neighbourhood areas to build up community spirit with all amenities within easy reach. (1) Landscaping. (1) Modern facilities. (1) Name of example. (1)
   (Up to 5 marks.)
   Total 25

8.1 *Environmental and human factors which influence land capacity*

1 Relief (1), climate (1), soil (1), water supply. (1) (2 of these.)

Climate (1), availability of labour (1), government policy (1), accessibility. (1) (2 of these.)

2 (i) Sandy soils blow away (1), sea air adds salt to soil (1), steep slopes (1), hummocky relief. (1)

(ii) Level land allowing use of machinery (1), roads giving access to markets (1), division into regularly-shaped fields for greater ease of mechanisation (1), no danger of flooding. (1) (4 developed points.)

3 (i) Artificial watering of the land. (1)

(ii) Water from Blue and White Niles (1), using natural slope of land (1) to take water to the fields (1) by means of canals. (1) (Up to 3 marks.)

(iii) Lack of capital for improvement (1), difficulty in obtaining good quality seed and livestock (1), poor communications (1) making access to market difficult (1), poorly educated (1), poor knowledge of new techniques (1), no fertiliser available. (1)

4 Payment of grants for improvement. (1)
Guaranteed price subsidies to farmers. (1)
EEC quotas. (1)
In centrally administered economies like the USSR, direct government control (1) of agriculture on collective farms and state farms. (1)
Income tax levels. (1)
Tax allowances for buying machinery and plant. (1)
(Reserve at least one for example.)
(Up to 5 marks.)

8.2 *Farm systems and decision making*

1 Huge ranches (1), few workers (1), low output per hectare (1), high output per farm worker (1), farms often owned by companies. (1) (3 of these.)

2 (i)

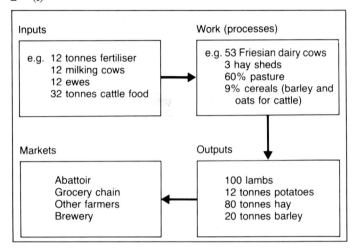

(Any 12 × ½ up to 6.)

(ii) Dairy farming. (1)

(iii) Rainfall over 750 mm which encourages good grass growth (1), mild winters over 0°C due to influence of North Atlantic Drift (1) and the modifying influence of the sea which allow grass growth throughout the year (1), so cattle can stay on fields longer (1), reducing the need for expensive winter fodder. (1) Large demand for milk and dairy products (1) to be sent away or for local tourist trade.
(4 developed points – up to 4 marks.)

3 (i) Inputs: market garden – labour intensive (1), plantation – capital intensive. (1)
Outputs – market garden – high yielding fruit and vegetables (1), plantation – high output. (1)

(ii) Perishable produce needs to reach the market quickly and regularly. (1)

(iii) Concentration on one major crop, (1) major infrastructure, (1) produce mainly for export. (1) (Up to 2 marks.)

(iv) Advantages of market garden: Polyculture (growing a great variety of crops on the same farm, so if one fails or does not sell well, others will still keep the farm profitable) (1), variety of foodcrops (1), produce sold locally. (1) Not overdependent on export trade. (1) Money stays in country. (1)
Plantation crop is mainly for export (1), and most of the profit goes to company owners, (1) but it provides regular employment for locals. (1)
(One mark for the decision, two marks for reasons.)

Total 25

8.3 Patterns of farming

1 Agricultural Gross Domestic Product. (4 × ½ mark.)

2 (i) India. (1)

(ii) Netherlands. (1)

(iii) The higher the percentage employed in agriculture (1), the lower the value of exports per head of population. (1)

3 (i) Modern intensive farming. (1)

(ii) Densely populated (1), lack of flat land/rugged terrain. (1)

(iii) Industrial nation, therefore need to produce as much food as possible (1), and reduce the need to import costly food. (1) Need to farm intensively to make fullest possible use of limited cultivatable land. (1)

(iv) Terracing to increase area of agricultural land (1), highly mechanised (1): miniature tractors. (1)
High-yielding crops (1) with large outputs. (1)
Labour and capital intensive. (1)
(Up to 4 marks.)

4 Reduction in number of farms. (1) Farms have tended to get larger (1) – increasing number of farms over 30 hectares. (1) General reduction in all forms of livestock (1), but pattern remains much the same in 1975 and 1966. (1) Increasing acreage under cereal crops. (1) Barley remaining single most important crop grown. (1)
(5 points made for 5 marks.)

5 Decreasing number of people living directly on the land or exclusively dependent on agriculture. (1) Increasing industrialisation throughout the world. (1) More and more farmers becoming more commercial (1) with the growth of international trade (1) and greater interdependence of different parts of the world. (1)
(Up to 4 marks.)

Total 25

8.4 Improving agriculture in developing and developed areas

1 (i) Rearing animals in warm sheltered conditions with the correct diet for rapid fattening. (1)

(ii) Groups which act as middle men between the farmer and customer, to ensure a regular price. (1)

2 (i) Small fields (1), many plots (1), scattered (1), fragmented. (1) (Up to 3 marks.)

(ii) Subdivision of holdings (1), equal inheritance among all children on death of farmer. (1)

(iii) Less time wasted in travelling between fields (1), easier use of machines in larger fields. (1)

(iv) Hedgerows and trees are destroyed (1), spoiling the landscape and causing loss of wildlife habitats (1), also opening up the landscape to wind erosion because there are no windbreaks. (1)

3 (i) New roads (1), irrigation and drainage (1), new farms (1), redistribution of land so there is more for peasants (1), deforestation. (1)
(Up to 3 marks.)

(ii) E.g. a Chinese commune. Communist government took land from landowners and handed it to peasants (1) who were ordered to set up agricultural communes, administered through a people's council. (1) Council decides which crops are to be grown (1) and how the rest of the land is to be used (1), how much fertiliser is needed (1), what capital schemes are necessary (1), what the targets are. (1) (Any 4.)
(Two marks for each point clearly made and developed.)
Also give marks for sensible alternative points such as: radio and TV broadcasts (1), postal information to farmers and landless peasants (1), public meetings (1), tax incentives to encourage change (1), public education groups (1), grants to encourage change. (1) (Up to 4 marks.)

(iii) Governments may not have the money (1) or political support (1) to go ahead with land reform. Peasants may not respond (1) or may be unable to cope with the new demands put on them. (1) Government plans are often over-ambitious. (1) Major landowners will oppose plans. (1)

Total 25

9.1 *Resources, raw materials and fuels*

1 (i) (a) Bauxite. (1)
      (b) Water. (1)
      (c) Manganese. (1)
      (d) HEP. (1)

   (ii) The dam provided electricity (1) to smelt bauxite (1) and turn it into aluminium. (1)

   (iii) Water for irrigation (1), source of water (1), for towns and industry (1), transport route (1), fishing. (1) (Any 2 points.)

2 (i) Use of Ghana's resources at low rates. (1) Profit to American company. (1)

   (ii) Most profit goes out of the country. (1) Provides relatively few job opportunities. (1) Capital rather than labour intensive. (1) But unlikely to be exploited at all without foreign aid. (1)

3 (i) Example: oil. (1)

   (ii) Examples: tidal (1), solar (1), nuclear. (1) (Any 1.)

   (iii) Fossil fuels nearing exhaustion (1), over-dependent on imported raw materials (1), environmental pressure (1), greed factor (1), export technology (1) and hardware (1), lower costs. (1) (Any 5 points.)

   (iv) Still large resources remaining, for example of coal. (1) Very high cost of developing alternative sources. (1) Alternatives not as efficient in some cases. (1) Questions over safety (1), especially nuclear power. (1) Jobs involved in mining. (1)

Total 25

9.2 *Industry: a system at a variety of scales*

1 (i) Using a traditional craft with simple tools. (1) Labour intensive. (1)

   (ii) (4)

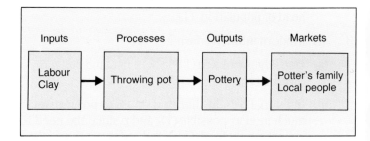

Inputs	Processes	Outputs	Markets
Labour Clay	Throwing pot	Pottery	Potter's family Local people

   (iii) Developed world craft industries geared towards tourism. (1) Often mechanised (1) using skills recently retaught. (1) Developing world examples are geared towards subsistence. (1) 'Likely to be appropriate technology' (1) using traditional skills. (1) (Up to 5 marks.)

2 (i) Secondary manufacturing. (1)

   (ii) (4)

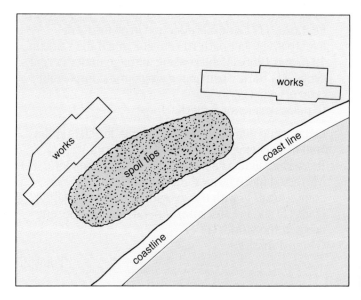

works

works

spoil tips

coast line

coastline

   (iii) Pollution controls (1), disposal of waste (1), environmental considerations. (1)

3 (i) A company with sections, branches or departments in several different countries. (1)

   (ii) Economies of scale. (1) Advantages gained from different parts of world (1), for example, research and development (1) in a highly developed part of world and assembly (1) in the developing world (1) where cheap labour is available. (1)

Total 25

9.3 Factors which influence the location of industry

1   (i)   Power supply – aluminium smelting. (1)
Source of materials – sugar beet refining. (1)
Large market – baking bread. (1)
Ready supply of labour – electronics manufacture. (1)

(ii)   Aluminium smelting: process requires vast amount of cheap electricity. (1)
Sugar beet refining: sugar beet cannot be transported far because it is bulky and deteriorates. (1)
Baking bread: perishable product which must reach the market quickly. (1)
Electronics manufacture: a large number of skilled and highly-qualified people needed for research and manufacture. (1)

2   (i)   Industries need not be specific to West Yorkshire. Credit any coalfield-based, heavy industry (1), for example wool (1) or cotton (1), coal mining (1), iron and steel. (1) (Up to 2 marks.)

(ii)   Decline of traditional coal-based industries (1), foreign competition (1), exhaustion of raw materials, out-of-date machinery (1), high unemployment rates (1), overdependence on a few basic industries (1), few opportunities for women. (1) (Up to 3 marks.)

(iii)   Good motorway links (1), near the ports of Liverpool and Hull (1), close to National Parks for recreation (1), plenty of labour in surrounding towns (1), central to west and east coast airports. (1) (Any 4 points.)

(iv)   Local authority regulations (1), planning controls (1), available buildings (1), labour relations (1), rates (1), government assistance available. (1) (Up to 4 marks.)

(v)   Advance factory building (1), tax relief (1), grants and loans (1), moving government departments to the area (1), improved communications (1), restrictions on industrial growth in other areas. (1) (Up to 4 marks.)

Total 25

9.4 From manufacturing to service industries

1   (i)   (a)   Primary – extractive. (1)
(b)   Secondary – manufacturing. (1)
(c)   Tertiary – service. (1)
(d)   Quarternary – information. (1)

(ii)   75 per cent. (1)

(iii)   40–42 per cent. (1)

(iv)   No credit for merely taking figures from the diagram. Highest percentage engaged in primary production (1), secondary occupations smallest percentage. (1) Tertiary sector relatively undeveloped. (1)

(v)   Small home market (1), small purchasing power of population (1), imports cheaper (1), foreign competition (1), poor infrastructure (1), unskilled labour. (1) (Up to 4 marks.)

(vi)   Likely to be very slow. (1) Associated with development of other branches of the economy (1) and of an infrastructure. (1) Likely to need too much capital (money) in areas which are short of cash. (1) Associated with development of an educated technical elite. (1) (Up to 3 marks.)
(*But* give mark for Arthur C. Clarke in Sri Lanka using high tech approach to writing science fiction!) (1)

2   (i)   Development of extractive industry on exposed coalfield. (1) Other raw materials found locally, for example, limestone (1), or readily-transported, for example, iron ore along the Rhine. (1) Movement of mining area northwards. (1) Exhaustion of resources. (1) Industrial inertia (1) but problems with out-of-date machinery. (1) Competition from other areas. (1) Abandonment. (1) (Up to 5 marks.)

(ii)   Unemployment (1), large market because of dense population (1), government innovations. (1) Industrial inertia (1) and closure of heavy basic industries. (1) (Up to 4 marks.)

Total 25

10.1 Transport and transport routes

1 (i) Pacific (½), Caribbean (Atlantic). (½)

   (ii) Severn. (½)

   (iii) Simplon. (½)

2 (i) Very few railways (1), majority run from interior towards the coast (1), very few cross political boundaries (1), no trans-continental railways. (1) Several countries with no railways. (1)
   (Up to 3 marks.)

   (ii) Burkina Faso (1), Ivory Coast. (1)

   (iii) Not shortest or most direct route, to avoid crossing into Ghana. (1)

   (iv) Gives landlocked Burkina Faso an outlet to the coast (1), avoids non-French territory. (1)

3 (i) Gave outlet to sea (1) to carry copper for export. (1)

   (ii) Increased trade through Dar-es-Salaam (1), open up the interior of the country. (1)

   (iii) As direct as possible (i.e. shortest) (1), having to avoid highlands as far as possible (1), avoiding Lake Malawi (1), linking up as many settlements as possible (1), taking shortest route through highlands. (1) (Up to 4 marks.)

4 Bridges crossing estuaries (1), e.g. Severn, Little Belt (Denmark). (½) Raised banks through marshy areas (1), e.g. Somerset Levels, Fens. (½) Tunnels through mountains (1), e.g. Alps. (½) Cuttings and embankments to keep level gradient for motorways (1), railways (1), hairpin bends on steep gradients. (1)
   (1 mark for each point, ½ mark for each example, up to 6 marks.)

   Total 25

10.2 Land transport: path, track, road and rail

1 (i) Motorway. (1)

   (ii) Wurzburg. (1)

   (iii) Many towns and cities (1) and a dense network of autobahns. (1)

   (iv) Faster (1), more direct (1), avoiding centres of settlements. (1)

   (v) Encourage cars and long distance coaches, vans and small lorries. (1) All these are small and quick. (1) Articulated lorries (1) with perishable (1) and low bulk cargoes (1) are better on motorways than on narrow roads. (1) Discourage very heavy cargoes (1), bulky cargoes needing convoys (1), dangerous cargoes (1) (should go by rail or waterway) (1), cyclists and pedestrians (1) who are at risk. (1)
   (Maximum of 2 for examples, 3 for reasons.)

2 (i) (Completed graph gives 5 × ½ mark for points, ½ mark for scale and labels.)

   (ii) General decline of all types (1) except passenger receipts (1), levelling out of coal and coke traffic (1) towards end of the period. (1)
   (Up to 3 marks.)

   (iii) Competition from other forms of transport (1), increasing passenger fares (1) mask reduction in passenger journeys. (1) Decline in coal and iron and steel industries (1) reflected in decline in use of railways. (1) (Up to 3 marks.)

3 Boy will lose job (1) as traffic is transferred to road. (1) Opening up of interior (1) and hilly areas (1) with better transport facilities. (1) Better for trade to and from hilly areas. (1) Destruction of the environment (1) with great engineering constructions necessary. (1) (Up to 4 marks.)

   Total 25

10.3 Transport by air and water

1   (i) (a) Roll-on roll-off (1), traffic can drive directly on or off. (1)

(b) Large box-like object (1) in which cargo can be easily moved between ship and a lorry or train. (1)

(ii) Ease of loading and unloading (1), saving time and money. (1)

2   (i) New Waterway. (1)

(ii) Oil. (1)

(iii) Petroleum havens (harbour/docks) marked on map. (1) Shell oil storage facilities. (1) Oil tanker. (1)

(iv) Large bulky commodity (1), non-perishable (1), time in transit not important as long as there is a continuous supply (1), cheapest form of transport for bulky commodity. (1) (Up to 3 marks.)

(v) At mouth of River Rhine (1) so has transit trade to the countries in the Rhine basin. (1)

3   (i) Rapid increase in aircraft movement (1) because of the growth of leisure (holiday) industry (1), greater mobility of people (1), shorter working times giving more time for leisure (1), increased international trade and co-operation. (1) (Up to 3 marks.)

(ii) Look for balance between advantages and disadvantages. (1) Reduce congestion at Heathrow and Gatwick (1); increased employment in rural area (1); spin-off into other areas of employment (1), e.g. building (½), tourism (½); increased noise and congestion (½); loss of property values. (1) (6 developed points for 6 marks.)

Total ⟦25⟧

10.4 Route patterns and transport networks

1   (i) Road (1), rail (1), water (lake). (1)

(ii) $\text{Beta index} = \dfrac{\text{Number of routes} (1)}{\text{Number of nodes} (1)}$

(iii) $\text{Beta index} = \dfrac{6 (1)}{11 (1)} = 0.54 (1)$

(iv) Very low figure. (1) Not a very well connected network. (1)

(v) 2/3 (1)

(vi) No railway link north of Kumasi (1) so north of the country remains isolated. (1)

(vii) More links to be built. (1) Railway link along coast. (1) Road/rail network becomes more integrated. (1) More east-west links. (1) Railway extended northward. (1) More feeder routes. (1) (Up to 3 marks.)

2   (i) One is simplified with no attempt to make it appear realistic, no coastline. (1) Topological map shows time of journey. (1)

(ii) St Pancras. (1)

(iii) 2 hours 30 minutes. (1)

(iv) English is a much more integrated network (1) with high level of connectivity. (1) Northern Ireland, one single link: Londonderry – Belfast – Dublin. (1) Wales only routes along north and south coasts. (1) Scotland no route north of Glasgow on west Coast. (1) Greater physical obstacles in Wales, Scotland and Ireland (1), also more sparsely populated and less demand in mountainous areas. (1) (Up to 5 marks.)

Total ⟦25⟧

11.1 *What is 'quality of life'?*

1 (i) Life expectancy: the number of years a person is expected to live. (1)
Literacy: ability to read and write. (1)
Infant mortality: the number of young children who die before reaching a certain age. (1)

(ii) Australasia (Oceania) (0 for Australia), Europe, North America. (2 of these for 2 marks.)

(iii) Portugal. (1)

(iv) Africa. (1)

(v) Large areas with difficult physical environments, e.g. desert, tropical rain forest (1); poor agricultural techniques (1); lack of fossil fuels (1); political instability (1); governmental incompetence (1); poorly developed infrastructure (1); lack of welfare (1), medical and social services. (1) (Any 4 developed points for 4 marks.)

(vi) Represent average figures for the whole population. (1) Great variations in earning power within population. (1) Often economic elite (1) based on class/colour who enjoy good quality of life. (1) (Answers need not be specific to South Africa or India.) (3 developed points for 3 marks.)

(i) Examples: average calorie intake of food (1), consumption of energy (1), number of people per doctor (1), unemployment rate. (1)
(Up to 3 marks.)

(ii) Examples: average calorie intake of food (1) – people with high intake are generally well fed and nourished (1); lower incidence of disease (1); greater life expectancy. (1)
(Up to 3 marks.)

(iii) Recognition of problem from surveys (1); provides money for basic requirements of life (1), i.e. food, shelter (1); when basic requirements satisfied, improve welfare facilities (1) to keep quality of life high (1); provide leisure facilities. (1) (5 developed points for 5 marks.)

Total $\boxed{25}$

11.2 *Human welfare*

1 Absolute poverty: when people have no home (1), no food and no medical help. (1) Relative poverty: have basic requirements of life (1) but poor compared with neighbours. (1)

2 (i) Wealth created in a country per year (1) shared out equally among every individual in the country. (1)

(ii) Average income per person is the average amount of money earned (1) and received by each individual per year. (1)

(iii) Less than 100. (1)

(iv) Valle d'Aosta (1), Piedmont (1), Liguna (1), Lombardy (1). (Any 1 of these.)

(v) Highest income in the north west (1); medium in north east and west coast north of Naples (1); lowest income in the south and the islands. (1) (No marks for merely repeating figures.)

(vi) Higher proportion employed in agriculture in the south. (1)

(vii) Lower food consumption (1); fewer radios/cars/bikes (1); greater percentage below the 'poverty' line. (1)

(viii)

Rank	Electricity	Cars	Per capita
Abrussi-Molise	3	3	3 = 9
Campania	7	5	4 = 16
Apulia	4	6	5 = 15
Basilicata	1	1	2 = 4
Calatina	2	2	1 = 5
Sicily	5	6	5 = 16
Sardinia	6	4	7 = 17

(1 for ranking, 1 for totals, 2 for shading, 1 for key.)

3 Double the unemployment rate (1), lower average earnings (1), higher mortality rate (1), fewer staying on at school (1), greater percentage of houses 'below bedroom standard' (1), fewer cars owned per 1000 people. (1) (Up to 5 marks.)

Total $\boxed{25}$

11.3 Leisure

1 (i) People are earning more money (1), shorter working week (1), longer holidays. (1) (2 of these.)

   (ii) Likely to go up (1), more affluence (1), greater unemployment (1), increasing mobility of population. (1) (2 of these.)

2 (i) Hotels. (1)

   (ii) Sport and other recreations. (1)

   (iii) Make up for general decline in manufacturing industry (1), allow growth of employment in more remote parts of the country. (1) Leisure industries often lead to spin-offs in other forms of employment, e.g. building. (1)

3 (i) To preserve natural beauty of countryside (1) from other pressures like factory development, building, quarrying. (1)

   (ii) Walking (1), rock climbing (1), pony-trekking. (1) (Any outdoor activity accepted.) (2 of these.)

   (iii) Large numbers of visitors walking in fields may cause conflicts with farmers – leaving gates open, dropping rubbish. (1) Increased mobility and use of cars leads to traffic congestion, pollution from exhausts. (1) Many upland areas are also sources of mineral wealth/building stone (1) – leads to quarrying scars, waste tips (1). Prohibition of building houses/factories may reduce employment prospects for local residents. (1) Holiday homes being bought up by people from outside the area (1), often forces the prices up above those affordable by local residents. (1) (Any 4 developed points for 4 marks.)

4 (i) Temperature remains constant/very high temperatures. (1)

   (ii) 26 mm (½ if units omitted) (1)

   (iii) Guaranteed sunshine (1), beaches (1), scenery. (1) (Up to 2 marks.)

   (iv) No marks for Yes/No. All marks for reasons. Provides employment in hotels (1), important earner of foreign exchange. (1) Can suffer from changes in fashion and exchange values. (1) Look for balance between advantages and disadvantages. (1) (Up to 4 marks.)

   Total 25

11.4 Quality of life: sources of conflict

1 (i) 27.1 per cent. (1)

   (ii) 38.2 per cent. (1)

   (iii) No credit for repeating figures directly from the text. Inner city population tends to be younger (1), more likely to be unemployed (1), with higher concentration of ethnic minorities. (1)

   (iv) More money should be spent to improve living conditions (1), more employment opportunities should be provided to reduce the unemployment rate. (1) Attempts should be made to improve the relationship (1) between police and the young population. (1) Racial understanding should be encouraged. (1)
   (Five well developed points. Look for balance, a very biased view should be marked down to maximum of 2.)

2 (i) Great contrast (1) between rich and poor. (1)

   (ii) Huge revenue from oil (1), concentrated in hands of a few people. (1) Much of population not affected by income (1) gained from sale of oil. (1) (Up to 3 marks.)

3 (i) Burning of fossil fuels (1), industrial processes (1), motor vehicle exhaust. (1)

   (ii) Contamination of water supply (1), destroying vegetation (1), killing fish in lakes (1), possible deformities in children (1), contamination of food crops. (1) (Up to 3 marks.)

   (iii) Attempts at international agreement for pollution control. (1) Clean air acts (1), tighter pollution control by individual countries (1), lead-free petrol (1), smokeless fuels (1), filtration of gases released into atmosphere. (1) (4 developed points for 4 marks.)

   Total 25

12.1 Development can be defined and measured in different ways

1 (i) (a) GNP/person (1), energy consumption/person. (1) (1 of these.)
       (b) Daily food supply/person (1), percentage of people in higher education. (1) (1 of these.)

   (ii) GNP/person: the total output of agriculture and industry for the country, divided by the total population. (1)
   Energy consumption per person: the amount of energy consumed by the population for domestic and industrial purposes divided by the total population. (1)
   Daily food intake per person: the total food intake divided by total population. (1)
   Adult literacy: percentage of population who can read and write. (1) (Any one of these definitions.)

   Explanation – The higher the value, the higher the stage of development. (2)
   (1 mark for the definition, 2 marks for the explanation of what it tells you.)

2 (i) Scattergraph. (1)

   (ii) One of three in bottom left hand corner of graph. (1)

   (iii) Cross in top right hand corner of the graph. (1)

   (iv) Close link (1), the poorer the country the lower the energy consumption. (1)

3 (i) Examples: Malagasy Republic (1), Chad. (1) (Any one.)

   (ii) Examples: USA (1) or UK. (1)

   (iii) Africa. (1)

   (iv) There is a concentration on cash crops (1) which bring in an income (1), so food crop production is abandoned. (1) Accept reference to climatic (1) hazards (1), for example, drought (1) or pests like locusts. (1) (Up to 3 marks.)

   (v) Over-dependence (½) on one source of income (½) is not satisfactory (½) as agriculture is subject to great price fluctuations (½) due to climate or disease which may devastate the crop. (½) May lead to underemployment (½) because, apart from seed time and harvest, not much labour is required (½) and it is subject to fluctuations in demand. (½) Will increase the popularity of cash crops (½) at the expense of food crop production. (½) (Up to 4 marks.) (4)

4 Discussion of at least two criteria and suitable reasons, for example:
   (i) Criteria: Consumption of energy. (½)
   (ii) Reasons: If energy consumption is low it would suggest that industry is not well developed and so there is overdependence on agriculture. (1)

Also, there is a low standard of living if domestic consumption is low because there are few labour saving devices and little use of electricity or gas in the homes. (1) (Two such answers gives 2 × 2½ = 5 marks.)

Total 25

12.2 Development is related to physical, social and political conditions

1 (i) Large number of islands (1); mountainous areas (1) in western Sumatra, central Kalimantan, Java and Sulawesi (1); constant high temperature (1), high rainfall in all seasons (1), suggests very high humidity. (1) (Up to 4 marks.)

   (ii) Large areas of the country very remote (1), difficulty of transport (1) and administration. (1) Farming difficulties in mountainous areas. (1) High temperature and rainfall may produce an unhealthy (1), energy-sapping (1) climate. (up to 3 marks)

   (iii) Concentration of population in Java. (1)

   (iv) Concentration of population and probably development in Java (1) means less attention paid to rest of country. (1)

2 (4)

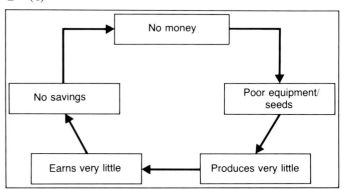

3 (i) Modern farming in poor countries using super seeds and fertilisers to produce high yields. (1)

   (ii) New higher yielding seeds give a greater output (1); disease resistant strains of seeds and animals. (1)

   (iii) Greater cost than old methods (1), over-dependence on the money lender (1), lack of technical knowhow (1) means many of new strains do not do well. (1)

4 Small schemes are labour intensive (1) and so employ many people (1) (who are readily available for work). (1) Large schemes are often very expensive (1) and are capital intensive (1), which a poor country cannot afford. (1) Frequently they do not produce many new jobs. (1) (Up to 5 marks.)

Total 25

12.3 Countries are interdependent in trade

1 (i) South East Asia. (1)

   (ii) West Africa. (1)

   (iii) 10 per cent. (1)

   (iv) Food. (1)

   (v) Primary. (1)

   (vi) Dominated by manufactured goods because poorly developed manufacturing sector. (1) Food imported because agriculture is dominated by primary cash crop production, for example coffee, cocoa. (1) (2 developed points for 2 marks.)

   (vii) Too dependent on one type of commodity, so if the price of the commodity drops there is a disastrous drop in foreign earnings. (1)

   (viii) Machinery and transport equipment exported. (1) Therefore there is a manufacturing economy. (1) But high value of manufactured goods (1) also suggests the high spending power of the population. (1) Imports raw materials for the manufacturing industry. (1) (Up to 3 marks.)

   (ix) Same for either country: Western Europe (North America/United Kingdom). (1)

   (x) Developing country is a source of raw materials (1) and cheap manufactured goods. (1) Preferential treatment for Commonwealth countries. (1) In return, developed country provides modern consumer items like cars. (1) (Up to 3 marks.)

2 (i) Completed bar graph. (10 × ½ mark = 5)

   (ii) The total value of trade from developing countries is very small (1) compared to developed countries. (1)

   (iii) Developing countries earn far less through trade than developed countries. (1) Developing countries trade in much smaller amounts than developed ones (1), also the value of trade in developed countries is much higher because it is mainly in manufactured goods (1), whereas developing countries trade mainly in raw materials (1) and other primary produce. (1) (Up to 3 marks.)

Total 25

12.4 Reducing inequality between and within countries

1 Bilateral aid is given by one country to another. (1) Multilateral aid is money from a number of countries which is sent to the poorer parts of the world. (1)

2 (i) Examples: high GNP per person (1), low dependence on agriculture (1), high literacy rate. (1) (Up to 2 marks.)

   (ii) Examples: large number of people per doctor (1), low energy consumption per head (1), few going on to higher education. (1) (Up to 2 marks.)

   (iii) 7/1000 of the total value of all production in the country. (1)

   (iv) Four. (1)

   (v) The Netherlands. (1)

3 (i) £7.92 (1)

   (ii) Christian Aid, Live Aid, Band Aid, Oxfam, World Vision. (2 of these for 2 marks.)

   (iii) Gain money for the charity (1) but must spend money on the advertisement. (1)

   (iv) Technical assistance (1), education (1), doctors (1), medical and welfare assistance (1), administrators. (1)

   (v) Values: food to prevent starvation (1), medicine/doctors to improve health (1), money to buy necessities (1), transport equipment (1), blankets or clothing for warmth (1), better agricultural equipment. (1)
   Dangers: over-reliance on food aid (1), reduces self respect (1) and the will power (1) to improve way of life (1), upsets economy. (1)
   (Look for balance – reserve 2 marks for values and 2 for dangers.) (Up to 6 marks.)

Total 25

Index